TALES
Tall & True

TO KNOW   TO UNDERSTAND   TO PARTICIPATE
THE CANADIAN HERITAGE IS YOUR HERITAGE

**ALBERTA HERITAGE
LEARNING RESOURCES
PROJECT**

A Project of Alberta Education
Funded
By
The Alberta Heritage Savings Trust Fund
and
Dedicated to the Students
of Alberta
by the
Government of Alberta
1979

Grateful acknowledgment is extended
to those who assisted in the development
of the Alberta Heritage anthologies

Members of the Selection Committee

Theresa Ford / *Edmonton Catholic School District*
Michael Allen / *Calgary Catholic School District*
Tom Gee / *Alberta Education*
Marg Iveson / *Edmonton Public School District*
Gloria Limin / *Calgary Public School District*
Lorne MacRae / *Calgary Public School District*
Maureen Ross / *Edmonton Catholic School District*

Western Canadian Literature
for Youth

TALES
Tall & True

Theresa M. Ford
Managing Editor

Alberta Education
Edmonton

Alberta Education
Devonian Building
11160 Jasper Avenue
Edmonton, Alberta
T5K 0L2

ISBN 0-920794-04-1

Project Director / Dr. Kenneth Nixon
Design / David Shaw & Associates Ltd.
Publishing Consultants / Hurtig Publishers, Edmonton
Illustration / Rene Zamic
Typesetting / The Albertan, Calgary
Printing / Lawson Graphics Western Ltd., Calgary
Binding / Economy Bookbinding Company Ltd., Calgary

To The Reader

The art of story-telling is as old as the language of mankind, as complex as the range of human emotions, as appealing as life itself to young and old alike. *Everyone* loves a story!

Sometimes, however, fact *is* stranger than fiction as you will observe when you read some of the true accounts in this book. At other times, the truth has been altered or embellished to such a degree in the telling of the story that the resultant narrative bears little relationship to the original event. Then, too, there are the tall tales in which the author's creative imagination holds free sway. Intermingled throughout *Tales Tall and True,* you will also find a treasury of Indian and Inuit legends which form such an important segment of the literary heritage of Western Canada.

So sit back — and enjoy!

5

Contents

MAN & THE ELEMENTS

LARGER THAN LIFE

People

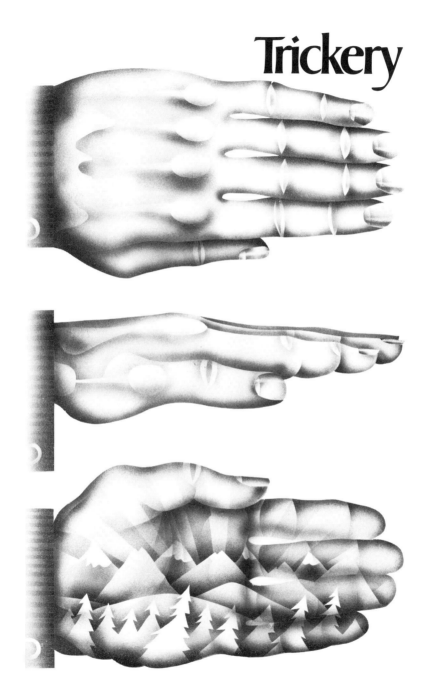

Trickery

Character as Trickster

The Race

George B. Grinnell

Once Old Man was travelling around, when he heard some queer singing. He had never heard anything like this before and looked all around to see who it was. At last he saw it was the cottontail rabbits singing and making medicine. They had built a fire, and got a lot of hot ashes and they would lie down in these ashes and sing while one covered them up. They would stay there only a short time though, for the ashes were very hot.

"Little Brothers," said Old Man, "that is very wonderful how you lie in those hot ashes and coals without burning. I wish you would teach me how to do it."

"Come on, Old Man," said the rabbits, "we will show you how to do it. You must sing our song and only stay in the ashes a short time." So the Old Man began to sing and he lay down, and they covered him with coals and ashes, and they did not burn him at all.

"That is very nice," he said. "You have powerful medicine. Now I want to know it all, so you lie down and let me cover you up."

So the rabbits all lay down in the ashes, and Old Man covered them up, and then he put the whole fire over them. One old rabbit got out and Old Man was about to put her back when she said, "Pity me, my children are about to be born."

"All right," replied Old Man, "I will let you go, so there will be some more rabbits; but I will roast these nicely and have a feast." And he put more wood on the fire. When the rabbits were cooked, he cut some red willow brush and laid them on it to cool. The grease soaked into these branches, so even today if you hold red willow over a fire, you will see the grease on the bark. You can see, too, that ever since the rabbits have a burnt place on their backs where the one that got away was singed.

Old Man sat down, and was waiting for the rabbits to cool a little when a coyote came along, limping very badly.

"Pity me, Old Man," he said, "you have lots of cooked rabbits; give me one of them."

"Go away," exclaimed Old Man. "If you are too lazy to catch your food, I will not help you."

"My leg is broken," replied the coyote. "I can't catch anything and I am starving. Just give me half a rabbit."

"I don't care if you die," replied Old Man. "I worked hard to cook all these rabbits and I will not give any away. But I will tell you what we will do. We will run a race to that butte, way out there, and if you can beat me you can have a rabbit."

"All right," said the coyote. So they started. Old Man ran very fast and the coyote limped along behind, but close to him, until they got near to the butte. Then the coyote turned round and ran back very fast for he was not lame at all. It took Old Man a long time to go back, and just before he got to the fire, the coyote swallowed the last rabbit and trotted off over the prairie.

The Dancing Lodge of Chief Little Mouse

Frances Fraser

One day Na'pe, the Old Man, was out on the prairie travelling from somewhere to somewhere else when he heard little voices singing. He followed the sound and found that it came from an elk's skull, which was lying on the ground.

He looked inside and found a large nest of mice having a party. They were singing and dancing and having a very good time. Na'pe was envious, so he said, "Little Brothers! Little Brothers! Let me sing too!"

The mice said, "Well, Old Man, we don't mind. Sit there and sing!" But no, Old Man didn't want to do it that way. "I would not make a guest sit outside *my* dancing lodge!" he said.

"Oh, very well," said the mice. "You may put your head in and sing with us that way, but you must not go to sleep. If you go to sleep, you will not be able to take your head out again. You'll be sorry!" said the mice.

"Oh, yes, yes," said Na'pe impatiently, and he put his head into the elk skull and began to sing with the mice.

The dancing continued till far into the night, with Na'pe keeping time to the singing with his head, shaking it back and forth. He began to get sleepy and he forgot all that the mice had told him about not going to sleep. Na'pe slept.

The mice laughed and laughed. Then they gnawed all his hair off and ran away.

When Na'pe awoke, he found that the little animals had told the truth. He was quite unable to get his head out of the elk skull. He wandered off over the prairie searching for someone to help him out of the skull. Since his eyes were covered by the skull, he could not see where he was going and he was forced to rely upon asking his way from the rocks and the trees, because all things talk to Old Man.

He said to a rock, "Where do you sit?" The rock said, "I sit on the side of a hill, Na'pe. Walk above me, for below me is the river." Na'pe went along his way. He bumped into a tree. "Where do you sit?" he said to the tree. "Are you near the river?"

"I am very near the river, Na'pe," said the tree. "Walk away from me, lest you should fall into the water."

Late in the day he said to another tree, "Where do you sit? Are you near the river or far away?"

This tree was a liar. It said, "I am far from the river, Na'pe. Walk this way, Old Man."

So Na'pe walked past the tree and fell into the river. The current was strong, and the water deep. Na'pe found himself whirled out into midstream and carried along very rapidly down the river.

A little way downstream there was an Indian camp. The women were down by the river getting water when they saw Na'pe in the elk horns coming down the river. They ran to the camp shouting, "An elk is floating down the river! An elk! An elk!"

The men seized their bows and arrows and ran to the river bank. They were ready to shoot at him when Na'pe cried for help. They knew his voice, and said, "Why it is our old brother, Na'pe!"

They waded out and brought him in to the shore. Then they took rocks and broke open the elk skull, freeing Old Man. But no sooner had his head appeared than the women began to scream.

"Oh, look, look," they said, "He has no hair. It is not Old Man. It is a water person! Run! Run!" And they all ran away as fast as they could, leaving Na'pe alone. He went to another camp, but they too thought he was a water person and ran away.

So he had to go and camp by himself for a long time, till his hair grew out again. "Oh, well," said Na'pe, "I sang very well with those mice. I did, indeed."

How Coyote Stole Fire
Gail Robinson & Douglas Hill

Long ago, when man was newly come into the world, there were days when he was the happiest creature of all. Those were the days when spring brushed across the willow tails, or when his children ripened with the blueberries in the sun of summer, or when the goldenrod bloomed in the autumn haze.

But always the mists of autumn evenings grew more chill, and the sun's strokes grew shorter. The man saw winter moving near, and he became fearful and unhappy. He was afraid for his children, and for the grandfathers and grandmothers who carried in their heads the sacred tales of the tribe. Many of these, young and old, would die in the long, ice-bitter months of winter.

Coyote, like the rest of the People, had no need for fire. So he seldom concerned himself with it, until one spring day when he was passing a human village. There the women were singing a song of mourning for the babies and the old ones who had died in the winter. Their voices moaned like the west wind through a buffalo skull, prickling the hairs on Coyote's neck.

"Feel how the sun is now warm on our backs," one of the men was saying. "Feel how it warms the earth and makes these stones hot to the touch. If only we could have had a small piece of the sun in our tepees during the winter."

Coyote, overhearing this, felt sorry for the men and women. He also felt that there was something he could do to help them. He knew of a faraway mountain-top where the three Fire Beings lived. These Beings kept fire to themselves, guarding it carefully for fear that man might somehow acquire it and become as strong as they. Coyote saw that he could do a good turn for man at the expense of these selfish Fire Beings.

So Coyote went to the mountain of the Fire Beings and crept to its top, to watch the way that the Beings guarded their fire. As he came near, the Beings leaped to their feet and gazed searchingly round their camp. Their eyes glinted like blood-stones, and their hands were clawed like the talons of the great black vulture.

"What's that? What's that I hear?" hissed one of the Beings.

"A thief, skulking in the bushes!" screeched another.

The third looked more closely, and saw Coyote. But he had gone to the mountain-top on all fours, so the Being thought she saw only an ordinary coyote slinking among the trees.

"It is no one, it is nothing!" she cried, and the other two looked where she pointed and also saw only a grey coyote. They sat down again by their fire and paid Coyote no more attention.

So he watched all day and night as the Fire Beings guarded their fire. He saw how they fed it pine cones and dry branches from the sycamore trees. He saw how they stamped furiously on runaway rivulets of flame that sometimes nibbled outwards on edges of dry grass. He saw also how, at night, the Beings took turns to sit by the fire. Two would sleep while one was on guard; and at certain times the Being by the fire would get up and go into their tepee, and another would come out to sit by the fire.

Coyote saw that the Beings were always jealously watchful of their fire except during one part of the day. That was in the earliest morning, when the first winds of dawn arose on the mountains. Then the Being by the fire would hurry, shivering, into the tepee calling, "Sister, sister, go out and watch the fire." But the next Being would always be slow to go out for her turn, her head spinning with sleep and the thin dreams of dawn.

Coyote, seeing all this, went down the mountain and spoke to some of his friends among the People. He told them of hairless man, fearing the cold and death of winter. And he told them of the Fire Beings, and the warmth and brightness of the flame. They all agreed that man should have fire, and they all promised to help Coyote's undertaking.

Then Coyote sped again to the mountain-top. Again the Fire Beings leaped up when he came close, and one cried out, "What's that? A thief, a thief!"

But again the others looked closely, and saw only a grey coyote hunting among the bushes. So they sat down again and paid him no more attention.

Coyote waited through the day, and watched as night fell and two of the Beings went off to the tepee to sleep. He watched as they changed over at certain times all the night long, until at last the dawn winds rose.

Then the Being on guard called, "Sister, sister, get up and watch the fire."

And the Being whose turn it was climbed slow and sleepy from her bed, saying, "Yes, yes, I am coming. Do not shout so."

But before she could come out of the tepee, Coyote lunged from the bushes, snatched up a glowing portion of fire, and sprang away down the mountainside.

Screaming, the Fire Beings flew after him. Swift as Coyote ran, they caught up with him, and one of them reached out a clutching hand. Her fingers touched only the tip of the tail, but the touch was enough to turn the hairs white, and coyote tail-tips are white still. Coyote shouted, and flung the fire away from him. But the others of the People had gathered at the mountain's foot, in case they were needed. Squirrel saw the fire falling, and caught it, putting it on her back and fleeing away through the tree-tops. The fire scorched her back so painfully that her tail curled up and back, as squirrels' tails still do today.

The Fire Beings then pursued Squirrel, who threw the fire to Chipmunk. Chattering with fear, Chipmunk stood still as if rooted until the Beings were almost upon her. Then, as she turned to run, one Being clawed at her, tearing down the length of her back and leaving three stripes that are to be seen on chipmunks' backs even today. Chipmunk threw the fire to Frog, and the Beings turned towards him. One of the Beings grasped his tail, but Frog gave a mighty leap and tore himself free, leaving his tail behind in the Being's hand — which is why frogs have had no tails ever since.

As the Beings came after him again, Frog flung the fire on to Wood. And Wood swallowed it.

The Fire Beings gathered round, but they did not know how to get the fire out of Wood. They promised it gifts, sang to it and shouted at it. They twisted it and struck it and tore it with their knives. But Wood did not give up the fire. In the end, defeated, the Beings went back to their mountain-top and left the People alone.

But Coyote knew how to get fire out of Wood. And he went to the village of men and showed them how. He showed them the trick of rubbing two dry sticks together, and the trick of spinning a sharpened stick in a hole made in another piece of wood. So man was from then on warm and safe through the killing cold of winter.

Kajortoq and the Crow
Maurice Metayer

Kajortoq, the red fox, was strolling along the edge of a cliff when she chanced to see a moose grazing on some moss. Approaching the moose Kajortoq said, "I know of a place near here where there is wild fruit. It is on a narrow ledge of rocks which we can reach by following the path halfway up the cliff."

The moose followed Kajortoq without hesitation, and jumping over rock hollows, soon found himself in a precarious position on the edge of the precipice. The fox, who had moved ahead of the moose, turned and warned, "Be careful here. It is easy to lose your footing. Take care not to fall. Jump quickly to this side!" The moose did as Kajortoq directed but when his hooves landed on the slippery rocks they struck a loose stone and he fell to the bottom of the cliff. When Kajortoq reached the bottom she found the moose dead and proceeded to make a meal of her victim.

Days later she had finished all of the meat and set out to continue her hunting. Eventually she spotted a bird sitting on its eggs in a nest at the top of a tree. She called up to the bird, "I want to eat some eggs. Throw one to me!" Although the bird valued her eggs, she was frightened and allowed one of them to fall to the ground. Kajortoq ate it quickly and moved away from the tree.

Soon she was back demanding more eggs. This time the bird replied, "No, I will not give them to you." At this Kajortoq screamed, "If you don't give me some of your eggs I will take them all for I shall cut down this tree with my axe!" Intimidated, the poor bird let a few more eggs fall to the ground and the fox ate her fill and moved on.

Tulugaq, the crow, had been watching these events and now he came to speak to the bird. "Why did you let that renegade fox eat your eggs?" he asked. The bird explained that if she hadn't given Kajortoq a few of the eggs she would have used her axe to cut down the tree and all the eggs would have been lost. Tulugaq replied, "That fox is nothing but a liar; she has no axe! She is only trying to frighten you."

When the crow had gone, it was not long before Kajortoq returned demanding still more eggs and threatening once more to cut down the tree. This time the bird spoke without fear or hesitation.

"I will give you no more eggs. I am keeping them for myself."

Kajortoq was suspicious. "Who has been telling tales about me?"

"The big crow told me that you have no axe and cannot cut down this tree where I have my nest," replied the bird. "I shall give you no more eggs!"

The red fox moved off muttering, "That crow is nothing but a chatter box." She headed toward an open field where she lay down, pretending to be dead. Curious, Tulugaq approached the fox's still form, cawing noisily and pecking at her buttocks and hind feet with his beak to see if the fox would stir. With great difficulty the fox remained perfectly still until Tulugaq, certain that Kajortoq was dead, moved toward her head in order to peck out her eyes. Suddenly the crow found himself imprisoned in the fox's strong jaws.

Kajortoq carried her victim to a small hill and prepared to eat him. However before she could begin her meal, the crow spoke.

"Where is the wind coming from?" the crow asked.

The fox thought, "Are you crazy to ask such a question?"

She opened her mouth wide to say so and the crow flew away.

Din's Back Room

J. A. Jackson

"Anyway," said Father Murray, O.M.I., missionary and pastor of the mining town of Forest, B. C., "if there's nothing good one can say about the Irish" — and he smiled amiably — "at least they are a hospitable people." Then, having first whetted my appetite for debate, he rose, went over to the woodbox in the corner of his two room mansion, and dropped some slabs into the air-tight heater. The temperature outside was a mid-January 32 below. We had just finished washing the supper dishes, after a hard day sawing cord wood in the bush, and now sat, with easy consciences, as close to the stove as the temperature warranted.

"Oh! yes," he resumed, rocking himself slowly in his chair, "whenever I meet an Irishman, I remember the first of your race I ever met, and a choice specimen he was. No doubt about that. It happened in the neighborhood of about 15 years ago, when I came to this town first. It was just a name on the map, a railroad station and some shacks around, with a small store, but recently a rich deposit of ore had been struck in the mine, so overnight Forest became a boom town. Into it from all corners of British Columbia and Alberta came a steady influx of French, Scottish, Swedes, hoping to strike it rich, and before you could say "zero" why, more than 4,000 people were putting up with its 10 feet of snow and its temperatures of as much as 60 below — buoyed up by the thought that tomorrow — always it is tomorrow — a lucky strike, and Cadillacs and champagne for the rest of his days. Such a swarm of humans was bound to have its percentage of Catholics, and no resident priest to take care of them. The first I knew of it was a brief note from the Bishop asking me to go to Forest and to take up my station there, and see what could be done for them. I packed my bag and went.

"You can picture a mining town rested in a canyon between two huge rocks with overhead conveyor chains and buckets that shovelled the ore and brought it overhead into the smelters; a scurrying mass of men hurrying here and there through the snow, knocking together crazy shacks; a saloon or two; a small cafe; two hotels; and a population with only one thing in mind — get rich and if you can't get rich, why, get drunk. There was no church of course (that was one of my first chores, to get one started) and as far as law or police were concerned, well, you know how these places go! There was a thriving business in bootlegging going on; and though nobody seemed to know anything about it, nobody was very thirsty for long. As I had a room in a hotel I had lots of painful experience of what a thirsty bunch the natives of Forest could be. From 6:30 in the evening that saloon door banged open and shut, forty times an hour, so that by 10 or 11 at night between the singing and brawling and banging the battered piano that went on downstairs in the bar, I can tell you my room was anything but a fit place for meditation. The fighting that went on on

Saturday nights especially, the number of panes of glass that were broken there each weekend mounted up so fast that the town got quite a name for itself, even in the north-west. A new sergeant of police was drafted in — a big gangling six footer, with an eye of ice and a fist as big as a ham: and one by one the bootleggers began to appear in court, paid their fines, and the Saturday fights in the hotel climbed down to a mild dozen or so. Bootlegging became quite a thrilling pastime; and was no longer the respectable business it had been in the good old days! And this is just where my friend the Irishman, came into my story.

"The hotel was so full of anything but saints it was my custom to go to a nearby frame house, with eight large rooms in it, every morning at 7:30 and say Mass there in one of the bigger rooms. The owner was a hospitable Irishman, from County Kerry, I believe, whom we'll call Din O'Connell. Din himself every morning got me my breakfast with his own hands: a pot of coffee, toast and bacon and eggs. One morning, at breakfast, Din carefully closed the door after him and sat down at the table, gave me a big cigar and showed unusual signs of reverence.

" 'Arrah, sure, Father, that's an awful place for a priest to be living in. That hotel, full of drunks and characters, and curses and fighting of all kinds. Sure you can't have a minute's peace between the lot of them now — isn't that right? Did you never think of coming over here and living in my place: sure I'll be always glad to let you have a room all to yourself, and it needn't cost you a cent.' And before I could say 'yes' Din was showing me through the house to a big room at the back. 'Bring your things along this evening, Father, and we'll have everything ship-shape for you in two shakes of a lamb's tail.' I can tell you I was perfectly overwhelmed by his hospitality. A dollar's a dollar especially on these poor missions up north and the hotel bedlam was costing me, — apart from headaches — two and a half dollars a day. So, fearing he'd change his mind, I hired a truck and appeared before Din's house in less than an hour: and there on the outside of the door was a neatly printed card — Rev. Fr. Murray, O.M.I. — for all the world to see. From that day onward, to say I was treated like a lord is only the stark truth. Din was like a shadow to me: whenever I moved out to go down town, he opened the door for me, and bade me 'good-bye', and 'mind the street cars, Father.' Likewise, when I returned, Din opened the door for me, and led me, in person, to my room, opened that door, and led me in with a kingly gesture. It was really a wonderful change for the better, especially as every house in town, at this time, was being practically torn asunder by the police stamping out the bootlegging trade. My old hotel had been raided and the proprietor fined $500 for bootlegging; why the police even came in one day and made a great commotion through all the rooms of his place. I was busy that afternoon in my room, and heard a great banging of doors, and heaving about of beds: but as I was sewing some buttons on my trousers I didn't investigate, but simply turned the key in my lock and stayed quiet. Eventually, footsteps echoed through the hall, and a large voice (I recognized the sergeant's) said 'So! Father Murray stays here! That's all right, boys: there's nothing in this room.' They moved off; and the usual afternoon quietness settled down again.

"For 8 or 9 months this went on, this period of quiet. I got my little church built, and each morning walked around the corner and said my Holy Mass, returning usually about 8:30 and breakfasting at Din's expense. Until one morning, returning earlier than usual, as I walked down the long hallway in the centre of Din's house, I noticed my room door was opened: looking in, there was my bed pushed back, and wonder of wonders, the venerable Din, dust all over his trouser-legs, was standing gaping at me, and I at him. Three long floor-boards had been raised and in the space beneath rested as mouth-watering a selection of bottles as anyone could desire. At the rates the bootleggers charged in Forest, there was a good thousand dollars worth of stuff there. I looked at Din. Din looked down anxiously at his boots. Then he pushed back his cap on his bald head, and shook himself. 'Arrah, sure, what am I doing, standing here; have I taken leave of my senses. Come right in Father, and have a drop of stuff to keep the cold out of your stomach.' And to think that I'd been mounting guard over Din's cache of liquor for a good six months, and not to know a thing about it." Father laughed a big hearty guffaw: and then concluded. "I got the biggest kick of my life out of this incident, some two years later when I moved to another parish, 250 miles south. In the cafe one day who should come in but Sergeant McIntosh, ex-Forest policeman. We fell to talking about old times. 'Y'know,' said the sergeant, with a puzzled frown, 'that Forest outfit got me beat. We rounded up every known bootlegger in that outfit and clamped them all in jail: but darned if the liquor wasn't as plentiful as ever. I had my eye on old Din and searched every room in his house, but never found a thing there. Yes, it sure has me puzzled.' But," concluded Father Murray, with a chuckle, "he looked a lot more puzzled at the remark I made to him as I rose from the table and said good-bye to him: — 'I guess what saved old Din was — his Irish hospitality.' "

The Eagles' War-Bonnet
Frances Fraser

This is a story from a long time ago, when the eagles wore long plumes on their heads and the magpies had short fluffy tails.

One day in the middle of summer the Old Man, Na'pe, was sitting in the middle of the shade of a cutbank trying to keep himself cool. It was hot and he wasn't succeeding very well. "Oh, I wish I were up there in the north where it is always cold," said Na'pe.

"If you wait till winter it will be cold," said Coyote, who was lying on the ground beside him trying to think up some amusing sort of trouble-making. "And when it was cold you complained something awful about *that*."

"I did not! I did not! *I did not!*" yelled Na'pe jumping up and down with rage.

Na'pe's yells attracted the attention of a pair of eagles who were sailing around in the sky. "Why, that's our old brother Na'pe," said the eagles. "What is he screaming about!" So they came down to see.

"Aie, Little Brothers," said Na'pe. "Take me up north, where the Big Ice is."

"Well, Old Man," said the eagles, "we can do that, but you'll be sorry, because if you don't wish to come back when we do, we will leave you there."

"Oh, yes, yes, yes!" said Na'pe impatiently.

"You *will* be sorry, you know," said Coyote, going off laughing.

The eagles came down and Na'pe grasped their legs, one leg in each hand, and away they flew to the north.

They came to where the cold began. "This is far enough, Little Brothers," said Na'pe, "I am cool enough now."

"Oh, no, no," said the eagles. "You wanted to go up where the Big Ice is. So we'll take you right there." They flew on a bit farther.

"This is far enough now, Little Brothers," said Na'pe.

"Oh, no, no," said the eagles. "You wanted to go where the Big Ice is. We are taking you there." And they flew on a bit farther.

They came to the Big Ice with Na'pe yelling and screaming "Let me down! Let me down!"

"Now, Old Man," said the eagles, "you don't want to get down here. You can't stay here. You'll freeze."

"I am Old Man!" said Na'pe. "I am too clever to freeze!"

"We are glad to hear it," said the eagles, "but we do not wish to leave you here all the same."

"Oh, you don't want to leave me here!" said Na'pe. "Very

well then, I *shall* stay here!" As they were passing an iceberg with icicles hanging down from the top of it, Na'pe reached out and seized an icicle in each hand and hung on to them. The eagles flew on without him.

The icicles began to melt in Na'pe's hands. "Come back, come back, Little Brothers," he called. "I will go home with you."

"Oh, no," said the eagles. "We told you if you let go of us we would not wait for you. So now we go home without you."

Oh, how Na'pe yelled. But the more he yelled, the farther away the eagles flew, and Na'pe was left hanging on to the icicles which grew smaller and smaller. The eagles went back to the south country.

Coyote saw the eagles flying south. "What have you done with my old brother Na'pe?" he called to them.

"Oh, we left him here or there, here or there!" said the eagles, laughing.

"You must go back and get him!" said Coyote.

"Oh, no," said the eagles. "We told him, and he did not listen. Now he can be sorry!"

"I've got a good mind, too, to leave him there," declared Coyote, "but I would miss my old brother Na'pe . . . I think." So he asked the geese to get Na'pe off the iceberg, but the geese had had a quarrel with Na'pe and they refused.

He asked the ducks to go, but the ducks said, "We are travelling another way, Brother Coyote," and they refused.

So he called the magpies. The magpies laughed and said, "It would be funny to see Old Man hanging on to an icicle. We will go just for that!", and away they flew. When they came to the place where Na'pe was, they began to laugh. They laughed so hard they could not pick Na'pe up. And the last bit of the icicle was melting.

As they flew by, Na'pe reached out and grasped a tail in each hand and hung on tight. The mami'as sika'miks flew away to the south country. But they still kept on laughing and this made Na'pe very angry. "If you don't stop laughing, you fools, I'll pull your tail-feathers out!" he said in a rage. The mami'as sika'miks laughed harder than ever.

While the magpies were laughing, their fluffy tails were stretching and getting thinner, and, after a while, Na'pe's hands slid right off the ends of their tails. That is why, even to this day the mami'as sika'mi has a long thin tail.

But there was Old Man lying flat on the ground. The eagles came back and flew over him a few times. At last they decided he was dead, and they came down and walked up and down his body. "Well, well," said the eagles. "Poor Old Man! Our old brother Na'pe is dead!"

"I think we should sing a mourning song for our old brother Na'pe," said one eagle.

"Indeed, yes," said the other eagle. "Certainly we will sing a song of grief for this dear friend of ours! But first I think we should eat him, lest some other hungry person should come along and we should have to invite him to share our meal."

"Yes," said the first eagle. "We will eat him and *then* we will mourn for him."

So the eagles began to eat Na'pe. They each took a large bite out of him.

"Oh," said one eagle, "he is so old and tough that I can hardly chew him!"

"Yes," said the other eagle, "and he tastes simply terrible, too!"

This made Na'pe very angry. He sat up and seized both eagles by the topknot of feathers on their heads.

"Now!" he said. "After this, the war-bonnets will be worn by us Indians!" He pulled all the feathers out of their heads, and the eagle-people have been bald ever since. The Indians have worn the war-bonnets.

"Enough is enough!" said Na'pe.

Ko-ishin-mit and Son of Eagle

George Clutesi

Ko-ishin-mit loved to copy and imitate other people —
especially the clever people. He would watch them doing their
tasks, then he would go home and imitate them, no matter how
hard it might be. He loved to go around visiting his neighbours
at meal-time, looking for free meals. He would walk for miles
for a feed. Oh, how Ko-ishin-mit loved to eat! Ko-ishin-mit
would eat anything put before him, he was so greedy.

One fine, lovely morning in the spring of the year Ko-ishin-
mit was sitting by the river. He watched the beautiful swallows
as they swooped and skimmed the surface of the water while
they picked up flies and insects. The swiftly-flying birds would
sometimes come so close over his head that he would fall
backwards as he followed their flight.

All of a sudden, and very near to where he sat, a salmon
broke the calm surface of the pool. It was a very large hissit,
sockeye salmon. Ko-ishin-mit was on his feet in an instant and
peering into the pool. To his great excitement he saw that there
was a school of salmon passing. They were swimming with ease
up the lazy river.

"Oh, how I wish I could have sockeye salmon for my
dinner," he drooled.

Ko-ishin-mit knew very well that he couldn't catch one. He
hopped along the bank following the school of salmon.

"How can I? I know. I know — I'll go and visit Son of
Eagle. Yes! I'll visit Son of Eagle. He always has fresh salmon
for dinner."

Son of Eagle lived very far away. His house was far, far
down the river. He lived at the mouth of the river but Ko-ishin-
mit did not mind that at all. Without waiting to see more
salmon, Ko-ishin-mit started down the river. He walked and
he walked. After a long, long time he sensed the smell of salt

in the air. He knew the Eagle's house was near the sea. At last he reached the place. There was the house. How hungry he was! He had walked far.

Near to the house was a tall, tall tree. Its topmost branch seemed to reach to the blue sky above. On this tall tree Son of Eagle loved to sit and watch for the salmon as they went upstream. The sly Ko-ishin-mit pretended to be passing by. He knew very well he would be invited in because he was so far from his own home. So he sauntered by the house humming a song just in case Son of Eagle should miss seeing him. He was very, very hungry by this time.

All of the people, he well knew, had been taught never to let anyone, whoever he might be, pass without inviting him in for a meal. Son of Eagle was said to be among the most generous in this way. Ko-ishin-mit sang louder than he really needed to. His voice was never sweet, at its best. Son of Eagle heard him from far off.

"Ho, Ko-ishin-mit! Where are you going so early in the day? Come in for a while and warm yourself by the fire," called the Eagle in a clear, strong voice. Son of Eagle was a big person and very handsome.

The greedy Raven came hopping in as fast as politeness permitted. "Choo, choo, choo. All right, all right," he said in his most cordial manner, "Choo, choo, choo."

"Sit down and warm yourself," said Son of Eagle, "while I go out and get us our breakfast." He put on his great wings and flew with the greatest of ease to the tall, tall tree.

Ko-ishin-mit watched out of the corners of his beady little black eyes. "I can fly too," he boasted under his breath.

Once on the top of the tall, tall tree Son of Eagle could see for a very great distance. Indeed, he had the sharpest eyes in all the land. He had such sharp eyes that he could spy the smallest fin of a salmon break the surface of the waters. A fat sockeye salmon dimpled the calm surface of the pool for a breath of air. He nosed up very slowly and most quietly. On his descent into the pool a tiny part of his small fin showed for a split second.

"Seek, seek, seek," sang Son of Eagle as he sailed down from his tall, tall tree and with his great talons he picked up the salmon, and in one graceful swoop he circled the wide area of the pool and sailed back to his house. All the while the beautiful, silvery salmon was wiggling helplessly in his strong talons.

Ko-ishin-mit watched and pretended not to be interested. "I can sail in the air too," he boasted to himself.

Mamma Eagle roasted the salmon over the hot, live coals she had already prepared for it. Mamma Eagle was very good at roasting salmon. It smelled so good Ko-ishin-mit dribbled and slobbered in his greed. The sweet aroma of roasting salmon wafted into his big nose. He shifted around with impatience and hunger. At last the salmon was cooked. Mamma Eagle set it on a huge wooden platter and placed it before Ko-ishin-mit.

"Slurrrp, slurrrp," the greedy Raven did not wait for his hosts to sit down with him. He gobbled and choked down the delicious, fresh roasted salmon. Ko-ishin-mit was greedy. He ate all the salmon himself. He ate so much that he fell asleep beside the open fire. The good Eagles let him sleep undisturbed.

Ko-ishin-mit awoke with a start. He roused himself and meekly murmured that he should be going home. He shook himself and the white dust of the fly-ash from the fire clouded off his coat. Thanking the Eagles he set out for his own home. If he was greedy, and sometimes ill-mannered, he was always thankful for his free meals.

Very early the next day, Ko-ishin-mit summoned his little wife.

"Pash-hook," he commanded in his most important but croaky voice, "I want you to go over to the Eagles' place of abode and say to them that I, Ko-ishin-mit, do invite them both to be my guests of honour at noon. Go now before you forget." He felt very important indeed.

Pash-hook knew well that they had no food in the house, but she went anyway without question. She always did what her husband asked of her cheerfully. She was always obedient to her husband.

It was Mamma Eagle who greeted her when she finally came to their home. "Pash-hook!" she exclaimed. "It is Pash-hook. Come in. Come in," she invited with delight. "Do tell me what you may be doing so far away from your home," she asked politely.

Pash-hook would not go in. Instead she looked over to where Son of Eagle was sitting and very solemnly announced in her tiny voice, "Ko-ishin-mit — invites you — Son of Eagle — and your mate — to be — his guests of honour — at noon — today." Little Pash-hook was so nervous that she almost sang her message in one breath.

Son of Eagle looked over to where his mate was before he answered, "We shall be honoured to be your husband's guests at noon today."

"Now Pash-hook do come in and have a little bite to eat before you start back for your home," Mamma Eagle's kindly voice persuaded. "You must wait for us and we shall accompany you," she added after she had looked over at her husband.

When they arrived at Ko-ishin-mit's little abode the other guests were arriving. Soon the small house was completely filled. Ko-ishin-mit was very gracious indeed. "To the end of the room. To the end of the room," he repeated as the Eagles entered. As the other guests arrived he bade them sit according to the the way they arrived. "Sit down while I go and catch a salmon," he said with gusto as he flitted and fumbled with his wings.

Ko-ishin-mit hopped and flitted, and finally away he flew.

Up to a tree he flew. He sat on a dead limb of a half-dead tree that stood beside his little house. He sat there — and sat — and nothing happened. He strained his weak, little beady eyes to espy a salmon. The glare from the noonday sun on the water hurt his eyes — and still nothing.

"I must get a salmon. I must get me a salmon," Ko-ishin-mit murmured desperately.

The noonday sun was hot. His poor eyes were tired. Ko-ishin-mit had a wonderful sense of smell, but his eyesight was very, very weak. While he perched on the dead limb many sockeye had passed by, but of course he had seen none of them.

Then, in the middle of the pool there was a ripple. It remained in the same spot. It grew bigger, and bigger still, until it was a strong disturbance in the otherwise placid pool. It made an especially big splash and Ko-ishin-mit finally saw it.

"Kootch, kootch, kootch." He plummeted like a stone. His wings were folded tightly to his sides. He hurled himself downwards, and then — Wham — his beak hit the disturbance in the middle of the pool.

Flap, flap, flap. Ko-ishin-mit was floating downstream. His wings were weakly flapping, flopping, slopping upon the surface. Flop, flop, flap.

"Ahhhhhhhhh," cried the womenfolk. "Ko-ishin-mit has done it again."

"Tu-shack? What has happened? He's floating down the river. Someone save him. Someone get him," cried the older men.

Strong Son of Eagle sailed out gracefully and picked up the unfortunate young Raven and carried him in his strong talons. Pash-hook put him to bed.

The tide in the river had receded during Ko-ishin-mit's watch and a big rock had pushed its hard nose above the surface of the water, and the increasing current had caused the disturbance that the weak-eyed Raven thought to be a big fat sockeye. Ko-ishin-mit had hit his nose so hard against the big rock that it swelled and swelled until it was a very big nose indeed.

The Eagles returned to their home without a meal.

The old men of the village chuckled. It is not good to copy other people.

In the spring of the year, when the swallows skim
Upon the surface of the river calm,
It is time for the Hissit to ascend
The rivers and streams, fed by the lake.
On the tall, tall tree, near the sea
Sits Tzith-wa-tin the eagle strong
To sing, Seek, Seek, Seek, as he sails with grace
To snatch in his talons strong a Hissit for his mate.

Author as Trickster

Spike Drew

Robert E. Gard

Spike Drew was a man to whom anything in the world could happen. Spike was going across country quite late at night. He was walking along when suddenly he heard a noise behind him. He looked back and saw several pairs of ferocious eyes. He knew they were the eyes of timber wolves, and he began to walk a little faster. The wolves kept right behind him. Spike tried all the old tricks of dropping his gloves, and other articles of apparel and food which he had with him. This didn't do any good, and the wolves began to close in on him. Finally Spike saw a lone tree standing away down ahead, and he made a break for it.

Just as he was shinnying up, one of the wolves made a leap for him and snapped the heel of his boot. For a time, however, Spike was safe. He climbed to the top of the tree while the wolves gathered around the trunk in a circle and looked up at him.

Spike sat and waited. So did the wolves. Finally some of the wolves began to get discouraged and drifted away. Eventually they all left except two. These two wolves just kept sitting, looking up at Spike. Soon these two sniffed noses a bit, then went away. Spike thought he was saved. He waited a suitable time then started to crawl down. He'd come about half way down when he saw a terrible sight. The two wolves who had waited so long were coming back, and to his horror Spike saw that they were carrying a live beaver between them! Alas, Spike knew he was lost!

A Fishing Story
Article from Crag and Canyon

I'll spin you a yarn. Yes, sir, it's the truth. Last summer I was rubbering down the Bow one day when all the sports were out, and the man I got on the end of a line was the biggest in the river. You just ought to have seen him. I've had plenty of luck, but this old fellow beat the record. I found him a little way up the river, not far from the creek, he was lurking there. My! but he was a gamey old rascal. I bet he weighed 300 pounds if he weighed an ounce.

I got a clear look at him when I started to play him and he was fully seven feet, with a beautiful red and purple color around the gills. And gamey? Say, he was something fierce!

As soon as I felt him strike I knew I had a tough proposition. For a time I thought he was going to have me in the air. But I held on and commenced to play with him in my best style. I knew I had him secure so he couldn't let go, and the only question was whether I could tire him out.

You can judge of his size when I tell you he hauled me clear round his boat twice, and I had to hold on tight or he would have got clean away.

Just as I began to feel that he was getting tired and I was beginning to think how fine he'd look in a photograph hanging up beside me, the line parted and I had to let him go. It was a shame, wasn't it? I'll never rely on those dinky little silk lines again. There'll be sport if ever I get him on the end of a line again. If any of you fellows think you've had fun with a fresh young guy, or one of those five-foot city dudes, wait till you see the man I nearly caught. I had him good and proper. And I'd have him up home now preserved in a frame and neatly varnished — if the bloomin' line hadn't broke.

Mice in the Beer
Norman Ward

One of the most thought-provoking spectacles to be seen in this country is that of a mouse in a beer bottle. The one I saw was in repose on his back, his hands all but clasped across his chest. His face was wreathed in smiles, and his ears were at a rakish angle. He was dead, but he had died happy.

Now these are days when anything that can be found out to the discredit of animals should be widely publicized, so as to make man seem a little better by comparison. Too much nonsense is written about the wisdom and industry of the lower creatures, and not enough about man's. As a result of the discovery of this sodden mouse, it can be reported with confidence that mice in Canada appear to be heavy drinkers.

The disclosure was made by a bottle-counter in a keg-and-bottle exchange to which I had assisted a friend to convey a few empties. On the way to the exchange we had noticed a peculiar odour hanging about, but we had taken it for granted as my friend has several children, all of them capable of fastening a dead cat under a car. The trained nose of the bottle-counter, however, quickly acquitted the children. "Mouse," he said tersely, expertly holding each empty up to the light as he counted it.

The man's assurance, and the fact that he was obviously accustomed to meeting mice, naturally led to interested investigation. It transpired that in addition to being an outstanding bottle-counter our man was also a well-informed mouse-finder with an inquiring mind.

Mice often crawl into empty beer bottles, he said, no doubt attracted by the malty smell. A mouse in a bottle, having lapped up the few remaining drops of liquid, commonly finds himself unable to negotiate the return journey to the outside world. A few drops for a mouse, our informant ventured to say, was roughly the equivalent of a pailful for an average-sized man.

This was not all our bottle-counter had to offer. His employment had given him a splendid opportunity to assess the drinking habits of mice over a vast area of the Canadian West, and it was clear to him that country mice are worse topers than their city cousins. Either the rural dwellers drink more heavily, he said, or the city ones are shrewder at knowing when to hit the road. Far more mice show up in shipments of bottles from scattered prairie oases than those brought in by urban people. My friend and I received the impression that we had acquired around the keg-and-bottle exchange a notoriety that would not soon leave us.

By a coincidence, that day's paper had carried a story about a speech made by one of the province's leading temperance advocates. Using one of those striking figures of speech that seem to fascinate the teetotal world, this citizen had allegedly asserted enough beer had been sold in our province during the past year to keep everybody over the age of fourteen drunk for three weeks. My friend had during the day made a number of unfriendly references to those who had got his share, but he was somehow cheered to think that it may have been the mice.

St. George
Nancy Senior

My dragon always loved walks
He used to go to the wall
where the golden chain hung
and take it in his mouth
laying his head on my lap
sideways, so the fire wouldn't burn my skirt

He looked so funny that way
with his legs dragging the floor
and his rear end high up
because he couldn't bend his hind legs
He was so well trained
always keeping his claws retracted
when he walked on the rug

With him on the leash, I could go anywhere
No band of robbers dared attack

This morning in the woods
we had stopped for a drink
where a spring gushes out of a cave

when suddenly, a man in armour
riding a white horse
leapt out of the bushes
crying "Have no fear, Maiden
I will save you"

And before I could say a word
he had stabbed my dragon in the throat
and leaping down from the horse
cut off his head
and held it up for me to see
the poor dead eyes still surprised

and mine filling with tears
He hadn't even had time to put out his claws

And the man said
"Don't cry, Maiden
You are safe now
But let me give you some good advice
Don't ever walk alone in the woods
for the next time you meet a dragon
there might not be a knight around to save you"

The Dinosaur
Bert Leston Taylor

Behold the mighty dinosaur,
Famous in prehistoric lore
Not only for his weight and length
But for his intellectual strength.
You will observe by these remains
The creature had two sets of brains —
One on his head (the usual place),
The other at his spinal base.
Thus he could reason *a priori*
As well as *a posteriori*.
No problem bothered him a bit:
He made both head and tail of it.
So wise he was, so wise and solemn
Each thought filled just a spinal column.
If one brain found the pressure strong
It passed a few ideas along;
If something slipped his forward mind
'Twas rescued by the one behind.
And if in error he was caught
He had a saving afterthought.

As he thought twice before he spoke
He had no judgements to revoke;
For he could think without congestion,
Upon both sides of every question.

The Chair
T. W. Gee

One fogbound, hoar-frosted evening last winter, I was sitting
in my den before a cosy fire reading from a book of short stories
when I happened upon a particular story that at first struck a
familiar note, then a chord of uneasiness, and finally an entire
symphony of spine-chilling sensations. It is only now, almost
a year later, that I can bring myself to set down what I learned
that evening, which explains so much of my past, and that of
my ancestors.

The story, written by Charles Dickens, was entitled *The
Bagman's Story*. In it was a passage describing a chair:

> . . . a strange, grim-looking, high-backed chair, carved
> in the most fantastic manner, with a flowered damask
> cushion, and the round knobs at the bottom of the legs
> carefully tied up in red cloth, as if it had got the gout
> in its toes. . . . There was something about this
> particular chair, so odd and so unlike any other piece
> of furniture. . . . The carving of the back gradually
> assumed the lineaments and expression of a shrivelled
> human face; the damask cushion became an antique,
> flapped waistcoat; the round knobs grew into a couple
> of feet, encased in red cloth slippers; and the old chair
> looked like a very ugly old man, of the previous century,
> with his arms akimbo.

You can imagine my shock and wonderment that night
when I realized, as I read on, that the supposed fictitious

description I was reading, and the setting into which that description was being placed, exactly matched our antique chair and its history. There, on the opposite side of the fireplace, its wooden parts gleaming with the high polish my wife had given them, rested the family heirloom, the "special guest" seat for "special-chair guests" only. Why, just the other night, our bank's director, Mr. McJarvis, sat in that chair listening enthusiastically to my plans for the merger of shipping interests in the Pacific, a merger of such magnitude that after five year's negotiations it is only now nearing fruition. But I must begin at the beginning if you are to know, as I now do, how it has come to pass that my name, and that of my family, is one whispered in awe, if it is mentioned at all, by the greatest financial wizards of the present century.

My great-great-grandfather, so the family story goes, was in his youth, before he shipped to the new world, an apprentice baker in a small, dreary hamlet very near Bristol. He received little money for his labours, and that, with the exception of a few pennies, he turned over to his ancient mother, who, when she'd finished hawking the bakeshop's produce, purchased what little food and mean lodgings their day's labours might provide. So you see, my family has always been connected with the bakery business; even the forebears of these wretched two had been in the business in one capacity or another for as far back as can be traced.

Now it chanced one Sabbath that, near the village, there was to be an auction of furniture from an old inn prior to its being razed. My great-great-grandfather, so the story goes, attended this auction seeking youthful diversion, and there he frivously bought for a few pennies a high-backed, damask-cushioned old chair in which he envisaged no doubt his tired old mother resting her weary bones at the day's end. It never came to that — it's reported she hated the thing on sight and refused ever to sit in it — and the chair collected flour dust and the droppings of rodents for some time at the back of the bake shop.

About a year later, however, a prospective buyer, set on expanding his holdings beyond the city's taxation limits, dropped into the shop to offer my great-great-grandfather's employer both a handsome price for his bakery and a managerial position over several bakeries which had been purchased in surrounding hamlets. As betokened his position, this buyer was offered the best chair, dusted of course, which was the only chair, in fact, in the shop, and that the chair whereof I write. On this occasion, great-great-grandfather was made an offer, unheard of in its generosity to a lowly apprentice, that of managing the bakeshop itself. He accepted, of course, and remained in the position fully ten years, by which time he had come, at the age of twenty-four, to be a man of some means in the village, married to the handsomest woman for miles around, albeit somewhat older than himself, and, despite his own colossal ugliness, a continuing familial nemesis to this day, father of two lovely daughters.

It was at his wife's insistence, so I have been given to understand, that great-great-grandfather finally decided to sell all and move to the new world. Opportunities and wealth were greater there, his wife insisted. And so, with a few sticks of furniture, including the chair in which she had grown especially fond of sitting of an evening, she suffered great-great-grandfather and the girls a most trying journey by water, by rail, and finally by ox cart to a settlement of tents and mud huts along the South Saskatchewan River.

Winter was fast approaching when they arrived; miles and miles of prairie wool cropped short by the last ranging herds of buffalo was all they had to feed their livestock, most of which soon died on this meager fare. To survive, great-great-grandfather set up his oven under a tarp and used his precious flour to bake loaves to sell to the Metis, the fur traders, the

Northwest Mounted Police, the whiskey traders, the Indians, the homesteaders, and any others who, when they were sober enough to bethink themselves of food, soon came to think first of great-great-grandfather's loaves. As the flour ran low, he bought the coarse-ground species of the Metis, regrinding it and sifting it as best he could. And so they survived that first year.

As years passed, and settlers continued to arrive, great-grandfather, a native son newly come to manhood, alternated between growing grain in summer, purchasing more land as he could to add to his father's original homestead, and baking bread in his own bakeshop in winter. The time came when he had built to his specifications a mill to grind his grain, and later elevators to store his grain, and finally a spur line from the new, transcontinental railway to ship his grain. When grandfather took over the family business at great-grandfather's death, the family name was already known to many businesses "back east". In fact, our family home had been graced by some of the more adventurous who had come to talk business, to sit in the guest chair and smoke large cigars and drink good sherry, and to return east duly impressed.

To great-grandfather's holdings, grandfather added section upon section of rich grain land, mills to east and west, rail cars and railway stocks, bakeries back east, and a vast company of employees to look after it all. My earliest memories of grandfather are intermingled with the smells of leather upholstery, of dust from the cool, dark red rugs, and of cigar scent from the damask cushions of the guest chair as I sat, in my velveteen Little Lord Fauntleroy suits, on the knee of some visitor's expensively tailored trousers. In those days, grandfather allowed me to remain, interrupting business discussions with questions of childish curiosity, at meetings from which even father was excluded.

My father still says he is in the bakery business, and maybe he is, but certainly I have never had any dealings with bakers.

He's a family throwback, I guess, spending most of his time "in the field". Meanwhile, I spend my days in the family business complex in downtown Calgary, discussing oil companies, steamship lines, South American cattle ranches, ores, textiles, entertainments, mergers, liquidations, politics, all the many facets of the family empire for which I was trained and educated since conception. Grandfather, may he rest in peace, saw to that, though I was unaware of it at the time.

But, on that awe-filled night last winter, all was at last made clear. The merger will be a success, and our business empire will, at last, be complete. That shipping interest was the last cog in the wheel. I couldn't understand how McJarvis had swung it. Lloyd's representative, old Stavely, was having nothing to do with it, and without his okay we were stymied. And no amount of sherry or Havana smoke seemed to influence him whatsoever. No, it wasn't until McJarvis brought him to the house and gave up his seat in the den, insisting Stavely would prefer it, that the tide began to turn.

It was the chair that did it. Dicken's chair! It's been the chair all along.

Munchausen in Alberta
Elizabeth Brewster

Our first winter in the settlement,
the old man said,
January was so cold
the flames in the lamps froze.
The womenfolk picked them like strawberries
and gave them to the children to eat.

That's the only time
I was ever a fire-eater.

"This May Hurt a Little"

Eric Nicol

I suppose some people actually do brush their teeth twice a day and see their dentist at least twice a year, but I don't. I brush my teeth once a day, with a brush whose few remaining bristles look hail-struck, and I never see my dentist until it's too late.

For some time, for instance, I have been bothered by pink toothbrush, sometimes right up to the wrist. At first I cleverly avoided the warning by using a pink toothpaste, but as the washbasin and nearby wall continued to look as though they had been the scene of an axe murder, I realized that I would either have to see my dentist or have the bathroom done over in a shade to match my blood (a sort of greenish cinnamon, the family didn't care for it).

Besides, while prowling around my mouth in search of scraps, the tip of my tongue had discovered several interesting cavities in my teeth, and often worried me by disappearing completely into a particularly spacious Carlsbad cavern at the rear. I had the impression it was storing food there for the winter. Clearly it was time to see my dentist, much as I would have preferred to see a charging rhinoceros. So I dropped in to Dr. Burcher's office one day and asked the nurse if I could make an appointment. Needless to say, I was reasonably certain that I couldn't. Dentists are terribly busy these days. You have to wait months. Maybe years.

Quietly whistling a gay tune and examining my fingernails, I waited while the nurse consulted her appointment book. She looked up brightly.

"You're lucky," she said. "Mr. Pockle has cancelled his appointment for tomorrow morning. The doctor can take you at nine-thirty."

For a moment I stared at her uncomprendingly, like Bette Davis when her lover tells her he's decided to go back to stamp collecting. Trapped. Tricked by somebody named Pockle. My spine quivered like a hurled javelin.

"Why can't Pockle make it?" I asked hoarsely.

"Why, I believe he said his wife was having a baby."

I hooted, two longs and a short.

"And you believed a trumped-up story like that?" I asked, perspiring freely. "You're going to let him weasel out of his appointment with a fairy tale like that?"

"I don't think there's any reason to doubt him," smiled the nurse, writing my name in the Doomsday book.

A wave of hatred for Mr. Pockle swept over me. With all my heart I hoped the new Pockle would be born with two heads and four sets of wisdom teeth.

Yet I couldn't help admiring the cunning of the man, and the superb timing which his alibi indicated. Pockle had me beaten, that was sure.

"All right," I said. "I'll be here."

As I was leaving I was shaken to note that Dr. Burcher's office had two doors, one for incoming patients, one for outgoing. These were shrewdly arranged so that persons waiting for their turn didn't see their predecessor leaving. He could drag himself sobbing downstairs, his face a bloody pulp, and they'd never be any the wiser. They couldn't even be sure that he ever left at all. For all they knew he may have been sitting in the Chair one minute and going straight through the roof the next, like a Nazi V-2 rocket.

At nine-thirty I sit down on the edge of one of the sumptous waiting room chairs and open a copy of the *Saturday Evening Post*. The first page shows a picture of a little girl looking as if she's just discovered a wasp in her drawers. "Mommy, didn't your teacher know anything?" the kid is asking. It seems the brat has found out that her old lady hasn't been massaging her gums with Ipana, and is raising a stink about it. I throw aside the *Post* and walk around the room a little. After a while the nurse comes in, her face wreathed in smiles. My face is just wreathed.

"We've been finishing up Johnny Adams," she beams. "He's only five years old and had three bad fillings. Didn't bother him a bit. Good as gold."

Next to Mr. Pockle, I decide, I hate Johnny Adams best. The normal, healthy reaction of an infant upon having its teeth filled would be to scream and holler. But not Johnny Adams. Johnny puts on a cheap hero act that I, only twenty-six years old, have to follow. I have to be as good as gold. Right now I feel as good as a chunk of cold porridge, getting colder every second.

The nurse leads me to the Chair, keeping up a chatter intended to distract the patient. Avoiding looking into the marble spit-basin to my immediate left, I ease into the Chair. My teeth seem to be chattering slightly. Fine, go ahead, fellows, it may be your last chance.

Dr. Burcher comes in while Nurse is bibbing me for the slaughter. We engage in gay banter, just as if I hadn't any idea he was going to crawl into my mouth and dynamite the old roots. Jittery, I open my mouth too soon and too wide. I shut it again while Dr. Burcher messes around in a drawer that clinks ominously. I don't know what he's after, but I'll bet it's the biggest of its kind.

Now he peers into my mouth with the little mirror. Poking around with a sharp instrument, he sees something he likes. He tries to drag it out. It puts up a battle, it likes it in there. Dr. Burcher plays it for a while, then throws a gaff into it. Something breaks off and I study his face carefully for confirmation that it is my jawbone.

"Quite a lot of tartar on your teeth," he says, and squelches my rebuttal by syringing water into my mouth. I spit, none too successfully, into the marble basin, and wipe off my chin for Round Two.

"I think I'll take a picture of those," he says, manipulating a fantastic machine which rears over me from the left. So, he's going to take a picture. For his file of Horrible Examples, no doubt.

Dr. Burcher wheels the machine over so that its snout is pointing into the side of my head.

"That's not my best side," I mumble, but already he's stuffing a negative into my mouth.

"Clench it between your teeth," he says, " and keep your tongue down."

My tongue doesn't want to keep down. Every instinct tells it to push the negative out of my mouth before it's too late, before the X-ray has a chance to record the fact that my gums are coming away from my face, or that my molars are all hollow and occupied by tiny animals.

But the camera buzzes briefly and Dr. Burcher has his pinkies in my mouth again, fishing for the negative. Now's the time to bite his fingers off. Nope, lost my nerve.

"I think I'd better fill that one at the back before it goes any further," says Dr. Burcher.

To back up this statement he throws a pick into the young cave behind the last molar on the lower left side. I wonder what Pockle is doing now. Cooing over his young, probably, the yellow rat.

Here comes the local.

"This may hurt a little," says Dr. Burcher.

I know what that means. Dentists give you that "may hurt a little" routine just to make you feel foolish when you jump onto the ceiling.

Dr. Burcher eases the hypo into the gum in easy stages, about half as easy and twice as many stages as I'd prefer. Hey. When's he going to stop? A little farther and he'll blunt that thing on my back collar button. Ah, now he's easing it out again, evidently with several nerves coiled around it.

Pretty soon my mouth is frozen and Dr. Burcher is digging his thumb into my chin, asking if I can feel it. I say, yes, I can feel it, so he starts anyway.

Here comes the drill, that evil, skinny, twisted steel arm. My tongue huddles in one corner of my mouth and a light dew springs out of my forehead. This is it, men. . . .

Half an hour later Dr. Burcher has been excavating with everything but a steam shovel. But the worst is over, he says, stuffing wads of cotton into my mouth. These wads soak up the blood so that you can quietly bleed to death without realizing it.

Setting the nurse to mixing cement — apparently enough to lay a small sidewalk — he fits a clamp over the molar and under the gum, and screws it tight. If he hadn't assured me that the worst is over, I'd swear this was it. Now he's jamming in the cement, tamping it down, scratching his initials on it.

"There," he says finally, "that should do it."

He holds up a mirror and I have a brief, horrifying glimpse of the inside of my mouth. What a ghastly thing to have handling my food!

But as I surge out of the Chair I feel the special satisfaction that comes only with a tooth well filled and a face still too frozen to feel it. I leave by the special exit, head high, a worthy successor to Johnny Adams. I could even forgive Old Man Pockle. In fact, I haven't a thing to worry about until a week from Wednesday, when I go back to have two more filled. A week to live!

The Drover's Tale of the Flying Bull

Watson Kirkconnell

Prologue

Caught by the blizzard, as it fell,
In that old Manitou hotel,
We sat and smoked around the fire,
Watching the birch-wood flames leap higher,
And told tall yarns to while away
The dull, interminable day.
We were a miscellaneous lot
Who thronged that parlour, wide and warm,
And deemed the place a pleasant spot
On such a stressful day of storm,
When all the roads were drifted high
And even trains had ceased to ply.
We were a dozen at the least:
A cattle drover, and a priest,
Two farmers, a country teacher,
A Lutheran Icelandic preacher,
The driver of the Grey Goose bus
(Whose stoppage caused uncommon fuss),
Two Mounties (both extremely tall,
A Sergeant and a Corporal),
A wholesale "drummer", pale and wan,
And I, a bashful college don.
Still others drifted in and out
From the small village round about,
For work that day was standing still
And they, like us, had time to kill.
There was a merchant, sleek and fat,
Likewise a lawyer, thin and seedy,
A doctor with a red cravat,

A clerk whose voice was high and reedy;
A butcher reared on brewers' nectar,
And a lean, wrinkled school-inspector,
While keeping all our talk in motion
With breezy jest and fertile notion
Was the hotel-man, Michael Casey,
A big, stout fellow, free and racy,
Whose native Irish *savoir faire*
Had freshened in our Western air
Into a bluff and hearty way
That made his guests delight to stay.
    He and the drover had been cronies
For many a year in Winnipeg;
Together they had played the ponies;
Each loved to pull the other's leg;
And each in his own virile fashion
Could tell a tale of manly passion.
So, as with breakfast done we sat
About the fire in quiet chat,
He hailed the drover with conviction
And tried to stir him up to fiction:
"Patrick," he said, "you're much the least
Of all men living given to lying.
Tell us the truth about yon beast,
The Angus bull that took to flying!"
    The drover dusted off his vest,
And spat, and gave his pipe a pull,
And then began with quiet zest.
His story of the Angus bull:

The Drover's Tale

"The toughest bull I ever saw
 Was on a farm near Neepawa,
 Where an old cowhand, Dave MacMeans,

Kept a big herd of Aberdeens.
Dave was a rough and wrinkled Scot,
With bulbous nose and sunset whiskers;
He liked his whiskey neat and hot —
When young he'd frisked among the friskers.
And sixty years had left him cursed
With stomach ulcers and a thirst.
Two things he'd loved in life's long battle:
Theology and Angus cattle.
And while the Calvinist in him
Waxed fervent on predestination,
He'd argue long with equal vim
That black bulls were the farm's salvation.
    The pride of his own dusky herd
Was "Mumbo-Jumbo," bull supreme —
The biggest, grimmest, blackest-furred
Of all the brutes of Pharaoh's dream.
He was as black as Satan's dam,
And nigh as tall as Pilot Mound;
The rumblings of his diaphragm
Made thunder thirty miles around;
His ribs were like a Roman arch;
His back was level as the prairie;
His massive legs in stately march
Made a small earthquake through the dairy;
But of his eyes no words can tell —
Within them glowed the fires of hell,
Two lamps of livid yellow, lit
With anger from the nether Pit,
His cows had always found him kind,
But hatred smouldered in his mind
For all our human jacks and queens
Except his master, Dave MacMeans.
Yes, Dave he loved, beyond a doubt,
For the old sanctimonious sinner

Would often give his mammoth snout
A snort of whiskey after dinner;
And so a spirituous bond
Kept beast and man uncommon fond.

II

Now in the spring of '35
David was gathered to his fathers.
On Sunday he had been alive;
On Monday, fierce internal pothers
Brought on that final, fatal quiver
That ends cirrhosis of the liver;
And so by Wednesday night he lay
Dead sober in the graveyard clay.
  Then distant heirs and lawyers, dark as
The vultures at Gehenna's gate,
Came flocking in to share the carcass
of Dave's unfortunate estate.
Farming they held in cold derision;
So, to facilitate division
And settle up with one clean slash,
They auctioned everything for cash.
One August morning, hot and clear,
A leather-larynx'd auctioneer
Stood in Dave's farm-yard on a table,
Half-way between the house and stable;
And there, amid the throng of buyers,
He bawled the merits of each chattel,
From combines down to common pliers,
And last, not least, Dave's Angus cattle.
The cows and calves were sold with ease
In tempting lots of twos and threes.
('Twas known to every farmer there
How often, at the Winter Fair,

Dave's feeders carried off the Cup,
And with what golden-handed itch
The abattoirs had snapped them up
To grace the banquets of the rich.)
But offers were not plentiful
For Dave's notorious black bull,
Whose most unmitigated choler
Was reckoned dear at half a dollar.
In vain the auctioneer avowed
That any farmer might be proud
To own so vast a thoroughbred,
Most famous in his progeny —
For looking in his eye with dread
Each thought he'd let the monster be.
Just when it seemed the day would end
Without a bid for the old devil,
One quiet voice agreed to spend
A hundred dollars, on the level.
And thus was sold the brute unruly
To Deacon Williams of Plum Coulee,
A man as good as he was strong
And pious as the day is long.
But when at last each buyer sought
To drive away what he had bought,
A streak of dark satanic strife
In Mumbo-Jumbo came to life.
Perchance he blamed on all these men
The loss of his beloved master.
Perhaps there came into his ken
Some dim foreboding of disaster,
Or some distaste for dreary travel
By prairie trail or highway gravel,
Far from familiar scenes to stay,
Southeast, a hundred miles away.
Whatever maggot in the brain

Stirred him to frenzies of disdain,
He pawed the ground, he snorted fire,
And one could see him in his ire
Fiercely and visibly determine
To rid the farm of human vermin.
Straight at the human throng he charged,
Straight at these puny things of shame;
And frantic lanes of fear enlarged
To leave him passage as he came.
Over the fences did they leap
Grasshopper-like by tens and scores;
Shunning the bull's destructive sweep,
Awed by the bull's appalling roars.
Against such cars as had been left
Within the yard he turned his spite,
Venting on them his two-ton heft,
A thunderbolt of Hate and Night.
A dozen Fords were overturned;
He tore the fenders off ten Nashes;
Sparks from his onset lit and burned
A score of Pontiacs to ashes.
When nightfall closed the day's wild session,
It found the bull in full possession.
   But hours later, far from thence,
Good Deacon Williams, sad but trusting,
Invoked the aid of Providence
To give the Devil's bull a dusting:
'Humble his spirit to the earth!
Give me my hundred dollars worth!'
Then with an 'Amen' loud and deep,
In simple faith he turned to sleep.

III

After a night of breathless heat,
There dawned the hottest day that any

Had ever known. Rays seemed to beat
As from a vaster sun; and many
Thought of that final Day of Ire
When all should be destroyed by fire.
The leaves and grasses quickly wilted;
Cracks opened in the baking soil;
On homes that slowly warped and tilted,
The blistering paint began to boil.
Men took to drinking by the keg;
Dumb beasts cried out with moan and mutter;
And thirst-crazed dogs in Winnipeg
Drank melted asphalt from the gutter.
Small wonder was it no one went
On such a day to Dave's old farm
To see the bull's dark discontent
Or seek his frenzy to disarm.
Parched but triumphant, hour by hour,
He stood there in insensate power.
Alone, unchallenged, black as ink,
He scorned to bellow for a drink.
   Two hours past the gasping noon,
A dark cloud rose to west-northwest —
Slowly above a world a-swoon
It reared with thunder in its breast,
A roaring, swirling, cloudy funnel,
Black as the entrails of a tunnel.
But though the 'twister' nearer swept,
The Angus bull remained defiant;
Dauntless he stood to intercept
The black, intruding, cloudy Giant.
But all in vain: its mighty force,
Seizing him swiftly from the ground,
Propelled him on a skyward course —
A heavenly bull, southeastward-bound.
And with him went the shattered hulk
Of Dave's best barn, and sped from sight

Revolving round his darker bulk
Like some infernal satellite.

IV

An hour later by the clock,
The storm near Deacon Williams' passed,
So close to all his barns and stock
That the good brother stared aghast,
Then 'mid the tumult of the storm
He saw a black, Satanic form
Swoop down, as though on hidden wings,
And light upon the prairie clay,
While with diminished thunderings
The great tornado ebbed away.
   Not fifty yards from Williams' door
There lay a miry open slough.
From it now came a mighty roar.
Out rushed the Deacon, swift to view;
And there, by heck, stood Mumbo-Jumbo,
Up to his belly in the gumbo,
By 'act of God' delivered duly
To his new owner in Plum Coulee.
   What thoughts had thronged his heavy mind
During that epoch-making flight
No one can tell; but I'm inclined
To think he got a thorough fright.
For all the rest of his black life
He was most mild — most timid, maybe —
And often Deacon Williams' wife
Would leave that bull to mind the baby."

Man & the Elements

Kathleen

Robert W. Service

It was the steamer *Alice May* that sailed the Yukon foam,
And touched at every river camp from Dawson down to Nome.
It was her builder, owner, pilot, Captain Silas Geer,
Who took her through the angry ice, the last boat of the year;
Who patched her cracks with gunny sacks and wound her pipes
    with wire,
And cut the spruce upon the banks to feed her boiler fire;
Who headed her into the stream and bucked its mighty flow,
And nosed her up the little creeks where no one else would go;
Who bragged she had so small a draft, if dew was on the grass,
With gallant heart and half a start his little boat would pass.
Aye, ships might come and ships might go, but steady every
    year
The *Alice May* would chug away with Skipper Silas Geer.

Now though Cap Geer had ne'er a fear the devil he could bilk,
He owned a gastric ulcer and his grub was mostly milk.
He also owned a Jersey cow to furnish him the same,
So soft and sleek and mild and meek, and Kathleen was her
    name.
And as his source of nourishment he got to love her so
That everywhere the Captain went the cow would also go;

And though his sleeping quarters were ridiculously small,
He roped a section of them off to make Kathleen a stall.
So every morn she'd wake him up with mellifluous moo,
And he would pat her on the nose and go to wake the crew.
Then when he'd done his daily run and hitched on to the bank,
She'd breathe above his pillow till to soothing sleep he sank.
So up and down the river seeded sourdoughs would allow,
They made a touching tableau, Captain Silas and his cow.

Now as the Captain puffed his pipe and Kathleen chewed her
    cud,
There came to him a poetess, a Miss Belinda Budd.
"An epic I would write," said she, "About this mighty stream,
And from your gallant bark 'twould be romantic as a dream."
Somewhat amazed the Captain gazed at her and shook his
    head:
"I'm sorry, Miss, but we don't take *she* passengers," he said.
"My boat's a freighter, we have no accommodation space
For women-folk — my cabin is the only private place.
It's eight foot small from wall to wall, and I have anyhow,
No room to spare, for half I share with Kathleen, that's my
    cow."
The lady sighed, then soft replied: "I love your Yukon scene,
And for its sake your room I'll take, and put up with
    Kathleen."

Well, she was so dead set to go the Captain said: "By heck!
I like your spunk; you take my bunk and I'll camp on the deck."
So days went by then with a sigh she sought him out anew:
"Oh, Captain Geer, Kathleen's a dear, but does she *have* to
    moo?
In early morn like motor horn she bellows overhead,
While all the night without respite she snorts above my bed.
I know it's true she dotes on you, your smile she seems to miss;
She leans so near I live in fear my brow she'll try to kiss.

Her fond regard makes it *so* hard my Pegasus to spur. . . .
Oh, please be kind and try to find another place for her."

Bereft of cheer was Captain Geer; his face was glazed with
   gloom:
He scratched his head: "There ain't," he said, "another inch
   of room.
With freight we're packed; it's stowed and stacked — why even
   on the deck.
There's seven salted sourdoughs and they're sleeping neck and
   neck.
I'm sorry, Miss, that Kathleen's kiss has put your muse to
   flight;
I realize her amber eyes abstract you when you write.
I used to love them orbs above a-shining down on me,
And when she'd chew my whiskers you can't calculate my glee.
I ain't at all poetical, but gosh! I guess your plight,
So I will try to plan what I can fix up for to-night."

Thus while upon her berth the wan and weary Author Budd
Bewailed her fate, Kathleen sedate above her chewed her cud;
And as he sought with brain distraught a steady course to steer,
Yet find a plan, a worried man was Captain Silas Geer.
Then suddenly alert was he, he hollered to his mate:
"Hi, Patsy, press our poetess to climb on deck and wait.
Hip-hip-hooray! Bid her be gay and never more despair
My search is crowned — by heck! I've found an answer to her
   prayer."

To Patsy's yell like glad gazelle come bounding Bardess Budd;
No more forlorn, with hope new-born she faced the foaming
   flood;
While down the stair with eager air was seen to disappear,
Like one inspired (by genius fired) exultant Captain Geer.
Then up he came with eye aflame and honest face aglow,
And oh, how loud he laughed, as proud he led her down below.

"Now you may write by day or night upon our Yukon scene,
For I," he cried, "have clarified the problem of Kathleen.
I thought a lot, then like a shot the remedy I found:
I jest unhitched her rope and switched the loving creature
    round.
No more her moo will trouble you, you'll sleep right restful
    now.
Look, Lady, look! — I'm giving you . . . *the tail end of the
    cow."*

Children of the Moon
Ella Elizabeth Clark

Many years ago, a chief who lived along the Pacific Ocean was
one day walking on the beach. He was on his way to a forest,
to look for a suitable tree to make a canoe. On the shore he saw
a small round log that seemed to have been washed up by the
waves. It was quite smooth, without any bark, and one end was
bigger than the other. Around the middle was something black
and hard. As he examined the log, he found that the hard piece
was loose and could be easily taken off.

When it lay in his hand, he thought, "I believe I can cut
with that."

So he hammered it with a large stone, broke it, and
flattened it into a straight piece. When he tried to cut with it,
he found that it would go entirely through a piece of wood. He
was delighted. He could use it in making his canoe. With a
leather thong he fastened a wooden handle to it and so made
a good knife.

"This is my secret power," he said to himself. "I will tell
no one that I have this power."

He found a good cedar tree, felled it, and began to build
his canoe. Inside and outside, he made it so smooth with his
new knife that his friends wanted to know how he was making

it. The man only laughed and replied, "My spirit has given me great power."

"Let us see the sign of your power," his friends asked.

But the man refused, and he would not work while they were watching him. So after a while they left him alone.

One day when the man was out hunting, he lost his power. He searched and searched but could not find it. He would not ask his friends to help him, for he was afraid they might find it and keep it. Grieving, he lost interest in everything. He could not eat and he could not sleep. At last he decided he did not want to live longer, and so he climbed the mountain behind the village, planning to die on its summit.

When he reached the top, he turned round to take one last look at the ocean. He saw the moon rising in the distant sky. On the moonpath, a few minutes later, he saw a beautiful big canoe, bigger than he had ever seen. It had large white wings, like a giant sea-gull flying.

"The moon's canoe!" the man exclaimed. "The children of the moon must be coming down to the earth. Something unusual is going to happen. Will all of us die, or are our enemies coming to attack us?"

As he watched, marvelling and wondering, the big canoe slowly moved out of sight. And the man forgot that he had climbed the mountain in order to die there, alone. He hurried down the mountainside, jumping from rock to rock. Breathless, he rushed into the village. "I have seen the canoe of the moon!" he shouted.

People laughed at his message. They laughed at the story he told them. "You have been dreaming," they said. "Some spirit has been deceiving you."

But the very next morning, when they awoke, they saw in their own bay the beautiful big canoe the man had described to them.

"Now you know that I told you the truth," he said. "Come. Let us visit the moon's children in the canoe."

But the people were afraid.

"Let us call a meeting of the council," they cautioned. "Our wise men should decide what we should do."

The council talked and talked. At last they decided to select twelve men, clean in body and in heart, who should go to visit the moon's children. So they made ready one of their large war canoes, and the twelve young men stepped in. As the boat pushed off, the man who had first seen the moon's canoe jumped in. So great was his curiosity he could not wait for a report from the others.

The young men paddled round the giant canoe, finding it longer and higher than they had realized.

"How can we get on it?" they asked each other.

Then they saw that long pieces of something like cedar-bark rope were dropped down the sides of the big canoe. Above, hands were motioning them to take hold of the ropes and climb up. The men did so. And when they were inside the boat, the chief of the children of the moon came to greet them. His face was white, his eyes were blue like the summer sky, his hair was like grass when it is yellow.

He looked friendly and made signs to them not to be afraid. When the Indians obeyed his motion to sit down, the children of the moon placed in their hands some bright, shining dishes. In each were bones and blood. With signs, the men were told to eat from the dishes.

The Indians shook their heads and talked among themselves. How could they eat blood and bones? But one of the moon's children took a piece of bone, dipped it into the blood, put it into his mouth and ate it. Then one of the Indians, more daring than the others, followed his example. He smiled and licked his lips.

"Good! Good!" he said to his companions. "Eat it!"

So they all fell to and ate with relish. They had never tasted anything like that food.

When they had finished eating, the moon's people passed

their fingers over the Indians' clothes, which were made of sea-otter furs. They seemed to like the feel of the fur so much that one of the young men suggested to the others, "Let us make them a present of our clothes."

So all of the Indians took off their fur garments and laid them down in front of the strange white men. With signs they indicated that the furs were gifts for the moon's children.

Seeing a flock of ducks flying overhead, one of the white men took a long stick and pointed it at the birds. Something made a terrific noise. The Indians were startled by the sound, and when they saw smoke pouring out of the long stick, they fell on their faces in terror. Then they heard a thud on the floor of the boat — a dead duck had fallen near them!

In wonderment, the Indians asked to see the fire-stick. Then they asked to have it. With signs the white men agreed to trade the fire-stick for furs.

Some of the Indians then went down the ropes to their own canoe, paddled back to shore, and told their people of the strange things they had seen. Back they came to the giant canoe, loaded with bundles of sea-otter skins. These they laid down by the fire-stick, which they used as a measure.

Taking the furs, the white men gave them the fire-stick and showed them how to use it.

"Now we have something better than bow and arrows," they said among themselves. "Now we can kill all the bears we want."

The chief of the white men gave them the shining dishes, saying, "You may take these to your people." The Indian chief hung them up in his lodge, where they shone brightly, just like the moon. Over and over again, the twelve young men told the story of their visit to the wonderful canoe, where they saw the wonderful children of the moon.

That was the first time any of them had seen white men or tin dishes, the first time they had handled a gun or tasted molasses and biscuits.

The Search for the Unmapped Lake
Mary T. S. Schaffer

The route over Nigel Pass and down the Brazeau River to
"Teepee Camp", near the mouth of Brazeau Lake, was like
returning to our own again. The old bunch of horses of 1907
seemed to have communicated to the new ones the fact that
there was great feed at the latter place, and the moment the
river was crossed there was great hustling along. As we pointed
out this small corner of real estate to the Botanist, he agreed
that in spite of the cold rain, — it was the most ideal camp-
ground he had ever seen, and also that the adjacent hills
had better be inspected the following day for plant specimens.

They made an interesting climb, though scarce covering
3000 feet, and we found the steep hill-slopes a perfect mass of
flowers, with game-trails running in every direction. So fresh
were some of the signs that we concluded the exodus of the
game had taken place only upon the arrival of our large party
in the valley below. Just before reaching the summit we passed
over a carpet of the bluest of blue forget-me-nots and flush
pink daisies. In some places they lay freshly broken and
crushed to the ground, and I could not help wondering a little
if it had been given these children of the hills to feel some of
this great beauty about them. Alas, I suppose the green grass
was all they asked, and to a mother sheep her child would look
no fairer for sleeping in a bed of blue and white blossoms on
the hill-tops. But they had vanished as the frost from the grass,
or the sun behind the clouds; our coming had breathed terror
in their hearts.

On the heights we got a fine view of Brazeau Lake, and
decided that a gap in the hills west of the lake was probably
the pass through which we were to make our way to the lake
of which we were in search — the Pobokton Pass. To merely
look into it was to be seized with the excitement incidental to

reaching new regions to explore, so, after gathering several rare alpine specimens, we faced about, longing for the morrow to start on our year-old quest.

By 8:20 the next morning (June 30th), the whole outfit was strung along the trail heading for the outlet of Brazeau Lake, and for a land of which we had not the slightest knowledge. We might find sustenance for ten or a dozen horses, but twenty-two was another proposition. On all the previous days Chief had known exactly where he was going to find feed for so large a family; did he have any fears now? If so, his face did not show it, but still there was an absence of joking, there was no whistling in front or warbling of the latest popular song in the rear — that was all.

Crossing the Brazeau at the very outlet of the lake was much easier than we had expected to find it, and as soon as we were over we took up Dr. Coleman's old trail of 1892. A sharp detour was first made to avoid some rock-bluffs jutting out to the water; and then for a half mile on the lake shore we encountered bad going. A few of the old stagers, grown wise at the game, scuttled along close to our heels to have the advantage of the leader's guidance, half a dozen others got more or less mired, and how the foolish, unthinking Twins ever came out alive, no one but their luckless driver in the rear knows, but they did not fail, either then or any other time, to turn up eventually safe and sound.

I think "M's" diary sums up the approach to Pobokton Pass to perfection, as we found it that initial day of our experience on it, and as others will find it unless they cross it later in the season: "The trail was a little fierce, quick changes from burnt timber to rock-climbing, muskeg, quicksand, scree slopes and mud slides." Late in the afternoon, after much tough work, we made camp at timber-line, where the horses went mountain-climbing for their suppers and we for flower specimens, getting some very rare ones among the rocks.

With the next day glaring clear and hot, we crossed the pass which our aneroid made 7400 feet, ploughing through deep snow which the horses hated nearly as much as muskeg. It was a hard climb up and over, and now that I have seen it I should never take the Pobokton Pass from start to finish for a pleasure trip; it is a miserable route, and one only to be used to accomplish an end.

The trail was a very well marked one till, on the second day's ride, it seemed to come to an abrupt end at the river's edge where there had been a large Indian camp at some time. At this point it became so indistinct that the men looked around for something more promising, and a few old cuttings decided us to take a sharp turn to the right and ascend a steep hill, where we continued to follow more or less of a trail for a couple of hours longer.

The Indians' map told us to leave the valley at the third creek coming in from the right. We had already passed a dozen of them and were now passing another, but no horse-feed was in sight. A short distance beyond, we reached an open stretch, found tepee-poles and stopped for the night. The feed was mostly moss, muskeg, and fresh air, lots of all three; but the lake was getting on the nerves of all the family, and the horses would have to put up with a little inconvenience themselves.

With tents in order, all went off in as many different directions as possible. The feminine contingent came back first, reporting "fine scenery but no pass as far as they could see." "K." appeared next; "he had been to the end of the valley from where the last creek emerged, but that was a matter of impossibility for horses." Then Chief arrived with the cheerful intelligence that "we could still advance; a good trail led down the hill and was probably the real Pobokton trail." Perhaps the river went through some impassable gorge at this point, to cause us to do such an amount of tall climbing all morning. It was a comfort to know we could go on anyhow, certain it was that no one wanted to stay there, and no one contradicted the coolness of the atmosphere. Far, far in the distance, at seven o'clock, we could see the sun just setting in a bank of angry clouds, the wind, which had not been any too pleasant all day, began to howl and sob, and caused us to prevail on "Chef" to leave his baking a few minutes and peg down our tent, as it threatened to go off with our entire belongings. A pocket-handkerchief soared away like a bird, and the collapsible hand-basin had already taken a short flight across the slough in front of our tent.

The morning of the "Glorious Fourth" was ushered in with a crackling fire at our tent-door and a familiar voice saying, "Hot water, thermometer somewhere about thirty!" It took a terrible lot of courage to emerge from the warm blankets, from which position we could note six inches of snow over everything, and every few moments the howling wind would send a fresh supply down upon us. In spite of "Chef's" extra trouble to keep the breakfast hot at our fire, and every one piling into our tent to eat it, the bacon was like candle-grease in the bitter cold, and the coffee barely warm. The packing was worse than the eating. The horses fidgeted and turned to avoid facing the wind, and, what with frozen tents, pack-mantles, and ropes, not to mention stiffened fingers, it was nine o'clock before we could get below the brow of that exposed hill.

For the next two hours the trail led us down a fire-swept valley where the chopping was incessant and heavy. Once more reaching the bed of the stream we again found old tepee-poles and a division of the way, one pointing to the Sun Wapta, the other leading into a notch in the hill with a northern trend. The stream from it really did seem as if it might be the one for which we were looking, and the opening in the hills the last possible one before reaching the end of the valley of the Sun Wapta, which we had occasionally seen to the north-west of us. The trail here was very steep and rough and, with the thought that we might be coming back over it the next day, very hard to keep on following. About half way up the hill, down came the snow, and every one said "Yes!" to the suggestion of stopping at the next suitable place.

The game was now on in earnest. The household was getting into a rather divided state of mind, the opinion not having been unanimously in favour of this particular valley. However, those who did favour it were to have a chance of exploring it. Consequently, Chief and "K." went off the next morning to see what was ahead and the rest of us, as usual, worked each in his own line.

At four o'clock the men returned; had found a good trail, crossed a pass, could see miles ahead, but no lake of any description could be seen. The decision was to push ahead; we always had the privilege of turning back, and the best of the summer was still before us.

The new pass was a duplication of all other passes, soft and spongy; our aneroid showed the altitude as 7200 feet. Long patches of snow made the travelling very heavy, but the pass was a short one, and, with the saddle-horses ahead breaking the way, we were not long in getting over.

Reaching the eastern slope, I think I never saw a fairer valley. From our very feet it swept away into an unbroken green carpet as far as the eye could see. The botanical department found a rare specimen of *pedicularis,* while Muggins captured a couple of ptarmigan, and then the cavalcade made a quick descent of about a thousand feet, tramping under foot thousands of blossoms of the *trollius* and *pulsatilla* which covered the way.

Two and a half miles below the summit, finding a bunch of tepee-poles — a hint we were now in the habit of taking from the Indians, — we made our camp. In the afternoon, I took a stroll up a near-by hill, hoping to be able to report having seen the lake on my return; but no such glory was in store.

The morning of July 7th was a perfect one, the green valley down which we made our way was ideal, and yet in spite of all these blessings we were distinctly dismal. When the outfit was too spread out for us to discuss the quite undiscussable geography about us, we certainly looked our thoughts and rode along in dead silence.

The trail was not well marked this day, but that was owing to the fact that a horse could travel almost anywhere. However, even in face of such depression, we were able to enjoy one particular cut-bank which we followed up to avoid a soft spot on the river's edge; it was a mass of forget-me-nots, great splashes of intense blue, as though a bit of the sky had fallen. Then on and on, up and down hill we crawled for about eight miles, till we came to a halt on the river's right in a fine bunch of spruce. The day had grown steadily warmer, and with it had come the first real instalment of mosquitoes, and, as we ate our lunch of bread and jam and tea, it took considerable vigilance to keep them from drowning in the tea or sticking fast to the jam.

With lunch over, up came the everlasting question: "Where is that lake? Do you think we are on the right track?" "K.", who had grown more and more solemn for days, suddenly jumped up and shaking himself violently said: "Well, it's two o'clock, but I'm going off to climb something that's high enough to see if that lake's within twenty miles of here, and I'm not coming back till I know!" Anxious as I was to go along, I knew he was in no mood to have a snail in tow, and then it was far more important to locate our quarry than that I should personally be in at the death. Besides, it would have taken a goat to follow him when he was as desperate as he was then. With aneroid, camera, compass and our best wishes, he left us, — he for the heights, and we to put in time below looking for flowers and fossils, tormented by hordes of mosquitoes. We found large quantities of the latter, and, after a short jaunt, returned to camp, where three of us donned the despised "bug-nets" from which we emerged only for dinner.

The hours went by, a smudge of damp moss assisted in

slightly allaying the pests, night settled down, but "K." had not returned. We were a dreary-looking crowd. It rained a little. In spite of the hot night, Chief made a rousing fire as a beacon for the climber, and we all sat listening for the first crackle in the bushes. Not till 10:30 did it come, then he staggered out of the black forest into the flaring light, looking thoroughly tired out. He said he had "kept hopping" the entire seven hours and, though tired and hungry, greeted us with the joyful news, "I've found the lake!" Ascending the ridge behind our camp, he dropped 2000 feet to another valley, then climbed a fine peak where the aneroid said 8750 feet. Reaching the top, he looked over and there lay the lake below. The quest was over, all doubts were at rest, so there was no turning back, we could go on. A sigh of satisfaction passed around the camp-fire. Every one had been on a strain for days; "K's" absence on the mountain had added to it; now that we had him and the lake safe, there was no noisy demonstration, just complete relaxation. He was regaled with bacon, tea, and cake; the campfire went down, the "bug-nets" went on, and the camp went to sleep.

The sound which woke our slumbers next morning was Chief shouting, "All aboard for the lake!" The expressions on all faces were comical. Every one got off a joke, no matter how stale, every one being in a particularly happy humor. "K." had reported the lake "just around the corner", a matter of six or seven miles; no one minded the mosquitoes and we "hiked" forth jubilant, still sticking to the river's right, though we had a line on Sampson's map telling us to cross to the left. But going was easy, never an axe was used, so why give up a good thing for an uncertainty.

In about two hours, after passing through a little very soft ground, we came out on the shores of Chaba Imne (Beaver Lake), but found our position too low to get much idea of its size, though even there it looked quite large enough for all the time and exertion we had spent on it. As we stood upon its shores, we looked across to the other side, wondered what it all held in store for us, then wandered around while the men looked for a good camp-site.

Indians, of course, had been there, but, unless a prospector or timber-cruiser had come in by way of the Athabaska River, we had reason to feel we might be the first white people to have visited it.

From the moment we left the trail on Pobokton Creek, there had not been one sign of a civilised hand; the Indian is a part of the whole, the white man, with his tin-cans and forest-fires, desecrates as he goes. The unknown has a glamour indescribable; it creeps into the blood; it calls silently, but none the less its call is irresistible and strong.

Yes, the long quest was over, the object found, and it seemed very beautiful to our partial eyes.

The White Mustang
Edward A. McCourt

The boy had run all the way from the upland pasture and his thin eager face was damp with sweat. His father was standing at the shady end of the barn sharpening a mower knife, and the grating noise of granite drawn over steel sounded loud in the afternoon stillness. The boy stopped directly in front of his father, shoved his hands deep into the pockets of his faded blue denim overalls and spat in the dust that lay thick around his bare feet. Some saliva dribbled over his chin and he quickly wiped it away with the back of his hand, hoping that his father had not noticed. "Dad — what do you think I saw way up on the hog's-back?"

His father held the mower knife upright and began methodically testing the triangular blades with his thumb. "What, Jed?"

"A horse — a grey horse! I figger maybe it's the one the

Judsons lost and Mr. Judson said he'd give $5 reward to anyone who found him! Gee, Dad, can't I ride up and see? If I got the $5 I'd be able to send for the .22 in the catalogue. It only costs $6.35 delivered and I've got a dollar and a half now."

The words burst out with a kind of explosive force that left the boy breathless and red in the face. He inhaled deeply, making a sucking noise, and scuffed the dirt with his bare feet. His father picked up the sharpening stone and eyed it critically.

"Not today, son," he said. "It's a long way up to the hog's-back on a hot day like this."

Jed turned away and looked at the big poplars down by the creek and tried not to think of anything at all. "But maybe tomorrow," his father said. "You could start right after breakfast. Only — "

"Gee, Dad, — that'll be great; I could be back for dinner easy."

"Only you see, Jed, I can't figure how Judson's horse could have got up to the hog's-back. Not from their side anyway. It's a mighty steep climb and there's no grass to lead a horse on. You're sure you saw one up top?"

"Gee, yes, Dad, just as plain as anything — standing right on the skyline. Honest it was a horse. Grey, nearly white I guess, just like the Judsons'. I was 'bout half a mile up in the pasture picking strawberries when I saw him."

His father leaned the mower-knife against the wall of the barn. As if a cord holding them in place had suddenly given way, his long limbs relaxed and he collapsed on the ground, his back miraculously against the wall of the barn, his legs straight out in front of him. From his overalls' pocket he pulled out a blackened pipe, held it between thumb and forefinger and looked at it without saying anything. Then his eyes crinkled at the corners.

"Son, I don't figure that was the Judson horse you saw at all."

Jed knew that his father was playing a game. Dermot

O'Donnell loved to play games. Jed laughed out loud and sprawled in the dust at his father's feet. "Then whose horse was it?"

"No-one's Jed. You've seen the white mustang."

"What white mustang, Dad?"

Dermot's heavy eyebrows shot up and threatened to disappear into his hairline. "Child, child, what do they teach you in school anyway? Nothing that matters or you'd have heard of the white mustang!"

He tamped down the tobacco in his pipe and struck a match along the left leg of his overalls, all the time wagging his head slowly from side to side. "There's hardly a puncher in the plains country clear from the Rio Grande to Calgary who hasn't seen the white mustang at one time or another. Mostly at night of course, when the moon is shining and he looks more silver than white. You can get close to him too, but not very close at that. But sometimes you see him in the daytime, only way off, and he doesn't stand long then."

"And has nobody ever caught him?"

"Not yet, Jed. You see, he's no ordinary horse. Seems like he never gets any older. And some fools have shot at him, but they either missed or the bullets went right through him and did no hurt at all. Anyway, no-one has ever even slowed him up. And you can't catch him on horseback. Once, so they tell me, they took after him in relays — down the Texas Panhandle it was — and chased him three days without a stop. But the white mustang never turned a hair. At the end of the three days two horses were dead and a lot more windbroken for life. But they never got within a half a mile of the mustang and every so often he'd turn around and laugh at them the way a horse does if he's feeling extra good. Last I heard he was down in Wyoming working north. Way I figure it, no ordinary horse could get up the hog's-back from the Judson side. I guess it's the white mustang all right."

"Will you give me $5 if I catch him?"

"$5 is it? $5?" The pain in Dermot's voice was almost real. "Jed, if you ever catch the white mustang, you'll find him tame as a turtle-dove. And when you get on his back he'll take you away — just like flying it'll be, I think — to a country you've never seen where the grass is as green as the spring feathers of a mallard. And in a little glen so close to the sea you can hear the waves wash on the rocks, you'll find a beautiful princess with long golden hair waiting for you. And she'll get up behind you and put her arms around your middle and the white mustang will bring you back like he's a flash of lightning. And I'll build a house for you and the princess in the poplars down by the creek, and the two of you will be able to help your mother and me. And all your children — you'll have a grand houseful of them in no time — will learn to ride on the back of the white mustang, and when their time comes they'll ride away on him to be kings and queens all over the world. But mind you, Jed, no-one has ever yet laid a rope on the white mustang."

Jed spoke thoughtfully. "I think I'd sooner have $5."

Jed's father was the most wonderful man in the world and his laughter was the most wonderful part of him. He laughed now, silently at first, then in a series of staccato explosions that culminated in a sustained gargantuan bellow. Jed laughed too; he always did, listening to his father. Then he ran away and lay down on his back in the middle of the grove of poplars where his father was going to build the house for the princess, and looked up through the tree-tops at the blue sky and thought of the things he would do with the .22 rifle.

Jed did not ride up to the hog's-back the next day. For the heat wave broke in a drenching rain that began as a thunderstorm over the mountains and spread out across the foothills in a steady, settled downpour. Jed tried not to show his disappointment. He knew that the rain was needed badly, that without it his father's small crop, already stunted and parched and clinging precariously to life, would have been burnt beyond hope of recovery in a week or less. But such considerations were theoretic and remote, of small weight beside the immediate loss of a day's adventure and $5 at the end of it.

Late in the afternoon Jed put on the high rubber boots and oil slicker which were among his most prized possessions and climbed up the path through the pasture and beyond until he was no more than a mile from the hog's-back, an immense arching hill-top that seemed as remote as a mountain-peak and almost as inaccessible. There was no path beyond the fenced upland pasture, and the long slope above was steep and treacherous underfoot. Jed had been up to the hog's-back only once; his father had taken him there one cool spring day and the memory of what he had seen from the summit was like a lovely haunting dream. Now that he had been granted permission to go alone, the delay seemed to eat at his stomach and leave a hollow ache unlike any other pain he had ever known. Once, when he looked up, the swirling mists far up the slope seemed to part for a moment, and he glimpsed a whiteness that was no part of the elements. It was a whiteness that you didn't see in horses very often, and its outlines, vague and indistinct though they were, suggested the existence of something strange, portentous behind the wavering curtain of mist. Then the clouds closed in again and there were no more breaks. At last, when the rain had penetrated his slicker at a dozen points and was running in cold rivulets down his back, Jed turned away and half walked, half slithered down through a tangle of undergrowth to the comparative level of the pasture below.

He was quiet at supper that night. His mother had made his favourite dish of beef stew with puffy white dumplings floating in the gravy, and for a while there was no time to talk. But when the dessert came — pie made of dried apples and Saskatoon berries — Jed stopped with the first mouthful impaled on his fork and looked at his father. "Dad, is the white mustang very big?"

Dermot chewed a mouthful of food and swallowed. "Not

big, Jed. A mustang is never big. But he looks big — like everything that's uncommon. Take Napoleon now. You'd measure him for a uniform and he was a small man, a runt — not much over five feet, I guess. And then you'd stand back and take a look at him and he was big. He was the biggest man you ever saw." That was another thing about Dermot — he made you feel that he had known Napoleon very well in the old days. Or Robin Hood or Brian Boru, or whoever he happened to be talking about.

Jed's mother filled Dermot's cup to the brim with strong black tea.

"What nonsense are you stuffing the boy's head with now, Dermot?" she asked. She was a small frail woman, the physical antithesis of her husband. But there was the same look in her dark eyes, a kind of remoteness in them that made her concern for the immediate seem casual at best.

"No nonsense, Mother, no nonsense at all. He hears enough of that at school."

"I wouldn't say that in front of the boy, Dermot," she said. "Maybe he'll learn enough at school to help him keep one foot on the solid earth. Dear knows it's more than he'll ever learn at home."

But she spoke without malice. And she looked at Dermot and Jed in a way that seemed to make no difference between them.

Next morning the sun shone from a clear sky and the mists rose from the earth in steaming exhalations that vanished before the cool wind blowing from the north-west. The ground underfoot was soft and spongy — muddy where there was no grass — and the grass itself washed clean of dust so that it looked as if it had turned green again overnight. Jed dressed quickly and hurried into the kitchen for breakfast. "It's a swell day, Dad," he said.

His father set a pail full of milk on the shelf in the little pantry adjoining the kitchen. "A fine day indeed, Jed. And I know what's in your mind. But I'll have to take Paddy and ride out to the far pasture this morning to look for the yearlings. They didn't come up with the cows and I'm thinking the fence may be down. But you'll be able to make hog's-back this afternoon. It'll be a cool day I think.

Jed did not protest the delay. He knew what his father was thinking, that the grey horse would be gone anyway and that half a day would make no difference. He swallowed the lump in his throat and ate breakfast quietly but without appetite. After breakfast, when Dermot had ridden off down the valley to the far pasture in the flats, he amused himself snaring gophers in the little patch of wheat just across the creek. But it was not a pastime he ever really enjoyed. He got a thrill from seeing the grey-brown head pop up from the hole in the earth — from the quick savage pull that trapped the victim — from the feel of weight at the end of the long piece of binder twine as he swung it through the air. But what had to be done afterwards was not so pleasant. Particularly he hated taking the string from the neck of the battered carcass, covered with blood and insides as it so often was. This morning his attempts were half-hearted and mostly unsuccessful. After a while he threw his string away and returned to the house. He felt hungry, and there were cookies in the big green tin on the bottom shelf of the cupboard, and milk in the earthenware jug that always stood in the coolness of the cellar steps. He poured out a cup of milk, sat down at the table and ate his way steadily through a plateful of cookies. His mother was busy at the small worktable by the window. Jed finished his last mouthful of cookie and pushed back his chair.

"Mom?"

"What is it, Jed?"

"Mom, did you ever hear about the white mustang?"

"Only what your father told you." Mrs. O'Donnell lifted a pie from the oven, using a corner of her ample gingham apron to protect her hands from the heat, and set it on the worktable.

She stood beside the table looking out of the window, and her voice was so low that Jed could hardly hear her.

"Your grandmother used to tell me a story about a white horse. The son of Finn rode away on him to a fairyland where he lived with a beautiful princess. They called her Naim the Golden-Haired. But he got lonely and rode back on the white horse to his own country. He knew that he shouldn't get off the white horse, but he wanted to feel the turf under his feet. And the white horse ran away and the son of Finn turned into an old man. That's what happens to people when they come back to earth."

Jed emptied his cup and set it on the table. "It's a funny thing, Mom. An awful lot of people believe in the white horse, don't they?"

His mother turned from the window without speaking. After a while Jed went back outside. He walked part way up the path to the pasture, then cut across to where the creek, rising from a spring far up in the hills, ran over rocks and gravel to the valley below. He sat on a flat rock and let the water trickle over his bare feet. The water was cold, but he liked the sensation of numbness stealing through his feet — first the instep, then the toes, heels last of all. Even better he liked the prickling feel of returning warmth when he drew his feet out of the water and warmed them on the surface of the rock. He stayed there a long time, until he heard his mother's high "coo-ee" and knew that it was time for dinner.

Dermot was late getting home. So late that Mrs. O'Donnell put his dinner away in the warming oven of the big range and brewed a fresh pot of tea. Jed waited stoically; but when he saw his father approaching up the valley trail he shouted at the top of his lungs and ran down to open the gate for him.

"Gee, Dad, I thought you were never going to get here!"

Dermot slid down from the saddle and stretched prodigiously.

"It was just as I thought — fence down and the yearlings miles away. Paddy's had a hard morning."

"He's too fat," Jed said. "He'll be all right in a little while."

He emptied a tin pail of oats into the manger feed box while Dermot unsaddled the sweating pony. They went into the house together without saying anything. Mrs. O'Donnell was setting Dermot's dinner on the table. "You're late, Dermot," she said.

"I am late, Mother, and I'm thinking it would be as well if Jed waited till morning now. Paddy needs a couple of hours' rest at least. And the grey horse is sure to be far away by this time."

Mrs. O'Donnell spoke with unusual sharpness. "Paddy can have his rest and there still will be plenty of time. The evenings are long and the boy will be home before dark."

Jed's heart gave a great leap. His father grinned at him. "And they tell you it's the womenfolk are over-anxious about their young," was all he said.

It was after two o'clock when Jed went to the barn to saddle Paddy. He threw the heavy stock-saddle over Paddy's broad back and pulled the cinch. You had to pretend you were all finished so the little sorrel would relax his distended belly. Then you gave the cinch strap a quick pull and took in about three inches of slack. As soon as the saddle was securely in place Jed shortened the stirrups and tied a lasso to the cantle. He could not throw a lasso very well, and anyway the Judson horse was a quiet nag that could be led on a halter shank. But the lasso looked impressive, and it was a good idea always to be ready for anything.

He rode Paddy to the water-trough and let him drink a few mouthfuls. His mother came to the door and he waved to her and she waved back and smiled. "Don't be late, Jed."

"I won't," he shouted. "So long, Mom!"

For nearly an hour he rode upward without pause, the pony stumbling often in the damp uncertain footing. The valley slid farther and farther away below him until at last Jed was able to see over the opposite side to the great plain itself. He stopped at last, not because he wanted to but Paddy was blowing heavily. He dropped to the ground and squatted on his haunches while Paddy stood quietly beside him with bowed head. Jed could no longer see his own house because of an intervening swell in the seemingly regular contour of the hillside, but other houses had come into view — Joe Palamiro's shack near where the valley ran out into the plain, and the Peterson place, easily identified because of the big windmill, right at the edge of the plain itself. And he could see, far out on the plain, a row of tall gaunt red buildings — grain elevators — standing like guardsmen on parade, and beyond them a second row, over the horizon itself, so that only the upper halves of the elevators were visible. Another time Jed would have been tempted to linger, trying to identify familiar landmarks when seen from an unfamiliar angle. But now, after only a minute or two, he stirred restlessly. Paddy tossed his head and began to nibble at a few tufts of grass growing around the base of a boulder. Jed leapt to his feet.

"All right, you old geezer," he said. "If you can eat you can travel. I'll lead you for awhile."

He unfastened the halter-shank from the saddle horn and started up the hill on foot, Paddy crowding close behind. There was no trace of path anywhere and Jed had to pick his steps with care along deep dry gulches channelled by the rush of water in springtime, over glacial deposits of shale and boulder, past dwarfed poplars and evergreen. There were flowers blooming on these upper slopes that he had never seen before, but he couldn't stop to look at them. In spite of the uncertain footing he went up quickly. The sweat gathered on his forehead and ran down his face in salty trickles, for the sun was hot now and the wind had almost completely died away. But the hog's-back was close at hand; already Jed could distinguish objects on the skyline — a stunted bush, a pile of rocks forming a natural cairn, a single tree as incongruous in its lonely setting as a human figure would have been.

Now that he was almost at the top Jed suddenly and unaccountably wanted to linger. For the second time he sat down and looked back. Below, the scene had spread out and yet diminished. The horizon had moved farther back; now he was high enough to catch a glimpse of distant emerald green where a river flowed between enormous banks, of towns so remote that it was impossible to conceive of their having actual being. There were mirages that would vanish with the shimmering heat waves that now hung above the level of the plain. Objects which half an hour ago had seemed close at hand — Joe Palamiro's shack and the Peterson windmill and the upright slab of granite at the mouth of the valley called, for no reason anyone knew of, the Dead Man's Needle — had somehow contracted, and slipped away as if carried on the surface of an outgoing tide. Jed sat for a long time until Paddy, dissatisfied with scanty pickings, came close and nuzzled his shoulder.

"All right, all right," Jed said. "We'll be moving."

He mounted and rode on. The ground was bare and brownish grey. Not even the drenching rain of the day previous could restore life to the few wisps of dry grass that lingered near the top, or the tall reedy stems of upland foxgloves that rattled mournfully in the wind again blowing across the foothills. His father was right, the boy thought, there was no feed up here for a horse. A horse like the Judson grey, he said to himself, in unthinking qualification.

And when he reached the very top at last and was able to look down the opposite side — down a slope that was strange and steep and menacing although he had seen it once before and it had not seemed menacing then — he remembered what his father had said about the inaccessibility of the hog's-back from the Judson side. Dermot was right. No horse could climb that slope. No horse would want to. Jed felt no regret but instead an unexpected lightness of spirit, a strange confusion of happiness and something that made him a little bit afraid. For he had seen a horse on the hog's-back — a horse more white than grey. He laughed out loud, then looked quickly at the sun. It was swinging low toward the mountains. It would be twilight in an hour and the dark would come soon afterwards.

He rode along the hog's-back until checked by the precipitous side of a dry gully, then returned to the highest point of the arching hill top, and again looked down the great slope that fell to the west. The world that looked different, hill rising above hill until at last they broke into the scintillating splendour of white peaks against a pale blue sky. For no reason at all Jed wanted to cry. Instead he shouted loudly at Paddy and drove his heels into the pony's fat sides.

Paddy trotted a few steps and slowed to a walk. It was then that Jed saw the trees. They were directly below him, just over the first big curve of the west slope. At first he could see only their tops, but as he went down they came completely into view — stunted Balm-of-Gileads that looked curiously unreal in their symmetrical grouping on the barren hillside. And low down, between two grey-green trunks Jed could see a patch of white.

He rode forward at a walk. Paddy snorted once and Jed pulled hard on the reins. He wanted to turn and ride back up the slope and over the summit toward home. But instead he went on slowly, and the dead weight that dragged at his heart made him faint and sick. He reached the circle of trees. Paddy could smell the water now, although the wind was blowing the other way, and snorted again. But Jed said "no" very quietly and with a funny quaver in his voice. He could see the white patch clearly now, above the surface of the water and partly on the ground. And he could hear the heavy buzzing noise made by the swollen blue-bottles as they rose in clouds from the carcass of the grey horse that had died — quickly or slowly, it did not matter now — in the treacherous sucking mud surrounding the hillside spring.

Paddy, scenting death, pawed the ground and whinnied. Jed swung the pony hard and slapped him with the ends of the reins. "Giddap-giddap!" he shouted. He rode over the hog's-back at a gallop and on down the other side. Paddy stumbled and almost fell. Jed pulled him in with a savage jerk.

"All right, you old geezer," he said. "Take it easy. No need to break your neck."

It was almost dark when Jed reached home. His father and mother were in the yard waiting for him. "I was on the point of starting after you," Dermot shouted, "when we saw you up there like a god against the setting sun." And he laughed a great booming laugh that echoed across the valley.

His mother kissed him on the cheek. "Your father will put Paddy away, Jed," she said. "I've kept your supper hot for you."

Jed washed very carefully and combed his hair. He had to comb it several times before he got the part right. His mother lit the oil lamp and set it on the table.

"You must be starved, Jed," she said. "I've got a lovely supper for you. Bacon and eggs and the strawberries you picked the day before yesterday."

Dermot came stamping into the kitchen. "And did you lay eyes on the white mustang, son?"

For a minute Jed did not answer. "He's dead," he said at last. "It was Judson's grey. He got bogged in a spring."

Astonishment showed in Dermot's face. "So you did see him day before yesterday! But how ever did he get up?"

"There's a stream running down from the spring. He must have followed it up. The grass would be good along the banks."

Dermot filled his pipe. "Too bad, son," he said.

He lit his pipe and blew such clouds of smoke that for a minute his face was almost hidden. "I figure, Jed," he said, somehow talking like one man to another, "that tomorrow you and I had better take a little trip to town."

Jed looked at his father quickly. Dermot blew another cloud of smoke. "The gophers are getting pretty bad. Doesn't seem like we'll be able to keep them down at all unless you get a .22. There's one in Heath's Hardware — nice little single-shot — for $7. I figure we can maybe swing it."

"Gee, Dad," Jed said, "that'll be great."

Suddenly he pushed away his plate. "Mom," he said, "I'm not hungry."

His mother laid her hand on his shoulder. "Would you like to go to bed?" she said.

Jed got up and turned away so his father could not see his face. He nodded jerkily. His mother spoke to Dermot.

"He's tired out. He'll be all right in the morning."

They went out to the little porch where Jed slept in the summertime. The night air was warm and still and full of rich scents that you didn't notice in the daytime. The moon had risen and a band of silver lay across the top of the valley wall opposite. Jed began to cry, silently. His mother put her arms around him without speaking and held him tight.

The door opened and Dermot came out to the porch. "Look at him, would you?" he said, and there was a petulant note in his voice. "All this fuss about a dead horse."

Jed's mother looked at Dermot. When she spoke he could hardly hear her. "Not just a horse, Dermot," she said. "Not an ordinary horse anyway."

And she repeated, matter-of-factly, "He's tired out. He'll be all right in the morning."

Dermot stared at her for a long minute in silence. Then he nodded soberly. "Sure, Mother," he said. "He'll be all right in the morning."

And he closed the door so quietly behind him that it made no noise at all.

At the Sign of the Buffalo

J. W. Grant MacEwan

As a young boy, Walking Buffalo heard the rich legends of his people. Like Traveller and Twist-in-the-Neck, he too participated in strange and mysterious events which were later woven into the fabric of Stoney history. It was from an early childhood experience that one of the most popular stories about him evolved. This tale became known as the "Grand Legend", and as can be expected, it centered around a buffalo motif.

According to the most common version of the story, Walking Buffalo was just learning to walk when he wandered away from the Stoney camp and became lost. In itself, this incident was not unusual; since the beginning of time, children have been running away and getting lost. In most instances, there is a brief period of parental panic after which the tot is located in good health, totally unconscious of any danger. With Walking Buffalo, however, the traditional search was unsuccessful. The youngster had simply vanished like a frog in a muddy pool.

Certainly there was an air of mystery about his disappearance. Wearing moccasins, buckskin shirt, and a dirty face, he had been playing with mongrel dogs beside his grandmother's tipi one minute yet had suddenly vanished the next. The woman called and then conducted a fruitless search. Friends joined to comb the tree-covered ground close to the Bow River more thoroughly, but the anxious searchers still found no clue as to the whereabouts of the missing boy. As darkness descended upon the mountains and valleys, the possibility of tragedy crossed the mind of each Stoney. Could it be that a hungry wolf or she-bear had emerged from its forest home to carry the child away? Could it be that the little one had fallen into the churning river, there to be swept to a cruel death by drowning? Or, did the possibility remain that little Walking Buffalo had simply used his unsteady legs to wander into a hiding place not far away where he would be discovered shortly?

Everyone, including the medicine man, tried to help. The next morning as daylight came again, the search was resumed and extended farther from the camp. The results were the same; no trace of the child. And so, after being forced to acknowledge his own failure, the medicine man counseled united appeal to the Great Spirit.

This was a solemn occasion, something like a great tribal prayer meeting or modified Sun Dance. A fire was built on a clearing of ground, and the Indians gathered around it in a circle. Scalps and eagle heads dangled from the medicine man's belt. As he advanced toward the fire, his painted face was partially masked by a headpiece made from crows' wings. His first act was to throw incense into the flames. Next, with the air of a man enjoying his authority, he demanded silence, then ordered singing and the smoking of pipes. Finally, at exactly the correct moment, the wise one called upon the Great Spirit to tell them whether or not Walking Buffalo still lived and, if so, where he could be found.

There followed a period of dramatic silence. Then as the evening wind moaned through the nearby trees, its sound was transformed into a human voice which said, "The boy is alive and will be found with the buffalo herd."

But many buffalo herds roamed the area. Where would the right one be found? Only occasionally did big herds penetrate the higher reaches of the Bow River. Generally when Stonies hunted buffaloes, they journeyed eastward to find herds on the plains. Hence, the medicine man next prayed for a clue as to the location of this particular herd. He did not have to wait long for an answer. Scanning the night sky, the wise one discovered a blue star in the east. This was his clue. Early the next morning, Stonies, both on horseback and on foot, followed the medicine man toward the plains.

Before going far, the Indians saw buffaloes, but these were

either too far north or too far south to interest the leader. He was adhering strictly to an eastward course. As the days passed, their travels brought the Stonies deeper into Blackfoot territory where attack was always imminent. Finally, a big herd was spotted directly ahead. The medicine man advised a cautious approach to allow for observation of the animals without causing them to stampede. Closing in on the herd, sure enough the Stonies spotted a small boy playing with buffalo calves. It was indeed the lost lad, uninjured and apparently quite happy.

The Indians, of course, were overjoyed, and Walking Buffalo's father impulsively called his child to him. The sound startled the animals, and with their tails held high in the air, they all fled, except for one old cow who stood close to where the small boy had been playing. Fearlessly, the cow faced the Indians, quite obviously trying to deal with this human invasion. But her thoughts were not focused entirely on the strangers; she repeatedly turned her head to observe the movements of the boy. The position of the child was clearly causing her anxiety.

After most of the buffalo herd had thundered away, the infant, instead of coming to his own people, tried to follow the animals. His small legs couldn't carry him very fast, but he was doing his best to catch up when the cow, having completed her assessment of the Indians, bounded after him and effectively blocked his escape until the Stonies could come closer.

Speaking to the Indians (as wild animals quite often did), she related the following events. She had found the waif alone in the foothills and had guessed that he required protection and food. Responding to his need, she allowed him to nurse along with her bull calf, and when the herd moved more deeply into plains country, the child followed. Now the cow was returning the little fellow to human care. Once she saw him back in the arms of his father, she turned and ran to rejoin the fleeing herd.

The child protested at not being permitted to go too. In his days with the wild stock, drinking rich buffalo milk, playing with the calves, sleeping with his body resting securely against the cow's warm flank, he had become a part of the animal community. Now the separation was unpleasant, even though the tribesmen were kind and were obviously concerned only with his welfare.

The medicine man was still in command. Because his intercessions had succeeded, he expected more respect than ever. He called for a ceremonial halt in order to remove any clinging buffalo traits from the boy's character and to restore, at the same time, his desire to be human. A fire was built, after which the medicine man uttered the necessary incantations. Tobacco smoke was blown in the boy's face, and for good measure a wisp of his hair was solemnly committed to the flames. Miraculously, the child relaxed, his ability to make human sounds and words returning. He was now glad to be back with his own people.

The legend about Walking Buffalo had a second version. According to it, the child was not found for some *months* after his mysterious disappearance. Stonies had finally been obliged to abandon the hunt. "The papoose is dead," they mourned resignedly.

Late in the autumn, however, as evening darkness was filling the mountain valleys, members of a Stoney family squatting in their tent heard the trample of heavy feet above the noise of the wind in the pines. They placed their ears on the ground and soon identified the sound as the footsteps of a buffalo. Surprised that the animal would venture into the circle of tipis, especially during this late season, the mother listened again to confirm her suspicions. "I hear more," she remarked, "I hear a papoose whimpering. We must see what this is all about."

Going out in the chilly night, the woman was startled by the sight of the indistinct figure of a small boy nursing at a buffalo cow. Strangely enough, however, the cow didn't bolt as do most wild animals. Rather, she spoke to the squaw and told her of finding this small and helpless infant searching for something to eat in the hills. Out of pity for the pathetic child, she had allowed him to nurse, thus saving his life.

"Now," concluded the cow, "I return the care of this papoose to you." With these words, she turned and wandered into the darkness of the forest, while the boy, after being identified as the child lost long months before, was returned to his overjoyed kin.

Walking Buffalo never forgot his debt to the generous buffalo. An affection for these animals never left him. In fact, he later adopted the painted figure of a buffalo as the insignia for his family tipi.

Romulus and Remus, legendary founders of Rome, were supposed to have been mothered by a she-wolf. To have been raised by a buffalo cow on the Canadian prairies is no less plausible and no less romantic.

Chinook
Lillian A. Maze

Lovely ribbon of sky-blue light,
Advancing scout of a warm soft wind.
Old legends tell that a maiden fair
Wandered afar on her swift white mare;
The bravest warriors searched in vain
Until a breeze blew in from the West,
Warm and gently it softly caress't.
"'Tis the breath of Chinook, our sister fair,
Kissing our cheeks and touching our hair."
When the sky dresses up in her blue-beaded dome,
Chinook, for a little while, is home.

The Bear Who Stole the Chinook

Frances Fraser

In this long-ago year, the snow came early, and lay deep, the wind blew from the north, cold and bitter, and the Chinook did not come. The Indians shivered in their lodges, for the snow made it hard to get wood for the fires. After a while, their food was gone. The children cried with hunger, and the hunters could find no game at all — everything had been driven away by the blizzard. Every morning, and every night, the Old Ones went out to look for the great, clear blue arch that tells of the coming of the Chinook. But the grey clouds lay flat on the mountains and the Chinook did not come. In this camp there was a poor orphan boy, living alone. He suffered even more than the others did, for his teepee was old and tattered, and his clothing ragged. The others in the tribe did not think much of him, and his only friends were the birds and the animals. He talked to them, and often they shared his scanty food. Now, he called upon them for help.

A-pe'si, the coyote, came and Se-pe'tse, the owl and his family, Ma-mi'as-sik-ami, the magpie, and A-pau, the weasel. They sat down in the poor boy's lodge, to talk. If it would only get warmer, they said. The magpie, you know, is a dreadful gossip. He goes everywhere, and sees everything and consequently, quite often he knows more than ordinary folk. So they asked him a question: What had become of the Chinook?

"For myself," said Ma-mi'as-sik-ami, "I do not know. But I have many relatives, and many of them live in the mountains. Some of them will know. I shall go ask them." And he flew away. After a while, he came back. "My relatives say," he told them, "that there is a great bear living far back in the mountains. He has stolen the Chinook, and he is keeping it fastened up in his lodge, so that he may be warm all winter."

The friends held a council of war. They decided that they would go to the mountains and set the Chinook free. They took a pipe, to make medicine smoke, and off they went. In the lead was Ma-mi'as-sik-ami, who acted as scout. The others caught birds and small animals for the boy to eat, and at night Coyote and his family lay all round him, and kept him warm. For days and days they travelled. At last Ma-mi'as-sik-ami told them they were near the den of the bear. Indeed, they could hear him as he snarled savagely. Se-pe'tse sent his wife to look through a hole in the lodge, so that they might know how the Chinook was kept. But the Bear was very watchful, and when he saw the owl's wife peeking through the hole in his lodge, he took his firestick and hit her in the eye with it. She flew away crying. Se-pe'tse sent his children, one by one. The same thing happened to each of them. Then, he went himself. The Bear poked him with a firestick, too, and he, too, flew away, crying. That is why, even to this day, owls have such big eyes.

"Let me go," said A-pau, the weasel. And he went to the lodge, and peeked through the hole as Se-pe'tse and his family had done. But A-pau, you know, moves very quickly, and when he saw the Bear look toward the hole, he ducked his head, and the Bear, seeing only his white fur, thought it was just a bit of snow, and he paid no more attention. And A-pau the weasel came back to his friends. "The Bear is huge, and very fierce," he said. "And he has the Chinook tied up in an elkskin bag, at the back of his lodge, farthest from the door. How we can get it, I do not know."

"I shall make a medicine smoke, and blow it into the lodge," said the boy. It will make the Bear sleepy." So he filled his pipe, and sat down outside the lodge to smoke. He smoked and he smoked. The Bear began to yawn, and nod his head. At last he went to sleep. Then coyote crept quietly into the lodge, seized the bag with his teeth and dragged it outside. But they could not untie it. And the thongs were tough, too tough for even A-pau's teeth to cut. While they were discussing what to do, they heard a small voice saying, "Ne-sa (brother), let me try." They looked and there was a prairie chicken.

"Very well, little brother," said the boy. The prairie chicken flew up on the bag and began to pick out the stitches along the side of it. When only a few of the stitches were broken, the Chinook poured out of the bag, and it began to blow over the country. Snow melted, and water began to run. When the prairie chicken flew down to the ground, mud splashed on his feathers . . . and that is why, even to this day, the prairie chicken has spots.

The Bear woke up, and came roaring out of his lodge, and the friends fled. But the Bear could never recapture the Chinook, and, ever since then, bears have slept all winter. And that is why, when they wake up in the spring, they are dreadfully cross. And ever since then, the snow can be deep, and the cold bitter, but, in a short while, the Chinook will come blowing over the mountains, and everyone is happy again.

The Cathedral Trees of Stanley Park
John S. Morgan

In the heart of Stanley Park, Vancouver, huge fir trees form a vaulted dome, unmatched in beauty by any cathedral fashioned by the hand of man. The subdued light that filters through their branches and the hush that pervades the forest suggest that the spirit of the Creator lingers over his handiwork. These trees, called the "Cathedral trees of Stanley Park", are the inspiration for an Indian legend.

Long ago, an evil witch haunted the region of our western coast. Like Medusa of Greek legend, who transformed to stone everything upon which she cast her baleful eyes, all life that came within reach of this witch-woman's evil eye withered and died. In her company, dread Disease stalked the land and pale Famine lingered over the Indian villages; berries and fruit withered on the branch, and abundant catches of salmon were memories of a happy past.

Then the Great Spirit, the Sagalie Tyee, resolved that if his creation, Man, were to survive, he must take action. To kill the witch-woman would not serve his purpose; her evil soul would live on. Therefore he summoned the four giants whom he used always to perform his work, and ordered them to turn the witch-woman into stone.

The four giants eagerly departed in their stone canoe. As they neared Prospect Point, they caught sight of the witch-woman. With a shrill laugh, she challenged them to do their worst. Then she fled into the depths of the forest (in what is now Stanley Park). Hurriedly beaching their canoe, the giants pursued her, each covering hundreds of yards at a single stride of his huge legs. In the heart of the forest, they captured her. Then the mightiest of the giants raised his huge arm and uttered these words:

"Since you destroy everything that comes within your grasp, changing the bountiful life of our woods and rivers into barren emptiness, you shall be changed to stone, which harbours no life within its dry surface and which even the moss and vine will shun."

Whereupon the witch-woman was immediately transformed into a huge stone.

The Indians believe that, since her evil soul could not be destroyed, it lives on, locked within this rock. As evil has a magnetic attraction for those who come within its range, so those who penetrate to the heart of Stanley Park can never break free from the spell cast by this evil stone. Forever and ever, their spirits are doomed to circle this huge rock whose surface is covered with black stains, each stain standing for one of the witch-woman's evil deeds.

Knowing that Evil can be overcome only by good, the

Sagalie Tyee decided to place at the entrance to the trail something so great and good that men could withstand the lure of Evil. He chose from among his people the kindest and most unselfish, whose souls were filled with love for their fellow-beings. These he transformed into the tall, stately trees whose branches form an arch for his cathedral.

Avalanches
Denise Fair

"Avalanche: A large mass of snow and ice, or of dirt and rocks, sliding or falling down a mountainside." An awful lot that tells you about avalanches! I know. I seen them, and what they can do to highways, railways, trains, cars and people, I'd hate to tell you. Sometimes they mangle 'em all up, and other times they just cover 'em up so you can't find 'em for days; people as well as them other things.

Actually, I never been in a slide, but, as I said, I seen 'em. I seen lots of them. Like that one in 1910, or maybe 1911. No it was 1910. I remember the date, though. March 4th. That's my anniversary. 'Course it weren't then, I weren't married back then. I'd just started working with the railway in the Revelstoke area. It was late at night, just before midnight, and me and the rest of the guys were real tired. *Real* tired. Then all of a sudden, someone ran in and said, "SAP on snowshed 17," and ran out again real quick. Now, like I said, I hadn't been with the railroad long, so I didn't know what SAP meant, but all the other guys started bundlin' up and running like they weren't tired at all, so I followed them. I asked someone what SAP was and he said that it meant "Soon as Possible". That's top priority in railroad talk.

Before I knowed it, we were on a train with our shovels, heading out there. Turned out there's been a big avalanche, or slide as we usually called 'em, and it'd buried a good number of people. A guy called Johnny Anderson was the road master there. He'd been calling in a progress report when it happened, and he didn't even know it until he went and didn't see no lights. He worked right along with the rest of us, but you could tell he was shaken up. To tell the truth, so were the rest of us. We kept finding bodies, and usually they were friends. It was hard.

Like I said, sometimes a slide mangles and sometimes it just covers. This one just landed plumb on top of 'em. I guess some of 'em had some warning, 'cause we found four bodies that looked like they were running. I guess one of them tripped on somethin', a root maybe, and then the other three tripped on the first one. We found 'em like that, one on top of the other, just like when the snow covered 'em.

Some just didn't get a chance to move. We found three guys standing up straight, just as if they were talking together. The snow just landed on top of them and they didn't have a chance. I seen lots of slides since then, but that one was the worst. Yes, sir, that one was the worst.

I never found out what caused that slide. Maybe someone else knew, but I never did. Most anything can start a slide. One a little while ago, January 1965 I believe, was started by an earthquake, but that's real uncommon. Downright rare as a matter of fact. More common were what we called dry slides and wet slides. A dry slide could be started by anythin'. A pebble rolling, a train goin' past, even the vibration from the wind in the trees. Anythin'. An' once it starts, it won't be stopped by anythin', at least not without an awful fight. Thing is, you can't predict a dry slide. If you're in slide country, you can expect to hear thunder any time, an' it won't be from lightning. Thunder is the sound of tons of snow falling down a mountain. Wet slides are easier to predict. They come in the spring, when the snow is melting a bit. See, the snow melts in the day, and at night the outer layer of water freezes first, and sort of forms a crust. When the inside freezes, it expands, and cracks the outer coat. That is sometimes enough to set off a slide. Sometimes, what happens is that the top snow melts first, and the water runs down and cuts a channel between the overhang and the main part of the snow. Pretty soon the overhang just kind o' gives way and starts his trip down the mountain.

Avalanches are awful. If you're a trapper, you got to watch every minute for snow tumblin' on top of you. Like I said, I never been in a slide, but I been told that just before it hits you feel a great big wind, like a hurricane, although I never been in a hurricane either, and if that hits ya, ya gotta hold on tight to something or else you'll get blown away. Matter of fact, that's what saved a guy's life in the 1910 slide. He was called Bill LeChance. The wind hit 'im and he was thrown sixty feet from his cab in the train. Good thing too. He got two broken legs, but he was alive, which is more than I can say for most of them men working there.

Them avalanches are dangerous things. Never can tell when they'll hit, and how many people they'll hurt or kill. Roger's Pass is a real bad place for avalanches. A real bad place. I never travel through it unless I have to. Too many bad memories. A lot of people have died there, and all over the mountains, from avalanches. Yes sir, avalanches are mighty dangerous things. The dictionary don't tell the half of it.

The Moon and the Seven Singers
Frances Fraser

Some of the oldest Blackfoot songs are sung to the bone whistle. The whistles are fashioned from the wing-bones of eagles or hawks, and are often beautifully ornamented. They are seldom seen any more, though some of the tribal elders still possess and cherish them. The Old Ones tell a story about how the whistles first came to our people — the legend of The Moon and the Seven Singers.

It was a long, long time ago, the Old Ones say, when the Sky People were somehow much closer to the Blackfoot than they are now, when the High Gods concerned themselves more with the affairs of men.

For many moons, the buffalo had gone from the prairie and the Indian people were starving. One by one the old people had gone away alone out on the prairie to die, knowing that while they remained in the camp the tiny store of food would be shared with them. Mothers wept for their children, who lay in ragged lodges, too weak now even to cry. Day by day, hunters went out in frantic search for food. They came back empty-handed, or with only a few tiny birds, or some small, poor animal.

Among the hunters was a young man, a warrior named Moon Eagle. He was younger than the others and they paid little attention to him. When the others had tried all their hunting skills and invoked all their medicine powers in vain, they said to Moon Eagle, "What is it that pities you?"

He said, "I am pitied by eagles."

The other hunters said, "The eagle sees everywhere. Perhaps he sees buffalo. Do you have pity for the children?"

Moon Eagle said, "I have great pity for the children. I will go."

He went away by himself out on the prairie to sacrifice to the Sky People and to pray for help. He cut off the ends of his fingers, and he called the eagle, his medicine-power, to come for his sacrifice. After some days, weak from thirst, hunger and the loss of blood, he had a medicine-dream, and the eagle came.

In his dream-vision the eagle ordered him to go to a certain place near the river where he would find a large rock with a hollow place on the top of it. In this depression he would find the skeleton of an eagle. He was to take the wing-bones and build a fire over the rest of the bones. He would let the fire die down, then build it up again four times, and on each fire he was to burn sweetgrass. During this time he was to fashion a bone whistle as the eagle directed.

Moon Eagle hastened to find the rock and to do as he had been directed. When the fire had burned low for the fourth time the whistle was completed. Moon Eagle put it to his lips and blew.

The first time he blew the whistle, the moon disappeared from the sky. Seven times more he blew it, and when the echo of the seventh had died away, he heard a strange, beautiful song. It drifted on the night wind, and to his mind came all the lovely sounds he knew — the wind in the trees, and birds singing, and little rivers running, and the laughter of children. And somewhere in it, a long way off, the weird, wild howl of wolves.

The singing came closer, and he saw, walking slowly toward him over the prairie, a beautiful girl dressed in strange, lovely feathered robes. A sparkle like sunlight on water glinted on her smooth braids and her feet in moccasins were ornamented like the wings of birds. She was followed by seven singers dressed in the same way, each carrying a small, ornamented drum.

"You called us," she said. "What do you want?"

"My people are starving," said Moon Eagle. "Give me food for them."

"Give me the whistle," she said.

"She blew the whistle four times, then handed it to the first of the singers. He blew it and gave it to the next in line. Four times the whistle was passed down the line of singers, and as each man blew it for the fourth time he turned into a large wolf.

"Bring me buffalo!" the girl commanded, and the singer wolves raced away across the prairie.

Soon Moon Eagle heard the sound of many running hooves.

"Your people will have food now," said the girl, smiling.

Then she took the whistle again and blew it four times. The seven wolves came running to her, and as they came the stars in the sky grew very bright. The Wolf Road, that pathway of stars the white man calls the Milky Way, swung around, and one end of it came down to touch the ground where they stood.

"Who are you?" cried Moon Eagle.

"I am the Moon," said the girl. "My singers are the Seven Wolves." Then she turned and, followed by the Seven Singers went back up the Wolf Road into the Sky Country.

The Moon and the Seven Wolves — the stars of the Dipper — shone brightly in the sky again. Moon Eagle summoned his people to the hunt, and the long famine was over. He kept the bone whistle, and, though never again could anyone call down the Sky People with it, it was used for many years in the rituals of our tribe.

The Owl and the Raven
Ronald Melzack

Long ago, when animals were still able to speak the Eskimo language, two old grandmother birds sat in a little bird-igloo and chatted. Grandmother Owl had big, bright eyes and a short nose. Grandmother Raven had a big, black nose and little beady eyes. And both wore plain dresses of drab white feathers.

Granny Owl said, "I wish you could make me look prettier. I feel so plain and ordinary."

And Granny Raven said, "I would like to paint you a pretty dress."

Granny Owl agreed, and the Raven took some soot from her oil lamp, and began to paint the spots which we still see on the Owl's feathers. Granny Owl was very patient while the Raven painted the lovely spots. When Granny Owl was told that the decoration of her dress was all finished, she jumped up and hooted with joy because she looked so young and pretty.

She danced a little jig — until she fell over, because she was really older than she looked.

Then Granny Owl asked if she could decorate Granny Raven's dress. Granny Raven agreed, and the Owl began to paint pretty designs on her feathers. Soon Granny Raven got tired of standing still and began to hop around. Granny Owl told her to stand still. The Raven tried, but she became restless. She just couldn't wait to see how young and lovely she would look in her pretty new dress. So she began to jump up and down with excitement. Granny Owl became angry and said that she couldn't paint well if Granny Raven didn't stay still. But Granny Raven still continued to hop from one foot to the other, jump up and down and move around.

Finally Granny Owl said, "If you don't sit still, I'm going to spill the lamp-oil all over you." Granny Raven tried to stand still, but she soon began to jump around again. Granny Owl became impatient, picked up the oil lamp, and poured all the black oil on poor Granny Raven. From that day on, Ravens have been black all over. And Owls and Ravens have never again spoken to one another — not to this very day.

How the Raven Brought Light to the World
Ronald Melzack

In the beginning, when the first Eskimos lived in the land of ice and snow, there was light from the sun as we now have it. Then because the Eskimos were bad, the sun was taken away. People were left on earth for a long time with only the starlight to guide them. The Medicine Men made their strongest charms, but the darkness of night continued.

In one of the Eskimo villages there lived an orphan boy who was allowed to make his home in the community hut. This little boy, like all orphans, had magical powers. He had a special black coat and peaked cap, and when he put them on he changed into a Raven. Then he was able to fly as the Ravens do. When he took off his coat and cap he again turned into a boy.

The village people were good to the little boy, and because he wanted to repay them for their kindness, he went off to search for the sun. He put on his black coat and cap, became a Raven and flew high up into the air. He flew for many days, and the darkness was always the same. But one day, after he had gone a very long way, he saw a ray of light ahead of him, and he felt encouraged. As he hurried on, the light showed again, plainer than before. At last he came to a large hill. One side of the hill was in bright light while the other side was as black as night. Close to the hill, there was a small house with a man nearby.

The boy silently crept closer to the house, until he could look into it. Through the ice window he saw a large ball of fire that glowed with a brilliant light. He had found the sun at last! The boy took off his coat and cap, and began to plan how to get the light away from the man.

After a time, he walked up to the man who was standing outside his house. The man jumped with surprise when he saw the boy, and said, "Who are you, and where do you come from?"

"It's so dark in our village that I don't like to live there. So I came here to live with you," said the boy.

"What! All the time?" asked the man.

"Yes," replied the boy.

"Hmm!" mumbled the man. "Well, come into the house with me and let's talk it over." He stooped down, and led the way through the snow tunnel into the house.

The moment the boy was in the house, he snatched up the ball of fire and ran out of the tunnel. He pulled his peaked cap over his face, and turned into a Raven. And he flew as fast as his wings would carry him. When he turned to look behind him, he saw the old man running after him on the ground. The old man cried out, "Give me my fireball! The Eskimos are bad and they musn't have it."

And Raven called back, "No! Now they're good. They work hard, and need light to hunt and fish." Then he flew off, holding the sun in his long, clawed feet.

As Raven travelled home, he broke off a piece of the fireball and hurled it through the sky. When it soared over the land of the Eskimos, they rejoiced, because at last they had daylight again. He went on for a long time in darkness and then sent another piece of the fireball hurtling through the sky, making it day again. This he continued to do at intervals until he reached his village. Once there, he took off his magical coat and cap, and celebrated with the happy villagers.

Nowadays, at Raven's village, day and night follow each other. Sometimes, the nights are very long, because Raven travelled for a long time without throwing a piece of the fireball. And so they have continued. For Raven threw pieces of fireball with such power that they continue to circle around the land of the Eskimos to this day.

How the Animals and Birds Got Their Names
Charlie Mack

This is the legend about what happened after the Great Flood. There were some people who survived, but all the animals and birds disappeared, because the flood lasted so long. At this time, the rabbit was chief. He was one of the survivors. The human beings who were left, started talking to each other. The chief said, "We are going to try and revive all the birds and animals. It will be an order for you to notify all the people who are not here."

The wolf, at this time, was a person named *Ka-wam*. The

chief said to him, "Wolf, you must go out and gather the people, and tell them what we are going to do." Wolf went around to the people and did what the chief asked of him. He told the people that they would have to bring back the deer, and all the other animals and birds. When Wolf had done what he could there were still some people on the other side of the mountain who hadn't heard the plan.

The chief sent his sons, as they were the only ones who could make it. There was a lot of fresh snow on the mountains. The rabbits tried, but they all came back; they couldn't make it.

The chief said to the porcupine, "Brother, you are the oldest brother we have. You better go up and bring those people down." The porcupine said, "Chief, you have tried all the strong men; do you think that I could do it? Alright, I'll go up and get those people." Porcupine started to climb, taking his time, ploughing through the snow. He got to the top of the mountain and rolled down to the bottom. He climbed up again, but once at the top, he rolled down again.

When Porcupine got to the people, he said, "We are having a big meeting and the chief wants everyone to come and listen. The rest of the people are over there waiting. "Alright," said the people. "Are you going to take us back with you? You know the way." Porcupine said that he would. "Follow me, we will go down there."

There was a good trail where Porcupine had rolled down, earlier. He took the people through. He hadn't rolled down the other side, so he curled up and rolled down, making a path. The people followed him and rolled down the deep, fresh snow. He got all the people down.

The chief was pleased that the porcupine had brought all the people down. "We are going to have a special gathering," said the chief. "Tonight, we will sing in the big house." These were underground houses.

The chief gathered all the people. "My dear people, I have

been thinking. Now there are no animals and birds. We are going to try and bring them back. We were saved because we were able to float around until the flood waters went down. All the animals and birds died; they couldn't make it. Everything that we lived on, died." At the meeting, they all sang their songs, for whatever power they had. Everyone sang.

A person said, "I am going to be a bluejay," and he made the noise of a bluejay. The people said that he could be a bluejay.

Another person made the sound of a magpie. The chief and the people said that he could be a magpie, as they had a lot of use for that bird.

Another person said, "I am going to be a deer, a fawn." He imitated the sound of a fawn and the people were satisfied. He was to be an ordinary deer.

Another person became a lark. He made the noise of a lark, and the chief agreed that he could be *Sh-kwi-la-tin*. This bird is similar to the woodpecker and lives in the mountains.

There were a lot of people at the special gathering, and they all turned into either a bird or an animal. The porcupine said, "I am the oldest brother; I am going to be a porcupine." He then sang a song. "When women need medicine, they can use my gall; it will be for that purpose."

The First Totem Pole
Hugh Weatherby

When Ramlaryaelk was very young, perhaps three or four years old, a medicine man told his mother that the boy would one day do something to make him remembered forever by the Indians.

As Ram — we will call Ramlaryaelk Ram for short — walked along the banks of the Footprints-in-the-shallow-water River near the upper reaches of the Skeena, he thought of the old prophecy, and how, even though he was nearly thirty, no chance had yet come for him to make himself famous. True, with his two brothers, he had engaged in many battles and proved his mettle, but all young Indian men fought like heroes in the never-ending wars. Perhaps, he thought, chuckling to himself, he would live to such a ripe old age that the tribal singers would make up songs about his doings and sing them to future generations.

His day-dreams were interrupted by a call from a nearby camp. "Ram," cried a stern voice, "take a basket and get some water from the Spring-that-always-boils."

Ram picked up a waterproof basket — the Indians wove baskets so fine they easily held water — and ran to do as he was bidden, for, as he and his brothers were only adopted sons of the Larsail, having once belonged to the Wild Rice tribe, they were made to do some of the unpleasant chores to show they were not quite as good as the Larsail men.

Ram found his two brothers sitting by the Spring-that-always-boils. It was late in the fall and quite cold, but the air around the spring was warm and comfortable. He greeted his brothers and they nodded in return, as was the custom, and then he stooped to fill the cedar-root basket with hot water. That move was never finished.

Before Ram's startled eyes a figure slowly rose from the middle of the spring. It seemed to be the statue of a man in a sitting position, with his hands pressed against his side. Seven young ravens rested on top of its head, which, like the rest of its body, was as bare of clothing as a new-born baby.

The three young men froze and stared, open-mouthed. Their feelings ran from fear to wonder and back to fear again. Ram was the first to recover his wits and he quickly turned towards the village and called for help, to bring the rest of the tribe to the scene so that there might be witnesses outside his own immediate family, for he realized, even in that short time, that the tale, unless others saw the strange sight, would be greeted with jeers and laughter.

All the villagers within earshot came pelting down to the

spring. As they arrived they, like Ram and his brothers, froze rigid for a second, their eyes bulging out, and then took up the chorus of "Ohs" and "Ahs" and gaped in amazement. The Indians cackled among themselves like a flock of geese disturbed by some prowler in the night. Surely nothing like this had ever before been seen by mortal man!

When the excitement died down a little, Ram sent a pair of his friends to bring tools while the rest of the tribe prepared to take the statue from the spring to firmer ground. "See," he said happily, "this is the beginning of the fortune the witch doctor told for me. From now on, with this at the door of our lodge, none will deny my brothers and me equal rights with the Larsail men."

"That is so," nodded one of the old men, "with such a totem before your door, who would dare say you should not have equal rights?"

The task of moving the figure to Ram's home proved more than any of them expected, and finally it was decided that the spring would have to be drained.

The work of digging drains took several hours, but at last the statue rested on dry, or at least fairly dry, land. The Indians hitched on their cedar ropes and made ready to pull the stone figure up the hill. Once again they found the figure too heavy, and, tug as they might, it moved not an inch.

After several attempts, and much grunting by the fatter Indians Ram raised his hand in a signal to stop. "We must have help," he said. "We will call in the Wolf, Fireweed and Larhaun tribes; we have helped them in the past and they will gladly help us now."

With the aid of the newcomers the figure was moved quickly up the hill and placed before Ram's door.

Ram looked it over with pleasure and satisfaction; pleasure because there was nothing else like it in the country and satisfaction because it meant equal rights for his brothers and himself with the Larsail men. Ram's breast almost burst with pride. Surely, he thought, this is the time to give a huge feast and show my find to the neighbouring tribes, and at the same time repay my own people for their help in getting the figure up here.

The news of the feast spread far and wide, as such news always does among the Indians, for they love a big feast or potlach, and, two days before the date set, members of some of the more distant tribes began drifting in. As more and more guests came Ram grew prouder and prouder; his fame would grow as the stories of the statue and feast were told and retold by his guests, till everyone on the river would know of Ramlaryaelk and the stone image he owned.

Ram stood before his lodge on the eve of the big feast and thought of the future with pleasure. From time to time he glanced fondly at the statue. Suddenly he straightened up, blinked his eyes, spat out the twig he was chewing, and gasped. The stone figure had moved! Slowly and surely it was sliding downhill! Even as Ram opened his mouth to cry for help, the statue gave another, harder lurch, picked up speed and slid with a grinding of stones and mad scattering of mud, past a few startled, staring Indian people, down the steep slope, and splashed into the lake. There was nothing left to mark its passing but a deep muddy ditch.

For a few seconds the poor man was too stunned to move, then he rushed to the water's edge, dropped to his knees; and peered hopefully into the green depths. There was nothing to be seen. The stone figure had already sunk from sight.

Ram tottered back to his lodge. He stumbled inside and sank down on a pile of furs, unable to believe his bad luck. He sat on his haunches and rocked back and forth, muttering to himself. "I am doomed! I am doomed! And just when I had a chance to become an equal member of the tribe. Surely the spirits are against me."

His mother heard his moans and looked in. After asking the cause of his grief, she sat down beside him. "Poor, poor Ram," she murmured, "to have this happen just when you were so near to success."

"If I could only find another statue, mother, to put in the place of the one I lost," he sobbed, "then it might not be so bad; but to have no statue to show, that is way beyond words. We will never live down the shame, it will follow us forever."

"Could you not carve one from wood?" the old woman asked.

Ram sat up with a jerk. That was the answer. A wooden statue carved as nearly like the stone one as he could remember. He jumped to his feet, patted his mother lovingly, and ran to ask the help of his brothers and his fellow-tribesmen. He knew they would all help, for, if no statue appeared at the feast, the honour of the whole tribe would be at stake.

The next day, the day of the big feast, Ram took his place beside the door of his hut, with his hand resting lightly on the head of the newly carved, grey-painted, wooden figure. As he greeted his guests, one and all remarked about the statue and to each he told the story of how he came by it. The last guest finally passed and not a soul, except the members of his own tribe, dreamed that the figure they admired was not the image dragged from the hot-water spring.

Ram watched the merry-makers through half shut eyes. This was indeed his big day, for now he was a full-fledged member of the tribe. Surely this was the day the medicine man spoke about, the one that would make him known to history.

Ram was right, too. That was his big day, but not, as he thought, because he gave a potlatch and displayed a statue to his friends, but because from that day on the Indians of the northern Pacific coast carved figures of wood. Ramlaryaelk had, without meaning to, invented the totem pole.

The Legend of the Thunderbird

Gail Ann Kendall

Many moons ago there was a tribe of Indians that lived on the coast of British Columbia. This tribe was blessed by the gods in numerous ways. In the forest there were deer and bear. Berries grew in abundance on the mountain slopes. Fishing was good. Indeed, they had everything they could wish for except a name. For this reason they were not recognized as a great tribe. Farther back than the oldest of the tribe could remember, the proud son of a great chief had disobeyed his father. He was disowned, and so with a small band of followers, he started his own tribe. Henceforth the tribe was nameless. As soon as a name was thought of, news came of another tribe which already bore that name. The nameless tribe had its pride too. It would not be called the Weasel Tribe, for instance! That was not their only worry. There was rumour that the God of the Sea was angry at them. Every third day great waves rolled high upon the beach. They were as deep as the tallest brave was tall, and came above the highest tide marker. Many children, even warriors, were carried away, and never seen again. Were the gods angry? Of course — how else could the people explain it?

One of the people lost to the waves was Brown Dove. Then Running Wolf, her husband, had been taken, trying to save her.

These were the parents of Lame Bear, so called because he was injured in a fight with a bear. He lived with his grandmother. They were a familiar sight in the village, an old woman and a lame boy, hobbling along the paths in search of food. Lame Bear was determined to avenge his father's death, though it meant a fight with the gods.

One day he climbed into his canoe. In the distance he could see the headland. From this direction the waves had come. It was easy in the cool morning, paddling quickly and smoothly, but as the sun rose higher and higher, his strokes were slower and slower. He decided to land, but because of his lame leg, he could not walk easily, so as soon as it grew cooler, he returned to the sea in his canoe. The water was calm now, but in one day and two nights more, the waves would start again. Darkness came on him quickly. Tired, hungry, and thirsty, he landed and sprawled on the beach. Soon he was fast asleep.

Next morning he awoke, and drank thirstily from a nearby spring. Then he paddled on. The point in the distance was growing larger, and he could make out an area of destruction. Evidently the waves came much higher here. He headed out to sea because he was going around the point. He hastened his paddling for the second night was descending upon him. Then when he was near the middle of the high cliff-like piece of land, he headed inward. Though it would be hard on his lame leg, he decided to walk across. Then he wouldn't be taking the chance of being caught in the waves.

He pulled his canoe high on the beach, and stared at the stark desolation. He limped higher on the beach, looking at the fallen trees and rotting debris in astonishment. Only a god himself could do such damage.

He climbed on, resting often, and making little headway. Finally he reached timberland. On and on he travelled. Then he reached the crest of the hill. His eyes widened in amazement. Here was even more damage than what he had just left! He ventured down farther, then sat down, well above the high tide mark, and waited. After a short while, a great shadow fell on the land, and Lame Bear heard a piercing scream. Looking up, he saw a large bird — surely the largest bird he had ever seen! Down, down, down it glided, and at last it landed. Lame Bear watched unbelievingly, as the great bird settled its wings.

Then the bird spoke!

"Do not be afraid," it said.

"Who are you?" cried Lame Bear, fearfully.

"I am called the Thunder Bird," it replied. "I am the

Maker of Storms. This is my sacred shrine. Every day I sacrifice a whale here."

It pointed its great wing, and for the first time Lame Bear saw bones bleaching on the sand. Then he understood. This was what made the waves, and it took them two days to get to the Indian Village.

The bird spoke again. "Where do you live?"

Lame Bear told it. Then he made a timid suggestion.

"Great bird, would you come to our village and be our god?"

After the bird thought for a moment, it agreed. Lame Bear was happy until he remembered his father. He had sworn to avenge his death. But Lame Bear had grown to like this huge flying creature, and what chance had he against it?

He spoke again. "Bird, the waves made by you have carried off many of our people, among them my father and mother. I have sworn by the sun, moon and stars that I will avenge their deaths."

"Oh, them?" said the bird. "I have them on my island. Climb aboard, and we will go see them."

The bird spread out its wings, and Lame Bear awkwardly clambered upon its back. There, exhausted by the bewildering happenings, he fell asleep on his feathery bed.

He awoke with a start — they had landed. Stiffly he crawled down, and stretched his cramped limbs. Ahead of him was a small, crude hut. The bird screamed loudly, and out of the hut came Lame Bear's mother, his father, and the other people of the village! His heart filled with joyous surprise. His father told him of good treatment and much food, and the kindness of the Thunder Bird.

"He has promised to come back and be our tribe totem!" said Lame Bear excitedly.

"Come!" cried the bird. "All of you climb aboard."

So up they got, and quickly they sped over the blue waters. Soon they saw their familiar village far below. Down they flew, and landed on the beach. The braves who had gathered there retreated fearfully. Imagine a great bird carrying those who were believed dead! But the chieftain advanced and said, "Let us have a council meeting, brothers."

A meeting was called. Old and young alike attended, and Lame Bear was called upon to tell his story. The Thunder Bird was taken into the tribe, and promised to protect the village for ever more.

And so it was. The carvings of the great bird can yet be seen on the totems of the Tribe of the Thunder Bird.

A Magic Bear
Edward W. Dolch & Marguerite P. Dolch

Long ago an old, old man and an old, old woman lived in an Eskimo village. The old man could not see very well. And the old woman could not hear very well.

The old man and the old woman had no children. There was no one to look after them. There was no one to go hunting for them and bring them food.

The old man and the old woman were very sad.

One day the hunters of the village killed many polar bears. There was great shouting and feasting. But no one came to the hut where the old man and the old woman lived. No one invited them to the feast.

The shouting was so loud that even the old woman could hear it.

"I cannot stand this noise any longer," said the old woman. "My ears are filled with noise. But my stomach is empty."

"There is nothing that we can do about it," said the old man. "No one comes to invite us to the feast."

The old woman was very angry.

"If I were a man, I would do something," said the old woman.

Now the old man was very angry.

"I will show you that I am still a man. I am going out. You put some water in the pot. Get the water boiling hot."

The old man went out, and the woman said to herself,

"I have never seen the old man so angry."

The old man was gone a long time. The water in the pot began to boil. Then the old man came back. He was carefully holding his hands together.

The old man did not speak to the old woman. He went to the pot and opened his hands. Three drops of blood fell into the pot. Then the old man put a small bit of meat into the pot.

All the time, the old man kept singing a magic song.

"What are you doing?" asked the old woman.

"You have spoiled my magic," said the old man.

The old woman looked into the pot. The pot had stopped boiling.

The old man did not know what to do. Suddenly he pulled out some of his wife's white hair.

The old man threw the white hair into the pot, and it began to boil again. The old man kept singing his magic song.

The woman watched. A little white polar bear came out of the pot. It was a Magic Bear. The old woman cared for it as if it were her baby.

The old man sat on the floor and tears ran down his face.

"I remembered, I remembered," said the old man. "When I was young, I was a great Shaman. I had great magic."

The old woman cared for the little polar bear all night.

In the morning the Magic Bear had grown to be a big bear.

The Magic Bear went hunting. In the evening he came home with a fat seal. The old man and the old woman had a feast.

Day after day, the Magic Bear went hunting. The old man the old woman had everything that they wanted. Then one day the old man said to the Magic Bear.

"My son, the old woman is tired of eating fat seals. She would like something else today."

"Would she like a fine fish?" asked the Magic Bear.

"No," said the old man. "She says that she would like a fine big piece of polar bear meat."

The Magic Bear looked very much surprised. He walked up and down. He looked very sad. But he did not say a word. At last he took the old man's bow and arrows. He went out to hunt. That evening the Magic Bear did not come back to the hut.

In the morning the old man and the old woman found a big, dead polar bear in front of their hut. It was meat that would last them a long time. But they never saw the Magic Bear again.

The Pilot of the Plains
E. Pauline Johnson

"False," they said, "thy Pale-face lover, from the
    land of waking morn;
Rise and wed thy Redskin wooer, nobler warrior ne'er
    was born;
Cease thy watching, cease thy dreaming,
    Show the white thine Indian scorn."

Thus they taunted her, declaring, "He remembers
    naught of thee:
Likely some white maid he wooeth, far beyond the
    inland sea."
But she answered ever kindly,
    "He will come again to me,"

Till the dusk of Indian summer crept athwart the
    western skies;
But a deeper dusk was burning in her dark and
    dreaming eyes,
As she scanned the rolling prairie,
    Where the foothills fall, and rise.

Till the autumn came and vanished, till the season
  of the rains,
Till the western world lay fettered in midwinter's
  crystal chains,
Still she listened for his coming,
    Still she watched the distant plains.

Then a night with nor'land tempest, nor'land snows
  a-swirling fast,
Out upon the pathless prairie came the Pale-face
  through the blast,
Calling, calling, "Yakonwita,
    I am coming, love, at last."

Hovered night above, about him, dark its wings and
  cold and dread;
Never unto trail or tepee were his straying footsteps
  led;
Till benumbed, he sank, and pillowed
    On the drifting snows his head,

Saying, "O! my Yakonwita call me, call me, be my guide
To the lodge beyond the prairie — for I vowed ere
  winter died
I would come again, beloved;
    I would claim my Indian bride."

"Yakonwita, Yakonwita!" Oh, the dreariness that strains
Through the voice that calling, quivers, till a whisper
  but remains,
"Yakonwita, Yakonwita,
    I am lost upon the plains."

But the Silent Spirit hushed him, lulled him as he
  cried anew,
"Save me, save me! O! beloved, I am Pale but I am true.
Yakonwita, Yakonwita,
    I am dying, love, for you."

Leagues afar, across the prairie, she had risen from her
    bed,
Roused her kinsmen from their slumber: "He has
    come to-night," she said.
"I can hear him calling, calling;
        But his voice is as the dead.

"Listen!" and they sat all silent, while the tempest
    louder grew,
And a spirit-voice called faintly, "I am dying, love, for
    you."
Then they wailed, "O! Yakonwita.
        He was Pale, but he was true."

Wrapped she then her ermine round her, stepped
    without the tepee door,
Saying, "I must follow, follow, though he call for ever-
    more,
Yakonwita, Yakonwita;"
        And they never saw her more.

Late at night, say Indian hunters, when the starlight
    clouds or wanes,
Far away they see a maiden, misty as the autumn rains,
Guiding with her lamp of moonlight
        Hunters lost upon the plains.

A Legend of the Rockies
John W. Chalmers

Blackfoot, Blood, Saulteaux, Sarcee,
Peigan, Stony, Sioux and Cree,
Courted they the chieftain's daughter;
Sought the hand of Running Water.

Ultimately three Blood brothers
Fought, defeated all the others,

Rising Smoke and Flying Cloud
And Falling Rock, brave men and proud.

How to choose the maiden's mate?
How to give the nudge to Fate?
Quoth the chieftain, "She'll espouse
The greatest hunter of your house.

"Flying Cloud, away you lope,
Bring me back an antelope.
Rising Smoke, a pinto horse.
Falling Rock, an elk, of course."

Fast the brothers sped away.
Two returned that very day.
"Where's the third one?" was the talk.
"What's become of Falling Rock?"

Still they seek the absent one
'Neath winter moon and summer sun,
Posting signs where tourists flock,
Urging, "Watch for Falling Rock."

The Golden Boy
Irene Craig

In 1951 the 5 ton lad on the top of the Dome of the Legislative
Building in Winnipeg, was outfitted with a new suit — a garb
of gold. This youthful figure carries a torch; the call of eternal
youth to join in the race. The Boy is poised on his left foot in
the pose of a runner and the tip of the torch he carries in his
right hand is 255 feet above ground. In the curve of his left arm
rests a golden sheaf of wheat. He is 13 feet, 6 inches tall
typifying "Eternal Youth" or "The Spirit of Enterprise" but
always fondly referred to as "The Golden Boy".

Sculptured by Charles Gardet and cast in Paris, the Boy was fashioned to complete architect Simon's beautiful design for the Manitoba Legislative Building, one of the finest in North America; but it was many a long day ere that took place. Before he ever glistened so enchantingly in the rays of a prairie sunset, this bronze figure, now clad in pure gold, had many adventures. At the outset the foundry was wrecked by German bombs; the Boy alone emerged unharmed.

Given the final touches he was stored in a freight ship, the first move on his way to New York. From there he would finish his journey by rail to Winnipeg. Lying snug in the hold he rested in his straw wrappings, making ready to start his race high up on the Dome. But when World War I was declared, at the last moment the freight ship was commandeered by the French Government to take on an emergency cargo of war supplies. The 5 ton statue remained in the ship as ballast. Continuing its war service, the vessel transported American troops.

Apparently forgotten, all during World War I the Boy in the hold voyaged back and forth, through submarine infested waters in the North Sea, the Atlantic, the Mediterranean, and in the English Channel. Not for several years did he disembark, as originally planned, at a pier in New York Harbour.

Finally, completing his journeyings on a flat car (of all things), the Golden Boy arrived in Winnipeg in August 1919, with plenty of time to relax; actually it was still several months later before he was hoisted to his perch 240 feet above ground level and symbolically placed, his gaze forever fixed toward the untold wealth of the northland.

Nearing 40 years of age, this Eternal Youth in his shining suit of 23 karat gold, perched on the Dome of the Manitoba Legislative Building, today looks younger than ever. Through the passing years, his added brilliance promising to become (if possible) still more radiant.

Where There's Smoke . . .

Jacques Hamilton

This story is set more than a hundred years ago, when the Cree and Blackfoot were still fighting, raiding north and south across the Red Deer River that separated their territories.

A party of Blackfoot had pushed north across the river, following the buffalo on their summer migration — and taking the opportunity to raid Cree camps for ponies and scalps.

The Blackfoot party, late in the summer, were camped on the banks of Pipestone Creek. The Cree were out for blood and had rushed a large force south to cut off the retreat of their enemies.

All day the Blackfoot sat in council of war, listening to the muffled drums of the Cree.

If the Blackfoot were worried by their position, there was nothing in their council of war to show it. Far from mapping out escape plans, they were hatching a scheme to raid the Cree camp by night and return home with even more horses and scalps.

It just wasn't Blackfoot nature to avoid a fight.

At that time, each of the tribes had a powerful young chief rising to leadership: Little Bear for the Cree and Buffalo Child for the Blackfoot.

When the Blackfoot were ready to scout the Cree camp to make the raid, it was Buffalo Child who was sent on the mission. By coincidence, the Cree were in the process of doing some scouting of their own, and Little Bear was doing it.

Being talented scouts, both men wanted to find the best vantage point from which to spy on the enemy's camp. Only, as it turned out, the best vantage point for both sides happened to be the same hill.

The two young chiefs stole up opposite sides of the hill at

the same time and, with a shock, suddenly found themselves face to face.

The two froze in their tracks, recognizing one another instantly. For a full minute they glared at one another, then Buffalo Child threw aside his rifle with a scornful smile.

"Dog of a Cree," he taunted. "See, I throw my gun away. I do not need it. With my bare hands I will break you in two."

With equal scorn, Little Bear tossed his knife aside. "No Blackfoot with the heart of a woman can get the better of Little Bear."

They circled warily, looking for an opening, spitting insults at each other. Then, like two great cats, they sprang and grappled.

The two were almost a match for size and strength and neither could gain an advantage. Locked in one another's grasp, they swayed and struggled. First the Cree would go down, then the Blackfoot, but neither for long enough to give his enemy victory.

For almost an hour, as the sun slowly set, the two struggled on in silence. Then, as though by mutual consent, they drew apart, panting and exhausted.

"You are a stout fighter," the Blackfoot admitted as he gasped for air. "Let us rest awhile and, later, we will renew the struggle."

Little Bear grunted agreement, and the two squatted facing one another. The fierce hatred in their eyes was now mixed with something almost like respect.

Buffalo Child fumbled at his belt and pulled forth a pipe and tobacco from a beaded bag. Little Bear followed his example, but found his pipe had been broken into three pieces during the fight.

Frustrated, he threw the clay fragments aside, then sat back enviously to watch his enemy smoke.

Slowly, the Blackfoot filled his pipe, lighted it, and began to puff complacently.

The sweet smell of "kinnikinic" smoke almost drove Little Bear wild. He smouldered with rage at his enemy's enjoyment of a pleasure that was denied him.

All this was not lost on Buffalo Child. It was a form of torture which an Indian could appreciate. He watched Little Bear with amusement. Suddenly, perhaps to heighten the torture, he held the smoking pipe out to his Cree opponent.

Before he could pull back his hand, Little Bear had snatched the pipe free, thrust the mouthpiece between his lips, and inhaled deeply.

Abruptly, he stopped with a strangled cough and stared at Buffalo Child. Buffalo Child, equally aghast, was staring back, mouth open with consternation.

An incredible thing had been done. Impulsively, through an act of fate, they had accidentally smoked together the common pipe.

It was the sacred pledge of amity and peace, made so by immemorial tradition, as unbreakable to them as the most solemn vow.

Finally, the Cree spoke. "My brother," he said softly, "we did not mean to do it, but we have smoked the peace pipe together. Henceforth we must be friends, and because we are chiefs of our tribes, our people also must be friends and think no more of war. Is it not so?"

Reluctantly, Buffalo Child agreed. He rose to his feet. "We must go back to the lodges of our people," he said, " and tell them of this thing we have done." He shivered in the growing darkness.

"I cannot understand it, but some great medicine must have been at work. Undoubtedly it is a sign; it must be the will of the Manitou. Let us go."

They turned on their heels, two dejected and bedraggled figures, and silently parted in the dusk.

The following morning, runners were sent from the camp of the Crees to summon the Blackfoot to council. During the night, on both sides, the older chiefs had listened gravely to the incredible story and shaken their heads in puzzlement. But all admitted that what had been done could not be undone.

Tradition could not be overridden lightly. And, without a doubt, it must be a sign from the Great Manitou.

In early morning, the council assembled on the hilltop where the struggle had taken place. Four chiefs of the Blackfoot and six of the Cree sat in solemn circle and passed the pipe of peace from hand to hand.

There were pledges of eternal friendship and peace, and the hatchet was buried with appropriate ceremony.

Ever since, outwardly at least, Cree and Blackfoot have respected the vows they exchanged.

And ever since, the hills outside one of Alberta's bustling communities have been known as "Weteskewin Spatinow" — the place where peace was made — Wetaskiwin.

The Creation of the Northern Rocky Mountains
Ella Elizabeth Clark

The Mackenzie River, which flows into the Arctic Ocean in the extreme northwestern part of Canada, was called by the northern Indians Too-Cha-tes, *meaning "Big Water". The stream which flows from the southwest and joins the Mackenzie near its mouth they called by a name that means "the river that flows from the country of the Big Man". Their name for Big Man was* Naba-Cha.

The Big Man, Naba-Cha, was one of the very largest men who ever lived. The lodge which was his home was made of three hundred skins of the biggest caribou that could be killed on the plains that lie north of his river. The dish from which he ate his meals was made of the bark of six huge birch trees. And it took one whole moose, or two caribou, or fifty partridges to feed him every day.

Big Man was known throughout the whole North Country, for he had often made war against the tribes of the north, the east, and the south. Northward he had travelled to the mouth of Big Water to fight the Snow Men, the Eskimos. Eastward, he had crossed Great Bear Lake to the country of the Yellow-knives. There he had seen the pure copper shining in the sands of the rivers that flow toward the Great Bear Lake and Great Slave Lake and toward the icy ocean.

Southward, he had travelled a long distance to the great plains, the country of the Crees, where he had seen many large animals. But westward he had never gone, because there lived a giant man, a man bigger than Naba-Cha.

Naba-Cha was not only big: he was wicked and very cruel. He was especially cruel to a Cree boy he had brought back from the south one time when he was on the war-path. The boy was an orphan without father or mother, sister or brother, to help him escape. His name was Caribou-footed.

The boy had one friend in the lodge of Big Man. That was Hottah, the two-year-old moose, the cleverest of all the northern animals. Swift he was, too. He had travelled, in one day, all the long distance from the mouth of Big Water to the home of Big Man.

Hottah liked Caribou-footed so much that he wanted to help him escape from Big Man. He knew that far to the westward, much farther west than Big Man had ever gone, flowed another river almost as long and wide as Big Water. The Yukon, it is called. West of the Yukon, he knew, lay safety for Caribou-footed. There lived Nesnabi, the Good Man.

So one day Hottah said to the boy, "We will go away. You take a stone, a clod of earth, a piece of moss, and a branch of a tree. Together we shall escape from the cruel Big Man. I will carry you on my back."

Caribou-footed gathered the things he was told to get, and soon the two were ready to leave. Hottah took the boy upon his back and carried him out of the great plains west of Big Water. But before long they saw Big Man coming behind them, riding his great caribou.

"Fling out behind you your clod of earth," said Hottah to the boy. Caribou-footed did so, and at once there rose behind them, between them and Big Man, great hills of earth. The hills were so high and wide that it was many days before Big Man came in sight again. During those days Hottah chewed the sweet grass that grew west of the hills, and Caribou-footed ate the ripe berries.

When Big Man came in sight a second time, Hottah called to the boy, "Fling out behind you your piece of moss."

Caribou-footed did so, and at once a vast muskeg-swamp lay behind them. For days the caribou and Big Man floundered in the muskeg, while Hottah and the boy moved on toward the setting sun. When Big Man appeared a third time, Hottah said to the boy, "Fling behind you your stone."

Caribou-footed did so, and at once there rose behind them, between them and Big Man, high rocky mountains. Up to the clouds they rose, white with snow, more magnificent than had ever been seen before. It was a long time before Big Man and his caribou had crossed the mountains and appeared again to Hottah and the boy. Then they were much nearer their goal, the great western river.

"Now fling out behind you your branch of a tree."

Caribou-footed did so, and at once arose a mighty forest, with trees so thick that Big Man and his gigantic caribou could not pass between them. Big Man had to cut his way through. And because its horns had stuck in the branches, the caribou was left behind.

By the time Big Man came in sight again, Hottah had carried the boy safely across the great river, the Yukon. Away toward the west it wound, through high rocky hills, foaming as it flowed.

Big Man reached the bank of the river and, seeing Hottah on the other side, called to him, "Help me, Hottah. Help me cross this turbulent river. If you will assist me to the country that lies beyond, I will do no harm to the boy. I promise you."

Without a word Hottah went to get Big Man. But as they were crossing the great river, Hottah dropped the giant into the water. Down he was swept by the swirling rapids of the river, on and on toward the setting sun.

Thus the wicked and cruel Bad Man, Naba-cha, was lost forever, and thus Caribou-footed was saved. And in the far Northwest, the foothills, the muskeg-swamp, the snow-capped Rocky Mountains, and the great forest remain where the Cree boy threw the clod of earth, the piece of moss, the stone, and the branch of a tree, long, long ago.

The Ballad of Yaada
A Legend of the Pacific Coast
E. Pauline Johnson

There are fires on Lulu Island, and the sky is opalescent
> With the pearl and purple tinting from the smouldering of
>> peat.
And the Dream Hills lift their summits in a sweeping, hazy
>> crescent,
> With the Capilano cañon at their feet.

There are fires on Lulu Island, and the smoke, uplifting, lingers
> In a faded scarf of fragrance as it creeps across the day,
And the Inlet and the Narrows blur beneath its silent fingers,
> And the cañon is enfolded in its grey.

But the sun its face is veiling like a cloistered nun at vespers;
> As towards the altar candles of the night a censer swings,
And the echo of tradition wakes from slumbering and whispers,
> Where the Capilano river sobs and sings.

It was Yaada, lovely Yaada, who first taught the stream its
    sighing,
    For 'twas silent till her coming, and 'twas voiceless as the
      shore;
But throughout the great forever it will sing the song undying
    That the lips of lovers sing for evermore.

He was chief of all the Squamish, and he ruled the coastal
    waters —
    And he warred upon her people in the distant Charlotte
      Isles;
She, a winsome basket weaver, daintiest of Haida daughters,
    Made him captive to her singing and her smiles.

Till his hands forgot to havoc and his weapons lost their lusting,
    Till his stormy eyes allured her from the land of Totem
      Poles,
Till she followed where he called her, followed with a woman's
    trusting,
    To the cañon where the Capilano rolls.

And the women of the Haidas plied in vain their magic power,
    Wailed for many moons her absence, wailed for many
      moons their prayer,
"Bring her back, O Squamish foeman, bring to us our Yaada
    flower!"
    But the silence only answered their despair.

But the men were swift to battle, swift to cross the coastal
    water,
    Swift to war and swift of weapon, swift to paddle trackless
      miles,
Crept with stealth along the cañon, stole her from her love and
    brought her
    Once again unto the distant Charlotte Isles.

But she faded, ever faded, and her eyes were ever turning
  Southward toward the Capilano, while her voice had
    hushed its song,
And her riven heart repeated words that on her lips were
    burning:
  "Not to friend — but unto foeman I belong.

"Give me back my Squamish lover — though you hate, I still
    must love him.
  "Give me back the rugged cañon where my heart must ever
    be —
Where his lodge awaits my coming, and the Dream Hills lift
    above him,
  And the Capilano learned its song from me."

But through long-forgotten seasons, moons too many to be
    numbered,
  He yet waited by the cañon — she called across the years,
And the soul within the river, though centuries had slumbered,
  Woke to sob a song of womanly tears.

For her little, lonely spirit sought the Capilano cañon,
  When she died among the Haidas in the land of Totem
    Poles,
And you yet may hear her singing to her lover-like companion,
  If you listen to the river as it rolls.

But 'tis only when the pearl and purple smoke is idly swinging
  From the fires on Lulu Island to the hazy mountain crest,
That the undertone of sobbing echoes through the river's
    singing,
  In the Capilano cañon of the West.

The Grey Archway

E. Pauline Johnson

The steamer, like a huge shuttle, wove in and out among the countless small islands; its long trailing scarf of grey smoke hung heavily along the uncertain shores, casting a shadow over the pearly waters of the Pacific, which swung lazily from rock to rock in indescribable beauty.

After dinner I wandered astern with the traveller's ever-present hope of seeing the beauties of a typical Northern sunset, and by some happy chance I placed my deck stool near an old tillicum, who was leaning on the rail, his pipe between his thin curved lips, his brown hands clasped idly, his sombre eyes looking far out to sea, as though they searched the future — or was it that they were seeing the past?

"Kla-how-ya, tillicum!" I greeted.

He glanced round, and half smiled.

"Kla-how-ya, tillicum!" he replied, with the warmth of friendliness I have always met with among the Pacific tribes.

I drew my deck stool nearer to him, and he acknowledged the action with another half-smile, but did not stir from his entrenchment, remaining as if hedged about with an inviolable fortress of exclusiveness. Yet I knew that my Chinook salutation would be a draw-bridge by which I might hope to cross the moat into his castle of silence.

Indian-like, he took his time before continuing the acquaintance. Then he began in most excellent English:

"You do not know these Northern waters?"

I shook my head.

After many moments he leaned forwards, looking along the curve of the deck, up the channels and narrows we were threading, to a broad strip of waters off the port bow. Then he pointed with that peculiar, thoroughly Indian gesture of the palm uppermost.

"Do you see it — over there? The small island? It rests on the edge of the water, like a grey gull."

It took my unaccustomed eyes some moments to discern it; then all at once I caught its outline, veiled in the mists of distance — grey, cobwebby, dreamy.

"Yes," I replied, "I see it now. You will tell me of it — tillicum?"

He gave a swift glance at my dark skin, then nodded. "You are one of us," he said, with evidently no thought of a possible contradiction. "And you will understand, or I should not tell you. You will not smile at the story, for you are one of us."

"I am one of you, and I shall understand," I answered.

It was a full half-hour before we neared the island, yet neither of us spoke during that time; then, as the "grey gull" shaped itself into rock and tree and crag, I noticed in the very centre a stupendous pile of stone lifting itself skyward, without fissure or cleft; but a peculiar haziness about the base made me peer narrowly to catch the perfect outline.

"It is the 'Grey Archway'," he explained simply.

Only then did I grasp the singular formation before us; the rock itself was a perfect archway, through which we could see the placid Pacific shimmering in the growing colours of the coming sunset at the opposite rim of the island.

"What a remarkable whim of Nature!" I exclaimed, but his brown hand was laid in a contradictory grasp on my arm, and he snatched up my comment almost with impatience.

"No, it was not Nature!" he said. "That is the reason I say you will understand — you are one of us — you will know what I tell you is true. The Great Tyee did not make that archway, it was — " here his voice lowered — "it was magic, red man's medicine and magic — you savvy?"

"Yes," I said. "Tell me, for I — savvy."

"Long time ago," he began, stumbling into a half-broken English language because, I think, of the atmosphere and environment, "long before you were born, or your father, or grandfather, or even his father, this strange thing happened. It is a story for women to hear, to remember. Women are the future mothers of the tribe, and we of the Pacific Coast hold such in high regard, in great reverence. The women who are mothers — o-ho! — they are the important ones, we say. Warriors, fighters, brave men, fearless daughters, owe their qualities to these mothers — eh, is it not always so?"

I nodded silently. The island was swinging nearer to us, the Grey Archway loomed almost above us, the mysticism crowded close, it enveloped me, caressed me, appealed to me.

"And?" I hinted.

"And," he proceeded, "this 'Grey Archway' is a story of mothers, of magic, of witchcraft, of warriors, of — love."

An Indian rarely uses the word "love", and when he does it expresses every quality, every attribute, every intensity, emotion, and passion embraced in those four little letters. Surely this was an exceptional story I was to hear.

I did not answer, only looked across the pulsing waters towards the Grey Archway, which the sinking sun was touching with soft pastels, tints one could give no name to, beauties impossible to describe.

"You have not heard of Yaada?" he questioned. Then fortunately he continued without waiting for a reply. He well knew that I had never heard of Yaada, so why not begin without preliminary to tell me of her? — so —

"Yaada was the loveliest daughter of the Haida tribe. Young braves from all the islands, from the mainland, from the upper Skeena country came, hoping to carry her to their far-off lodges, but they always returned alone. She was the most desired of all the island maidens, beautiful, brave, modest, the daughter of her own mother.

"But there was a great man, a very great man — a medicine man, skilful, powerful, influential, old, deplorably old, and very, very rich; he said, 'Yaada shall be my wife.' And there was a young fisherman, handsome, loyal, boyish, poor, oh! very poor, and gloriously young, and he, too, said, 'Yaada shall be my wife.'

"But Yaada's mother sat apart and thought and dreamed, as mothers will. She said to herself, 'The great medicine man has power, has vast riches, and wonderful magic, why not give her to him? But Ulka has the boy's heart, the boy's beauty, he is very brave, very strong; why not give her to him?'

"But the laws of the great Haida tribe prevailed. Its wise men said, 'Give the girl to the greatest man, give her to the most powerful, the richest. The man of magic must have his choice.'

"But at this the mother's heart grew as wax in the summer sunshine — it is a strange quality that mothers' hearts are made of! 'Give her to the best man — the man her heart holds highest,' said this Haida mother.

"Then Yaada spoke: 'I am the daughter of my tribe; I would judge of men by their excellence. He who proves most worthy I shall marry; it is not riches that make a good husband; it is not beauty that makes a good father for one's children. Let me and my tribe see some proof of the excellence of these two men — then, only, shall I choose who is to be the father of my children. Let us have a trial of their skill; let them show me how evil or how beautiful is the inside of their hearts. Let each of them throw a stone with some intent, some purpose in their hearts. He who makes the noblest mark may call me wife.'

" 'Alas! Alas!' wailed the Haida mother. 'This casting of stones does not show worth. It but shows prowess.'

" 'But I have implored the Sagalie Tyee of my father, and of his fathers before him, to help me to judge between them by this means,' said the girl. 'So they must cast the stones. In this way only shall I see their innermost hearts.'

"The medicine man never looked so old as at that moment; so hopelessly old, so wrinkled, so palsied; he was no mate for Yaada. Ulka never looked so god-like in his young beauty, so gloriously young, so courageous. The girl, looking at him, loved him — almost was she placing her hand in his, but the spirit of her forefathers halted her. She had spoken the word — she must abide by it. 'Throw!' she commanded.

"Into his shrivelled fingers the great medicine man took a small, round stone, chanting strange words of magic all the while; his greedy eyes were on the girl, his greedy thoughts about her.

"Into his strong, young fingers Ulka took a smooth, flat stone; his handsome eyes were lowered in boyish modesty, his thoughts were worshipping her. The great medicine man cast his missile first; it swept through the air like a shaft of lightning, striking the great rock with a force that shattered it. At the touch of that stone the Grey Archway opened and has remained open to this day.

" 'Oh, wonderful power and magic!' clamoured the entire tribe. 'The very rocks do his bidding.'

"But Yaada stood with eyes that burned in agony. Ulka could never command such magic — she knew it. At her side Ulka was standing erect, tall, slender, and beautiful, but just as he cast his missile the evil voice of the old medicine man began a still more evil incantation. He fixed his poisonous eyes on the younger man, eyes with hideous magic in their depths — ill-omened and enchanted with 'bad medicine'. The stone left Ulka's fingers; for a second it flew forth in a straight line, then as the evil voice of the old man grew louder in its incantations the stone curved. Magic had waylaid the strong arm of the young brave. The stone poised an instant above the forehead of Yaada's mother, then dropped with the weight of many mountains, and the last long sleep fell upon her.

" 'Slayer of my mother,' stormed the girl, her suffering eyes fixed upon the medicine man. 'Oh, I now see your black heart through your black magic. Through good magic you cut the Grey Archway, but your evil magic you used upon young Ulka. I saw your wicked eyes upon him; I heard your wicked incantations; I know your wicked heart. You used your heartless magic in hope of winning me — in hope of making him an outcast of the tribe. You cared not for my sorrowing heart, my motherless life to come.' Then turning to the tribe, she demanded: 'Who of you saw his evil eyes fixed on Ulka? Who of you heard his evil song?'

" 'I,' and 'I,' and 'I' came voice after voice.

"'The very air is poisoned that we breathe about him,' they shouted. 'The young man is blameless, his heart is as the sun, but the man who has used his evil magic has a heart black and cold as the hours before the dawn.'

"Then Yaada's voice arose in a strange, sweet, sorrowful chant:

My feet shall walk no more upon this island,
With its great, Grey Archway.
My mother sleeps forever on this island,
With its great, Grey Archway.
My heart would break without her on this island,
With its great, Grey Archway.
My life was of her life upon this island,
With its great, Grey Archway.
My mother's soul has wandered from this island,
With its great, Grey Archway.
My feet must follow hers beyond this island,
With its great, Grey Archway.

"As Yaada chanted and wailed her farewell, she moved slowly towards the edge of the cliff. On its brink she hovered a moment with outstretched arms, as a sea gull poises on its weight — then she called:

" 'Ulka, my Ulka! Your hand is innocent of wrong; it was the evil magic of your rival that slew my mother. I must go to her; even you cannot keep me here; will you stay, or come with me? Oh! my Ulka!'

"The slender, gloriously young boy sprang towards her; their hands closed one within the other; for a second they poised on the brink of the rocks, radiant as stars; then together they plunged into the sea."

The legend was ended. Long ago we had passed the island with its Grey Archway; it was melting into the twilight, far astern.

As I brooded over this strange tale of a daughter's devotion, I watched the sea and sky for something that would give me a clue to the inevitable sequel that the tillicum, like all his race, was surely withholding until the opportune moment.

Something flashed through the darkening waters not a stone's throw from the steamer. I leaned forwards, watching it intently. Two silvery fish were making a succession of little leaps and plunges along the surface of the sea, their bodies catching the last tints of sunset, like flashing jewels. I looked at the tillicum quickly. He was watching me — a world of anxiety in his half-mournful eyes.

"And those two silvery fish?" I questioned.

He smiled. The anxious look vanished. "I was right," he said; "you do know us and our ways, for you are one of us. Yes, those fish are seen only in these waters; there are never but two of them. They are Yaada and her mate seeking for the soul of the Haida woman — her mother."

No Mean Country
John W. Chalmers

"My home's between the Smoky and the Peace,"
He said. "That's where we raise the world's best wheat."
"So I've heard," was my reply. "You also grow
Barley, oats, and rye that can't be beat.

"No rivers run so deep, so clear and fleet
As those that Twelve Foot Davis' Land can show;
No clouds so pearly white, no skies so blue,
No other place such gentle breezes blow.

"No moose or bear so great, or laid so low
As those your wise and mighty hunters slew.
No grass so green as grows upon your leas,
No land on earth so fair or bright or new.

"No dawn or sunset with so rich a hue;
No timber ever came from taller trees;
No other girls as lovely or as sweet."
He smiled, "You've been there, I can see with ease."

Larger Than Life

Rene Zamic

People

The Most Stupid Boy
Ruth Young

Once upon a time, in a little village on the west coast of Vancouver Island, there lived the stupidest Indian boy in all the world.

His uncle was a chief, a strong man and a cunning hunter. His canoe fared far in pursuit of sea otter and whale, but the boy cared nothing for the honor of his tribe. All day long he lay on the beach. Sometimes his uncle would take him to hunt, then the boy would crouch in the canoe, whimpering with fear.

At last the tribe held a great council, and for a long time they talked.

The medicine man had a vision. The grandfather-of-all-whales alone could give the boy a strong heart.

The people prepared for a great whale hunt. The men fixed their harpoons; the women twisted stronger and stronger cedar bark rope. Idly, the boy watched the preparations; with stupid curiosity he saw the little fleet of canoes leave the harbor.

When the hunters returned they brought the grandfather-of-all-whales. They did not drag the great carcass to the beach, but anchored it in the harbor. The women paddled out in their canoes and cut a large piece of blubber from the whale. Then the people of his tribe stripped the stupidest boy and carried him to the whale and placed him in the hollow. While the medicine man chanted magics and the stupidest boy's grandmother (who loved him) cried and wailed, the people cut the ropes that anchored the great whale — and the boy drifted slowly away with the outgoing tide in his strange craft.

The stupidest boy cried with fear and he was very hungry and very lonely. As he drifted past a rocky headland he saw an eagle (the boy belonged to the Eagle tribe), and the eagle spoke to him and said: "Stupidest boy, eat, of the whale blubber beside you."

The boy scratched a little blubber from the whale and ate. He began to feel a strange strength surging through his body.

Four days he drifted on the waters, eating of the whale's blubber and getting a strong heart. At the end of the fourth day he found himself at his home. He went up to his house. The people scarcely recognized him — he was so tall and straight and strong.

Many proofs of his strength and cunning he gave to his people. He pulled up young trees by the roots; single-handed he brought in great whales. He devised cunning plans against their enemies. When his uncle died he became chief, and because of his magic-begotten strength and courage, the stupidest boy became the hero of his people — long remembered in legend and song.

The Legend of the Twin Sisters
John S. Morgan

This legend is told by the Indians of the British Columbia coast. Long ago, some say thousands of years ago, war's cruel hand laid hold of the tribes inhabiting the west coast of what is now British Columbia, and caused them to engage in fierce and bloody battles. The main opponents in these wars were the tribe dwelling in the region of the Capilano Canyon and the tribe living amongst the fjords and islands of the northern coast where the city of Prince Rupert now stands. Like all wars, this was a foolish war, for both tribes worshipped the same Great Spirit, the Sagalie Tyee, who had blessed them both by providing them with ample means to obtain a livelihood: from the salmon, a never-ending source of food that each spring braved rapids and even leapt falls in their journey upstream; from the fruits that grew in the fertile valleys; and from the animals that abounded in the forests. Yes, the Sagalie Tyee had been good to them; but both tribes, like selfish children, instead of living in brotherhood and harmony, sought to keep the other from hunting and fishing in the coastal region.

The time came when the twin daughters of the chief of the southern tribe reached womanhood. This was an occasion that called for much rejoicing, for the Indians regarded the miracle of birth as the supreme gift of the Great Spirit, and gave honour to the mother, the fount of life. It was through her that the tribe survived: valiant sons were born to defend the tribe, gentle daughters to give it life.

The southern chief was determined to make this occasion a great celebration, for he loved and cherished his daughters as a special gift from the Sagalie Tyee, which indeed they were. Endowed by him with unequalled grace and beauty and having been nurtured in the Capilano Canyon remote from war's cruel slaughter, they grew up not only beautiful and radiant as the sunrise but also meek and pure in heart.

Summoning all the elders and chief warriors of his tribe, the southern chief announced that he was going to hold a big potlach. He bade his people prepare food and special costumes for this event.

Weary of war, which had long darkened the land like a heavy cloud, the people responded joyfully to the chief's wishes. They busied themselves in making masks for the ritual dances; preparing food; and fashioning beads and ornate carvings, gifts for the maidens to be honoured.

Meanwhile the daughters witnessed the preparations made in their honour, not with gladness but with sorrow. As was their custom they first took their problems to the Great Spirit, the Sagalie Tyee, praying to him at the foot of the mountains which rose from the forests bordering their home.

They then went to their father with a request that they scarcely dared hope he would grant. The taller of the two girls spoke:

"Father, we appreciate all that you have done for us in the past, and are doing to honour us now. Nevertheless our hearts can never be made glad unless you grant us this, our request."

"O daughters, graceful as the aspen, beautiful with the beauty of sunrise, and gentle as the fawn, speak. What is your wish, that I may grant it?"

Again, the taller sister spoke, this time with greater assurance. "Father, we have now reached womanhood. Soon we shall be married and shall bear sons worthy to be called your grandchildren. But of what use is this if they are merely to be sacrificed to the cruel war that is casting its shadow over our land? We pray you, invite our brothers to the north to this, our festival, that they, too, may share our joy."

Amazed that they should even suggest bringing their enemies into the camp, the chief at first refused. But, when he realized that he could not bring them to his point of view, he granted them their wish.

Canoes were despatched into the regions held by the northern tribe. This time the young braves of the south bore, not weapons of destruction, but the invitation to attend the feast of the chief's daughters.

The warriors of the north responded in good faith. They cast aside their bows and arrows and war paint. Accompanied by their wives and children, and provided with stores of food and appropriate gifts, they set out on the southward journey.

The next few weeks witnessed the intermingling of the two tribes. Children of the north frolicked with their southern playmates on the beaches; as they prepared food for the festivities, the women of both tribes talked freely, as women do when they get together. The only rivalry exhibited among the men was in the stories they exchanged as they sat before the campfires.

Such festivities took place as had never been seen before. The tribes vied with each other in seeing who could offer the most food; games and contests were engaged in from dawn to sunset; singing and dancing continued until the pale finger of dawn touched the eastern rim of the sky.

But, just as day must yield to night and spring to summer, all things, even occasions as joyful as this, must have an end. The time came when the people of the south lined the shore to bid farewell to their northern comrades. As the canoes slipped away the cries of "Farewell Brother" and "Good-bye, Hunter of the North" echoed across the still surface of the water in the early dawn.

From that day forth, the tribes of our western coast have lived in peace and harmony, for what man can wage war with his brother? Who can quarrel with his friend?

And the Sagalie Tyee, having seen all that had happened, was content. How best could he reward the twin sisters who had been responsible for bringing peace to a land so long torn by war? He wished to build a memorial to them that would stand forever as a testimony to their gentle and selfless spirits.

The Sagalie Tyee took them in his hands and set them high on the crest of the mountains overlooking Capilano Canyon. There they stand to this day, in the full glory of their youth, unwearied by age, unwrinkled with the years. Just as the Sagalie Tyee had given them beauty and grace in their human form, so he now placed on their peaks a wreath of snow. Each day the sun changes at random the pattern of colours and tones — now vivid under his direct rays, now subdued by a soft cover of cloud, now veiled by pearly mists. Evening clothes them in rosy hues and night lends them her blanket of silver moonlight.

The Girl Who Married the Morning Star

Frances Fraser

On a hot summer night, in a long-ago time, three young girls were lying on the grass by the river, talking, as young girls do, of the men they would marry some day. One, daughter of a chief, the most beautiful of the three, found fault with every man suggested by the others. As last, exasperated, they said to her, "What do you want for a husband — a star? No man pleases you!"

The girl raised her eyes to the sky, where one star shone brighter than all the rest. "I would marry that star if he would come and get me. I wish he would! Please come, Star!!" The girls laughed, and returned to their tepees.

When night came again, there was need of wood to feed the camp-fires, and the girls were sent to gather some.

While they were picking up the dried branches, a young man dressed in beautiful feathered garments stepped out of a thicket, and said to the daughter of the chief, "Are you ready to go?"

"Go? Go where?" she said. "Who are you?"

"I am the Star you called last night," the stranger said. "You offered to marry me, remember? I have come to take you to my home in the Sky Country."

The girl looked at him. He was tall, and strong, and his eyes were kind. She turned to her companions, and said to them, "Tell my parents where I have gone." And the other girls, frightened, ran toward the camp.

The Star Man took a robe, made of feathers, and coloured like the rainbow, from his back, and, wrapping it round the girl, held her close against him. And they rose through the air toward the Sky Country.

It was a beautiful country. There were green grass, and

flowers, and berries, and quiet-running water. There was neither sickness, nor pain; the lodges never wore out, nor the clothing; there was always food, just by wishing for it — and the winter never came. The women had only to do what work they wished, and the men spent all their time on raids, and war. But those who were killed always, by daylight next morning, were alive again. And the animals were tame, and easy to hunt. It was a beautiful country.

The girl forgot all about her people and her life on the earth. After a while a son was born to them, and her happiness was complete.

Only one thing was forbidden. Her husband had told her that never was she to pull up a certain large wild turnip (ma'ase') that grew in a hollow near their tepee. For a long time she respected the restriction, but more and more she wondered, Why? What would happen if she did? The thought grew and grew.

One day her husband went hunting; and as she sat in the tepee with nothing to do, she thought of the ma'ase'. And she went to the hollow and pulled it up.

The ma'ase' left a hole in the sky, and looking down through it, she saw a circle of lodges, with the people going about the daily tasks of the camp. A wave of homesickness poured over her — a nostalgia for the life she had left, for the gossip of the women, the familiar tasks, the noise and smells of the camp. She replaced the ma'ase', and went, weeping, to her lodge.

Her husband, returning, found her sobbing in the tepee. "You disobeyed me," he said, sadly. "Now, I must send you back to your people." He sent messengers to gather hides and buffalo, hundreds of them, all the Star people had. Then they cut each hide into long stripes, and tied them together, making a long, long rope.

They lowered the girl and her baby down to the earth. But the baby was changed into a large mushroom, or puffball (which our people call "Star-Balls") since, being a sky-child, he could not live on the earth.

With her the girl also brought the Sacred Turnip, the ma'ase', and on her head she wore the holy Crown, the head-dress used to this day by the woman who makes the Sun Dance. (And to this day, the ma'ase' has a part in those rituals, and the poles of the Sun Lodge are tied with rawhide rope.)

The girl lived with her family, teaching the people much that she had learned in the Sky Country. She tended her Star baby.

But among the people were some who resented her teaching. And one day, these wicked ones took the Star baby, and cut it up into small pieces, and scattered the bits around on the ground.

The girl was heartbroken at the killing of her Star baby. When the Morning Star rose next, she went out on the prairie and called to her husband, asking him if the ones who did this could not be punished.

He answered her, and told her to have her father and other men build a raft of logs tied with thongs. When the raft was completed, they were to take a pair of each kind of animal on to the raft, and to warn the virtuous members of her tribe to go there too.

Then the Star sent moon after moon of rain, till all the earth was flooded. The people and animals on the raft were all that were left alive.

When the rain had ceased, the girl's father sent a young beaver to find land. The beaver never came back.

Later, the chief sent a duck out. The duck, too, did not return. He sent other birds, and other water animals, and they, also, were not seen again.

At last, the muskrat said, "Let me go." The chief protested. He was fond of the muskrat, and the others had not come back. But the girl added her voice to that of the muskrat and at last the chief consented, and the little animal departed.

Late in the night, a feeble splashing was heard alongside the raft. The muskrat, nearly dead from exhaustion, had come back, and clutched in one little paw was a tiny bit of earth.

The water was receding, and at last the green grass grew again, and the flood was over. (The water went into the rivers, and the lakes, and down into holes and crevices in the ground. That's why, when you dig a well, you get water.)

The girl saw her people happy again, leading lives of virtue, with due attention given to the things she had taught them. But she was lonely, and when the Morning Star shone bright, she went out and called him, and the Star Man came for her as he had before, and they went back to their home in the Sky Country.

Dance for the Devil
Edward A. McCourt

Coyote Gully isn't a place you'd notice twice, because it's like so many other districts in the Canadian West — flat, windy, dry — but thirty years ago, when the Reverend Dugald Cameron first came among the people, things were different. Coyote Gully was a name then that you might hear in parts far off; for nearly everybody who went there stayed only a little while and likely said hard things afterward about the place and its inhabitants. It wasn't a soil where you'd figure the Word would ever take root, and maybe it wouldn't have but for one thing, a thing the like of which isn't often heard in a new country. For the Reverend Dugald Cameron met the devil face to face in old Raftery's hut on the top of Dead Man's Butte and sent him packing. After that people did what he told them, not wishing to argue with a man who had faced up to the devil; and today you won't find a more respectable God-fearing community the length and breadth of the land.

In those days settlers were few and far apart — small ranchmen mostly, living along the foothills, for on the plain itself the soil was light and sandy and rain hardly ever fell. A queer and ill-assorted lot they were too. Blond restless Swedes from the Dakotas; a scattering of Englishmen, younger sons mostly, their veins flowing blue blood and alcohol; black-haired Slavs from Central Europe who wrested a living somehow from the sandy soil of the prairie itself; a settlement of Scots — not the dour industrious kind you mostly get on the Western farmlands, but dark wild men who were the riffraff of the Glengarry counties back East; and a family of slow-spoken loose-jointed Southerners who'd come up a year or two before from the hills of Georgia or maybe Tennessee. There were hardly any women; it wasn't a woman's country then, though of course things are different now.

There was no town to speak of in the district — just a general store at the crossroads run by Olaf Svenson, a big Swede who'd left the States for reasons you didn't ask about, and a stock corral alongside the railroad tracks where the ranch men loaded their cattle. The Mounted Police were forty miles away; the settlers pretty well made their own laws and ran their lives without interference from the outside. Sometimes, though, a policeman would come snooping round for a day or two, trying to figure out where the citizens got their liquor from; for those were prohibition days, and Saturday night and most nights in between, Coyote Gully flowed raw alcohol. Some of the liquor got as far as the Indian reserve up north, and that was bad, but the police never found anything. After a while they always got discouraged and went away, and everyone would celebrate by getting drunk again. That was the way things were when the preacher came.

He held his first service in the crossroads store. Nearly everyone turned out, for there wasn't much doing in Coyote Gully Sundays, the Scots having strong convictions about getting drunk on the Sabbath. Even the Graingers were there — the Southerners who'd moved in a couple of years before.

They kept to themselves mostly, and nobody knew much about them, for they raised no grain and kept no stock except a string of saddle horses, Kentucky bred, that they rode a lot at nights. Old Man Grainger looked like one of the patriarchs you read about in the Bible, if you could overlook the trickle of tobacco juice that ran out the corner of his mouth and stained his long gray beard. Six-feet-four, he must have been when he straightened up, pale-eyed, hawk-nosed, a mane of white hair hanging near to his shoulders. He sat up front at the end of a bench by an open window, and every minute or so, regular as clockwork, he'd turn his head and let fly. There wasn't a mark on the sill you could see afterward. His three sons slouched on the bench beside him. It was easy telling they'd be like their old man in thirty years, if they lived that long. Kitsy was different.

Kitsy was worth looking at twice. Often, if you were a man. She was small — maybe she favored her dead mother — with a waist you could buckle a hatband round. Her face was a golden oval studded with the bluest eyes you ever saw, under a shock of hair that looked like sunlight when she let it flow over her shoulders the way she mostly did. Today, though, she had it done up top in braids. She wore a gingham dress that was tight in places, the skirt crisped out so you could see a lot of white lace underneath. Not the kind of girl you'd find it easy to stand up in front of and talk about things of the spirit. Not when she kept her blue eyes fixed all the time on your face.

Maybe the Reverend Dugald Cameron didn't make much of a hit his first time up, but the odds were all against him. Nobody wanted him in Coyote Gully, not even the Scots. It's a wonder he didn't quit the minute he saw the manse where he was supposed to live — a two-room tumble-down shack half a mile from the crossroads, full of holes and mice and dirt. Standing up front he looked tired and rumpled, like he'd slept in his clothes. He was pretty young, and women maybe thought him handsome; only too thin, all joints and angles, his face lean and gaunt. You could see he needed a woman to feed him up.

The hymn singing wasn't much, for there were no hymnbooks. The preacher had a fine bass voice, and a few of the Scots strung along with him for a line or two, but they petered out pretty quick and he had to finish all by himself. By preaching time he was looking pretty discouraged. But after a while the fire in his eyes got fanned up and you could tell he was getting a grip on himself. He had nerve anyway. He told those people what he or any other God-fearing man thought of them. He talked about the way they scorned to make provision for their minister, having the manse in mind and forgetting that no one had invited him — he'd been sent by the church back East to reopen a mission that had been closed for twenty years. But it was liquor he had most in his mind. For a Scotsman he attacked it in a manner unexpected and violent. He told the people that their drunken carousals were the shame of the whole nation. He told them about what happened to Sodom and Gomorrah, and though he didn't go so far as to complete the comparison, you could see what he was driving at. He made it seem like a straight fight between himself and the Little Brown Jug, and long before he was through you had a feeling the jug was going to get smashed.

Even Old Man Grainger rested his cud and listened. Especially when the preacher got to talking about the devil. For he talked about him in an intimate, personal sort of way, as if he'd known him all his life. Near the end, the sweat was running down his face and he'd taken to pounding the counter so hard you could see Olaf Svenson was concerned about the tinned goods piled on top of it.

"Brethren," the preacher said — and how he could call that congregation "brethren" with a straight face was hard to figure — "the devil is here, among us! He lives and thrives in Coyote Gully! He must be driven out, wholly and forever! That is my task! There is nowhere room for the devil and the Word! I am the bearer of the Word! I shall not go hence while the devil dwells among us!"

He didn't call for a hymn to wind up with. He said the benediction in a subdued sort of way and stood there up front looking tired and white, the fire all gone out of him. Maybe he figured that what he said hadn't made an impression on anyone. He was wrong. Old Lauchlan Fraser, who all through service had been out of sight behind the flour barrel, got slowly to his feet.

"Mr. Cameron," he said, "if you're lookin' for the de'il, we all ken fine where you'll find him."

The fire came back into the preacher's eye. "I have found him," he said. "In this room."

"I'm no speakin' o' the de'il in any metaphysical sense," Lauchlan said. He had studied philosophy in Edinburgh before his brain went queer on him. "But perhaps ye dinna believe in him as a visible reality in the form o' the flesh?"

"Old man," the preacher said, "I am a Presbyterian."

The answer seemed to satisfy Lauchlan. "Verra weel, then," he said. "You'll find him nights in the old cabin at the top o' Dead Man's Butte."

A kind of shiver ran through the congregation then, and people looked at one another sideways. Old Lauchlan had spoken of things best kept quiet. For there was no denying something queer about the tumble-down log cabin on the summit of Dead Man's Butte. An old man had lived there till two years before — an Irishman named Raftery who claimed to be a descendant of the fiddler of Dooney; and it was true he played the fiddle the way that made you think he couldn't have learned it just by practice like ordinary folk.

" 'Tis the devil's gift," he used to say when he was drunk, which toward the end was nearly all the time. "He gave it to the family a long time back, a reward for faithful service. But it's myself is the last of the Rafterys, and when I'm gone there's none will fiddle like me, except the devil himself. For he'll take back his gift, you see. It's a way he has with men."

The night old Raftery died people heard music coming

from the cabin, wilder than they'd ever heard before, and when they went to the cabin next morning they found Raftery stiff and cold in his chair, his fiddle across his knee, bow broken on the floor beside him. And the strange thing was, so people whispered, that though they buried Raftery, his music played on. Clear, still nights they could hear the sound a long way off, and nobody ever went near the cabin anymore. For the devil had come to Coyote Gully — it was then that the liquor started to flow the way it hadn't done before — and set himself up in Raftery's hut.

Not that there was much talk about such things, for they weren't suppose to happen in a new country. That was why, when Lauchlan brought the devil's music out in the open before a stranger, people looked at one another from the corner of their eyes, furtive and half ashamed.

Old Man Grainger unbent himself and stood up. His face was dark and his thin lips twitched. "I ain't got time fer listenin' to loony talk," he said. "Hants don't skeer me none." And he stumped down the room and outside, his tribe at his heels.

All except Kitsy. She stood up before the Reverend Dugald Cameron and looked him over slow, from head to foot. All the time his face got redder and redder, till it looked like any minute it would catch fire.

"Preacher," Kitsy said, in that soft drawl of hers that always made men's blood run faster, no matter what they thought of her, "why don't you go home? Coyote Gully is no place for a man of God."

Maybe what she said was kindly meant, but the preacher didn't take it that way. The fire left his face and shot out from his eyes. "Child," he said, "on your lips the name of God is blasphemy."

For just a second Kistsy looked as if she'd been slapped hard across the face. Then she put her hands on her hips, thrust out her bosom. "Child, did you say?" She was smiling now in a way that didn't look natural. "I'm a woman, preacher. And there's no man here knows it better than yourself."

She went out then, chin up, petticoats aswirl, and for a minute the preacher just stood there up front, staring after her. Then he faced the congregation.

"Mr. Fraser," he said, "I will count it a great favor to be shown the way to Dead Man's Butte." And he went out without shaking hands with anyone.

Old Lauchlan came to the manse one night when the air was so still you could hear the smallest sound five miles away, and the moon shone now and then between great banks of cloud that hung low in the sky.

"The de'il's makin' music on the hilltop," was all he said.

The preacher never answered a word. He saddled the spavined old gray nag one of the Scots had sold him for a lively four-year-old, and followed Lauchlan across the prairie toward the foothills, till after an hour's riding they could see the queer humped outline of Dead Man's Butte rising from the level plain. At the foot of the hill Lauchlan drew rein.

"'Tis a dark business ye may be engaged upon, sir," he said. "A dark and evil business. And since a layman would be no help at all in exorcisin' the de'il, I'll be leavin' ye here. But perhaps this wee token may be a bit comfort to ye, gin the de'il is vulgarly no supposed to be susceptible to lead."

He shoved a Colt revolver into the preacher's hand. The preacher considered it in silence.

"Thank you, Mr. Fraser," he said after a while. "But I share the vulgar opinion." And he gave back the gun.

He tied his horse to a nearby sapling and started up the overgrown path leading to the top of the hill. What he thought about on the way up, there's no telling. Maybe, in spite of his calling, he was afraid; for the wind had risen across the foothills and made strange noises in the trees, and the moon shone through ragged edges of cloud and the light it cast was wild and beautiful and sad. He couldn't see the cabin, but he saw a dull glow up top, like a dying fire far off; and wind or no, he heard always the thin wail of a fiddle, an eerie outland sound full of queer trills and shivers like you'd expect to hear when the devil made music in the cabin of a sinful old man who had died.

The preacher reached the top and walked easier. He could see the cabin ahead, and the dull glow coming through a windowpane covered over with paper or maybe dirt. For a minute he stood still. The music was louder now — shrill, high-pitched, the kind of music you'd figure a bow held by man couldn't drag out of any fiddle ever made.

Then the moon shone clear and the music stopped and the preacher went on. There was a clearing on the far side of the cabin, and a wide track running away from it down the side of the Butte facing the foothills, but the preacher didn't stop to wonder why. He walked right up to the cabin door, pulled it open and stepped inside.

His legs carried him clear to the middle of the room before he was able to stop them. And by the time he'd stopped he knew it wasn't any use turning back. There were figures between him and the door, and they closed the door and for a minute there was no sound at all in the cabin except for the preacher's heavy breathing and the sputter of embers on the stone hearth that had been Raftery's pride.

The preacher drew a deep breath right into the bottom of his lungs and straightened his shoulders. He faced the figure sitting quiet in a broken-backed chair beside the dying fire.

"They told me," he said, "that in this cabin I would meet the devil face to face."

Old Man Grainger got up off the chair, moving slow and quiet, and stretched himself to his full height. "They told true," he said. He shoved his hawk nose close to the preacher's face. "Why have ye come here?" His voice had a rasp in it.

The preacher never turned a hair. "To drive you out of Coyote Gully," he said. "You and your spawn."

The shadowy figures behind the preacher moved away from the door and drew around him. They spoke no words, but looked at Old Man Grainger as if expectant of the sign that would move them to violence and blood.

"And destroy your works," the preacher said. He waved his hand toward the row of puncheons standing along the cabin wall.

The old man laughed, low and short, as if he didn't think what the preacher had said was funny. "Watch him close, boys," he said. "We'll settle him when the time comes."

They flushed the preacher for concealed weapons, dragged him to a chair in the corner and sat him down, a guard on either side. The preacher didn't say anything at all, but his lips moved all the time. Maybe he was praying; you couldn't tell from his face.

Old Man Grainger went back to his chair. He dipped a tin mug in the puncheon beside him and drank deep. Then he picked up the fiddle lying by the chair and drew a bow across it. The fiddle let out a melancholy screech. He tucked it under his chin and began to play.

He played a long time. But he played only one tune, over and over again; a wild haunting melody, plaintive and sad at first, but getting faster and faster till near the end you could hardly see the flash of the bow or the twinkle of the old man's fingers on the strings. But sometimes, when he played the trills and quavers that had lifted the preacher's hair when he heard them far off, the music broke for a split second and a false note would jar a man who had an ear for such things. And whenever that happened, the preacher's head would come up and he looked at Old Man Grainger with a gleam in his eyes that hadn't been there before.

The music snapped off clean in the middle of a bar. Old Man Grainger shot out of his chair as if a tack had stuck into him, and the words that came out of his mouth were the kind you'd figure the devil would say when he was upset. For the door had burst open with a bang that could be heard a mile off, and Kitsy stood in the middle of the cabin floor. Her hair was wild over her shoulders, her clothes wind-tossed and disheveled, but her smile was as gay as the morning. She stood right in front of the preacher, hands on her hips, and looked at him the way she did in church.

"So you've come, preacher," she said. "Lauchlan told me. I didn't believe him."

The preacher got up from his chair. "I said I'd come."

Kitsy stared him in the face for maybe a minute. Then her eyelids flickered. "How do you like the devil's music?" she said. "Does it make you forget the dreary hymns you sing through your nose?"

That wasn't fair, for the preacher had a big bass voice that rumbled around deep inside him before bursting through a wide-open mouth. He opened his mouth now and laughed till the rafters shook.

"The devil may be accomplished in evil," he said, "but he can't play a fiddle worth a tinker's dam!"

For just a second it was so quiet in the cabin you could hear a cat walking. Then Old Man Grainger grabbed Kitsy by the shoulder and flung her aside.

"So I can't play the fiddle!" he shouted. "I'm the champeen fiddler of seven counties — eight if the judges hadn't of been crooked!"

He stopped then and his face tightened up and the red went out of it. He held out the fiddle to the preacher.

"Mebbe you kin do better," he said.

The preacher took the fiddle and ran his hand over the back as if he were petting a favorite dumb animal. "It's a long time since I've practised," he said. "But if I can't play better than the devil, I deserve to go to hell."

He picked at the strings with long thin fingers and

tightened up a couple of pegs. "To a sensitive ear," he said, "this fiddle is out of tune."

The preacher sat him down in the devil's chair without a by-your-leave to anyone, and slid the fiddle under his chin. The very first notes he drew, a hush settled inside the cabin, and except for the music and the flash of the bow, there wasn't anywhere sound or movement. At first the preacher played only simple things, tunes that every Scotsman knows, and all the world besides, like "Annie Laurie" and "Lochaber No More" and "The Flowers o' the Forest"; and some that must have come from his land's far north or maybe the Outer Islands, weird wailing melodies in a minor key that called to mind all manner of things fanciful and sad.

All the time the devil and his sons sat quiet on the floor, and the devil didn't make even a move toward the puncheon. But Kitsy crept closer and closer to the preacher's chair, till she was sitting almost at his feet. And she looked at his face as if she couldn't draw away her eyes.

The preacher untucked the fiddle and laid it across his knee. " 'Tis a strange thing, Mr. Devil," he said, "a strange thing indeed that you should play so badly the tune which in my country they say you devised. 'Tis called the 'Devil's Hornpipe'. This is how it should go."

It was the tune men said old Raftery played the night he died — the tune the preacher heard while he climbed the path to the top of Dead Man's Butte. Wild and strange it was, with crazy trills and quavers and double-stopping even in the trills. It made you think of things that set the blood racing and the foot tapping — of things you wouldn't ever talk about to anyone, not if you wanted to be thought an honest God-fearing man.

Before the preacher had been at it a minute, everyone in the room was clapping hands in time to the music. All except the devil himself. He never twitched a muscle, but the sweat ran down his face in streams.

All of a sudden Kitsy got up off the floor. Her body swayed in time to the music, and the firelight cast queer shadows on her face. For a minute she stood in the middle of the room, swaying to the music. Then she began to dance. And that was strange, for they say that whoever dances to the devil's music is the devil's slave forever after. But Kitsy couldn't help herself. White, strained, with the kind of look you see on people in a trance or maybe going mad. She swung her hips like a woman of the streets, and her feet twinkled so fast under her long skirt you'd have sworn sometimes they weren't there at all. And all the time the music rose wilder, faster, so that it seemed no mortal feet could ever keep time to it.

Kitsy never missed a step. Not even when she dropped her skirt from her hips and kicked it across the room. She danced then in her lace petticoat. But the preacher never flicked an eyelid and his bow never missed a note.

Like a candle flares up bright just before it goes out, Kitsy spun in a dazzling pirouette, so fast she was just a blur, and crashed to the floor. The "Devil's Hornpipe" snapped off short, like a broken string. The preacher crossed the room in one jump and dropped to his knees beside the huddled heap on the floor. He slid his arm under Kitsy's shoulders and drew her close to him. Kitsy lay white and still against his chest; then her blue eyes opened and she smiled up into his face.

"Preacher," she said, "you played me down."

He gathered her up as if she were a child and set her in a chair. Then he picked up her skirt, which lay all crumpled in a corner.

"Make yourself decent," he said.

Old Man Grainger spoke in a voice so low that the preacher barely caught his words. "I never heerd the beat of it," he said, and his face worked strangely. "Go peaceable now and we'll do ye no harm."

The preacher drew himself up and his eyes flashed lightning. "I will go when my work is done!"

"What work?" You could tell from the way the old man spoke that he was afraid.

The preacher pointed to the puncheons ranged along the wall. "The destruction of the devil's brew," he said. "The brew you carry over the trails to the weak and the ignorant and afraid."

A great anger flamed in his eyes now and his voice rang out like a bugle. "Go home, old man, and pray! Leave off this trumpery masquerade which would not deceive a child, much less one armed with the Word! Go home and repent, all of you! And henceforth show yourselves not as devils, but as men!"

For a long minute the preacher and the devil faced each other, breast to breast, eye to eye. Without a word, Old Man Grainger turned away. He went out of the cabin, walking slowly — a man beaten, tired, old. The others followed, one by one, till the preacher stood alone.

He stood for a long time without moving. After a while he gathered up an armful of sticks and threw it on the fire. When the flames leaped up, he pulled bits of the blazing wood from the hearth and scattered them about the room. The floor and walls caught in a dozen places.

The preacher picked up the devil's fiddle and made as if to throw it into the fire. A hand caught his arm and he whirled about.

"Kitsy!"

"Dad will miss his music," she said.

The preacher smiled. "A fine fiddle," he said, "when well played."

He led her outside then, just in time, for the fire was blazing on three sides of them. They stood together in the shadow of the trees and watched the flames in the cabin grow brighter, shoot out through the windows, the roof, toward the sky.

"The devil brews good ale," the preacher said. "It burns well."

"You're a brave man, preacher," Kitsy said. She stood

close to him and her hand rested lightly in the crook of his arm.

"I'm a good fiddler," the preacher said.

"And I'm the devil's own now," Kitsy said. "For I danced his Hornpipe. But, preacher, I couldn't help it."

The preacher laughed the way he did before he took the fiddle from Old Man Grainger. You could hear his shout a mile away, above the roaring of the flames.

"Whoever dances the 'Devil's Hornpipe' belongs to the man who plays it!" And he swept her into his arms and kissed her the way no girl had ever been kissed in Coyote Gully or maybe the whole of the West.

That night the folk had gathered in the crossroads store from as far away as the second range of foothills, for word had got around that the preacher had gone to fight the devil in Raftery's cabin on the top of Dead Man's Butte. And though they laughed loud and drank hard, you could see a great fear was on them, though maybe the fear wasn't the same for all. They stayed in the store a long time while the night wore on and the liquor sank lower in the keg.

The Scots were talkative enough at first, but after a while they were dour and silent, for they were Covenanter stock and knew that the devil was real, no matter how much they denied him when the sun shone. The Englishmen from the ranches drank more than their share and quarreled noisily with the Swedes, but after a while they, too, were quiet, and wishing they hadn't come. All the time old Lauchlan Fraser slept behind the flour barrel. Or seemed to. But every now and then his eyelids lifted and his eyes gleamed sharp in the lamplight.

When they heard horses galloping, there wasn't a man of them not on his feet, and Olaf Svenson took a double-barreled shotgun from under the counter and fingered the triggers. When the preacher came in with Kitsy behind him, there was a sound like the night wind sighing in the treetops, which was only a great gust of breath coming all at once from men's lungs, and a shout went up that rattled the crockery on the shelves.

But the shout died away and men stared at the preacher, and the great fear came back. For the preacher's face was black with smoke and his eyelashes gone and his coattails singed and the smell of fire upon him. And through the open doorway they could see a blaze of light on the top of Dead Man's Butte — flames shooting to the sky and painting the clouds a fearful bloody red.

The preacher walked down the room and men gave back on either side. He stood with Kitsy beside him, and his face was dark and awesome to behold. "The devil is gone from Coyote Gully!" he thundered. "The devil and all his works!"

With one mighty sweep of his arm he hurled the keg of liquor from the counter. It was almost empty, but even so you could hear a groan rumble through the room, and men watched with anguished eyes the liquor run across the floor and form little dust-covered puddles in the worn places.

The preacher stalked back to the door, turned and stood with his long body framed in the doorway, the fire on Dead Man's Butte behind him. "I give you one week!" he said, and his voice chilled the blood of all who heard him. "One week, to make the manse fit for the minister's wife to live in!"

That was thirty years ago. The old manse is gone now, and there's a fine big new one on the best street in Coyote Gully. It needs to be big, for the Reverend and Mrs. Dugald Cameron have a large family, and besides, they're hospitable folk who keep open house nearly every night of the week. The preacher and Kitsy aren't often alone, and if you knock on their door almost any hour you're sure of a warm welcome. But sometimes if you go past the manse at night you'll hear music from the back room where the light is, and then you'll know not to knock, for there won't be any answer. It's a fiddle playing that you hear — wild, eerie music that lifts the hair on the back of your head if the night is dark. It couldn't be, of course, for it's the preacher who plays it, but if you heard that tune anywhere else, you'd swear it was the "Devil's Hornpipe".

My Friend Mike

John W. Chalmers

As I drive through the country these fall days and see the modern self-propelled combines and handsome trucks in the fields, I am reminded of my own experiences as a harvest hand in Manitoba almost a quarter of a century ago. As the excitement, the good food, the camaraderie and fellowship are recalled, those seem "the good old days". Minor evils such as icy cold and broiling sun, Canada thistle and animated dandruff, refractory horses and decrepit rigs — did they ever exist?

Typical of the outfits on which I worked was one powered by perhaps the last surviving steam tractor in the West. The crew included the separator man (the boss), the fireman, the water man, a dozen pitchers, and a few half-grown boys to haul the grain.

It was on this outfit that I met my friend Mike Popovec. Surely he deserves a place in our folklore comparable to that of Paul Bunyan or Old Stormaway. But because his lot fell among inarticulate wheat farmers, his exploits have been forgotten. Had he been a cowboy, a lumberjack, a sailor, his deeds would have been embellished, embroidered, adorned until his shadow would have stretched from the shores of that ancient Agissez Lake to the foothills of the Rockies. Instead, his only monument is perhaps this plain and factual memoir.

Although Mike seems in retrospect to have been ten feet tall, he couldn't have been more than six. And the width of his shoulders and depth of his chest made him seem almost squatty. He came to our outfit direct from the plains of Hungary, with no word of English, no means of communication other than his luculent smile. But it was enough.

At first, like all greenhorns, he made all the mistakes in the book. Then he added an appendix. He tried to unharness his team by unfastening the hames at the top rather than at the bottom, with the result that the harness fell around the horses' fetlocks. He tried to put the harness on upside down, inside out and backwards. The boss spent forty profane minutes straightening it out. Mike got his reins crossed, so that the team went gee when he pulled haw, and almost wound up in the big stock-watering tank. Or he so fastened his lines that the near horse headed in the direction of the rising sun whilst the other veered toward the Rockies. Once Mike angled a load of bundles over a fire-guard furrow and dumped sheaves, rack and himself on the ground precisely as the fireman was tooting madly for sheaves. In short, his maladroitness was such as to keep the boss, an old-country Belgian, in a constant state of profane near-apoplexy. There have been some masters of invective who could turn the air blue, but this old Belgian was the only man I ever saw or heard tell of that could give a cerise tint to the circumambient ether. I always figured this feat was possible because the old gentleman knew all the expletives in three languages: English, French, and Flemish. Just as steelmakers can gauge their molten brew by its colour, so could we judge the temperature and temper of our boss by the hue of the surrounding atmosphere. But Mike took it all in good part, answering with "Ja, ja, ja, ja," and his bright smile. And the storm would be over.

Mike learned. Soon he was skilled as any on the crew, never wasting a motion as he tossed his bundles from stook to rack, from rack to separator. Soon he was tossing, not single sheaves, but whole stooks onto the wagon. Then he graduated from a standard three-tined pitchfork to a five-tined stable fork. So strong was he that he had to stop his rig thirty feet from the stooks; otherwise he could not help throwing them right over the rack. Finally he dispensed with the rig altogether, and simply tossed the stooks from wherever they were in the field right on to the separator feeder. His record throw was four hundred fifty yards, but that was with a favourable wind. On a calm day three hundred yards was all I ever saw him do. Of course, that was a whole stook, and forty-five-bushel wheat in the bargain.

Soon Mike was handling one side of the separator by himself and the boss was able to lay off four teams and five pitchers. This decrease in personnel should have made the women-folk happy, for, as is well known, harvesting in those days was a ceaseless round of cooking and baking: pies, meat, buns, potatoes, pies, cakes, flap-jacks, pies, cookies, pickles, pies, biscuits, vegetables and pies. Three heavy meals a day to prepare, differing only in the time of day at which they were served. Mid-morning and mid-afternoon lunches that would have made a five-course dinner look like a bedtime snack. But the more Mike worked, the more he ate. Lunch used to be brought to the field about 3:30 p.m. in two cartons, each large enough to hold a young piano. One carton was for Mike, the other for the rest of us.

Mike's Olympian strength was useful in many ways. Anyone who has worked near a steam tractor will remember that it had to be fired up about two or three in the morning. Pressure mounted very slowly until enough head of steam had been built up to activate the automatic blower, after which the pressure increased rapidly. Our fireman found that he could get an extra hour or two of sleep by having Mike breathe gently through the bronchial tubes of the old boiler when it was being fired up. Such a draft was created that the pressure zoomed and the blower could function almost instantly.

Once our engine's mobile water supply ceased to function. With two hundred feet of garden hose water was siphoned from a nearby stream direct to the boiler. Mike's mighty lungs created the suction. Normally a siphon must have its outlet lower than its inlet. However, so effective was Mike's vacuum that it lifted the water thirty-nine feet and created such a flow that the siphon functioned for seven hours.

After threshing stopped for the night — or those three or

four hours of it when the dew made the grain too tough to thresh — Mike used to unload the odd 120-bushel grain tank. He would back the wagon up against a bin, remove the tailgate, and lift the front end. With his other hand he would practise the fine western art of cigarette-rolling.

I used to like that old steamer. For one thing, being old and infirm, it broke down often, thereby providing frequent opportunities for a smoke or a snooze. (We didn't get much opportunity for sleep at night as we weren't in bed long enough to get the blankets warm.) On the very last load of the season the old engine completely collapsed, three miles from the boss's home quarter. At my request, I was paid off then and there. And the last ever I saw of Mike was him trudging down the road, pulling the separator and waving me good-bye.

Tale of a Gunman
Andy Russell

My father told about a rancher who came into Alberta on a fast horse during the Wyoming range war between cattlemen and sheepmen. It was said that he had killed a sheepman in a fight, wherein self-defense was in some question. His relatives later trailed his cattle up across the boundary and he set up a ranch in Canada. For years this man was rarely seen that he wasn't heavily armed. He seldom came to town and was always suspicious of strangers. If he saw someone at a distance on the prairie, he immediately headed at a run for the nearest cover, where he would wait to find out the visitor's identity. Needless to say, nobody was inclined to approach him within rifle range, unless they had very pressing business. He married and raised a family, but to the day he died as an old man, he was always nervous and watchful — probably afraid that relatives of the man he had killed would show up looking for revenge.

In 1890 Harry Longbaugh, a quiet handsome young man, showed up at the Bar U ranch near High River looking for a job. He was an excellent rider and had no trouble getting work with Herb Millar, who was breaking horses for the ranch at that time. Nobody knew that back in Wyoming he was known as the Sundance Kid.

One day as Longbaugh stepped off a bronc and pulled off his saddle, Herb saw something glitter. While Longbaugh was roping another horse, Herb stepped over to the saddle for a look and saw that the glittering object was a hacksaw blade peeping out from under the woolskin lining of the skirt. He knew what that meant, but asked no questions and kept his mouth shut about it.

At the annual roundups, Longbaugh was rated a top hand and was a popular cowboy. Nobody knew that he was also one of the fastest and deadliest gunmen ever to show up in western Canada. He stayed around for two or three years and was respected as a good hand and a law-abiding man.

But then one winter he went into partnership with Frank Hamilton, a bully who owned a bar in Calgary. On several previous occasions Hamilton had taken partners to do most of the work; then when it had come time to split the earnings, he had picked a quarrel and beaten them up, thrown them out and kept the money. He tried it with Harry Longbaugh to his sorrow.

Harry was behind the bar when the row started. Moving with the grace and power of a cougar, he placed his left hand on top of the bar and vaulted over it in a twisting jump. When his boots hit the floor, a .45 six-shooter had appeared as if by magic in his other hand and it was jammed into Hamilton's middle. The money was not long in changing hands. The cowboy backed out of the place, got his horse and promptly disappeared.

He headed south into Montana, where he contacted some old friends, Butch Cassidy and Kid Curry. They set out on a ten-year-long trail of holding up banks and trains all through the western States. Finally, hard pressed by the law, they quit the country heading for South America, where they proceeded to raise hell in a similar fashion. Eventually they were cornered by a contingent of Bolivian cavalry and went under in a blaze of gunfire.

Akers and Purcell, Whiskey Traders
Andy Russell

Toughness ran to personality and violence on occasion. When the Mounted Police came west in 1874, the first duty they performed was to close the whiskey trading Fort Whoop-up on the St. Mary River. Two of the traders, Dave Akers and Tom Purcell, went into partnership in a ranching venture, but eventually quarrelled and split up. Dave Akers eventually relocated on a homestead up on Pothole Creek a few miles from its confluence with the St. Mary River, where my grandfather's ranch was located.

The broken partnership did nothing to smooth relations between these two frontier hardcases, and when they were in their cups at various bars, they both vowed to kill the other. Both were always armed wherever they went on the prairie, and Dave was particularly watchful, for he was afraid of Tom.

At daylight one spring morning, Dave was saddling a horse in his corral when Tom showed up suddenly, riding into the corral through the open gate. Cursing and calling Dave every bad name he could lay his tongue to, he rode at him with a heavy elk horn quirt reversed in his hand ready to strike. Dave was not carrying a gun, but he hastily backed up toward a corral post behind which he had a .44 Winchester rifle cached. He grabbed the rifle, dodged a blow of the clubbed quirt, levered a cartridge into the barrel and fired. The bullet caught the attacker in the flank and emerged at the base of his neck, killing him instantly. Dave knew he was in deep trouble.

My grandmother was alone in the house making breakfast that morning when she heard a knock at the door. Upon opening it, she saw Dave Akers, who announced without preamble, "I shot Tom Purcell!"

"You shot Tom Purcell," she exclaimed. "Is he dead?"

"Yes, missus!" Dave assured her. "He's deader'n hell!"

My grandmother called grandfather, who was doing chores, and Dave told him that he wanted to give himself up. So grandfather hitched up a team and drove him to the Mounted Police detachment in Lethbridge, where he was taken into custody to await trial. If there hadn't been so much threatening, Dave might have gone free on a plea of self-defense, but as it was he was sentenced to two years at Fort Macleod for manslaughter.

There is a sequel to this story. Dave was married to a Blood Indian woman and she, along with numerous relatives, often visited him in jail. One of his jobs there was to clean, oil and repair police harness and on various occasions he slipped a piece of harness to his blanketed visitors to be hidden and smuggled out of the fort. When Dave got out with some time off for good behavior, he had a complete, new set of harness for a four horse team. Of course this was a standing joke among the Indians, who were delighted with the prank, and the story was told around their fires for years afterward.

Baldy Red
Robert E. Gard

As my friend, Mr. Norman Soars, of Peace River says, "Nicknames are a Northern habit. Witness our celebrated bootlegger, Baldy Red — which is a sort of double-barrelled nickname; and I assure you that I once heard two fur-buyers talking: one said, 'One-eyed Pete's in town.' The other replied, 'Not One-eyed Pete from Deadman's Creek!' "

Yes, the names in the Peace River Country are certainly interesting and colourful. I heard names like Baldy Red, Society Red, Sad Sam, Gyp the Blood, Buckskin Annie, attached to persons of somewhat doubtful reputation, but who in their own line were beings of enormous stature, especially Buckskin Annie.

And then, too, you run onto towns with names like North Star, Bluesky, High Prairie, Grande Prairie, Driftpile, Beaverlodge, and Pouce Coupe.

Considering the characters I am convinced that Baldy Red is at least *one* of the best known names throughout the Peace River Country. Baldy's real name was George Yeoman, but very few people remember that. They do remember that he came from Eastern Canada, was of English stock, and some who knew him claim that Baldy was the son of a wealthy Montreal banker. They remember, too, that Baldy got his nickname from the fact that he was bald on top with a fringe of red hair and that as Baldy Red he was known from Calgary and the foothills north to Peace River.

In police court, when asked his business, he invariably described himself as a bootlegger. Bootlegging, however, he regarded more as a sport than a profession, since it appealed more to his sense of humor and sport than to his acquisitiveness.

He enjoyed his wide reputation and loved to tell stories about himself. He used to tell how he got over to England during the First World War in charge of a shipload of horses. "And when I walked down Piccadilly, every second man I met said, 'Hi ya, Baldy! How the hell did you get over here?' "

Among the innumerable yarns regarding Baldy are a few favorite tales that even the kids know in the Peace River Country.

The episode of Baldy and the foxes, for instance, took place at Grouard in the early days of the fox-farming boom. Grouard was then the metropolis of the North, and the country was full of buyers trying to pick up live silver foxes which were fetching fancy prices. Baldy got into conversation with a fur buyer in the hotel one night and casually let out that he knew where there were quite a bunch of foxes to be had.

"About three hundred or more," said Baldy, "a nice bunch, mostly reds with a few crosses and some good silvers amongst 'em."

After considerable haggling, Baldy finally named a price at which he told the buyer he could have them. A very reasonable price it was. "But at that price," said Baldy, "you will have to take 'em as they run, reds, crosses, and silvers."

The buyer by that time was thoroughly "sold" and when Baldy told him that to bind the bargain he must have twenty dollars, he promptly got it.

Next morning, bright and early, the buyer was waiting and suggested to Baldy that they go and look the foxes over.

"Me, I'm not going," said Baldy, "I'm too busy. You go and look 'em over."

"Where are they?" asked the buyer.

Baldy waved his arm around the landscape. "Out in the bush. You agreed to take 'em as they run, and boy, they're running!"

A popular story of Baldy concerns the time he was being taken out to the Fort Saskatchewan jail by a Mounted Policeman. An unfeeling judge had sentenced Baldy for stealing a cow, when all he had done was to pick up a piece of rope with a cow at the other end of it! Another prisoner was being taken to jail at the same time, convicted of stealing a watch.

Baldy, to pass the time, would every few minutes ask the other prisoner: "What's the time? Have you the time on you?"

Finally the other man, completely exasperated, snapped back: "It's *milking* time!"

Baldy's best known exploit occurred when he drove the

Grey Nuns on their collecting trip along the construction line of the Grand Truck Railway.

The nuns maintained hospitals in the construction camps and made trips collecting funds. Baldy went to them and explained that he was a poor man and couldn't afford to give them money, but that he would like to drive them and put a wagon at their disposal. The Nuns made the trip, never suspecting that they were sitting on a cache of booze, and while they preached and collected, Baldy peddled his moonshine without interference from the police.

He pulled the same stunt at Peace River town when he drove in two Anglican missionary ladies. He parked his wagon in front on the Mounted Police barracks and asked Sergeant Anderson, who was a devout Anglican, to keep an eye on the ladies and the belongings. The liquor on which they sat got through!

Baldy's outstanding trait was his sense of humor. He loved to tell of finding a cache of liquor at Crooked Bridge, and of how he washed off the label and sold it in Peace River to the bootlegger who had cached it at the Bridge.

He died at Grande Prairie, and in the Peace River Country they tell me that undoubtedly his sense of humor got him safely through the Pearly Gates.

The Old Man
Frances Fraser

One day the Old Man was taking a walk, when he saw a lot of deer playing. They were jumping down a little hill, and having a very good time. Na-pe began crying loudly. Said the leader of the deer to one of the others, "Go and see what Old Man is crying about."

"I am crying because you are having such a good time, and I am not!" said the Old Man. The deer, feeling sorry for him, invited him to join in their game.

He leaped down the hill a few times, then said to the deer chief, "I have been jumping down your hill. Now, since you have been good to me and have let me play with you, I will let you play with me. Come jump down my hill." And he led them to a cutbank!

"I will go first," said Na-pe; but instead of jumping, he ran round to the bottom of the bank, and lay there laughing heartily.

"Why are you laughing?" called the deer, peering over the edge.

"Oh, it is so much fun!" said Na-pe. "The hill is wide; you can all jump at once. Come down here with me!"

So the poor silly deer all jumped at once, and of course, were all killed. Na-pe gleefully skinned them, cut the meat in strips and put it up to dry. He had just finished arranging all the tongues on a long pole, when along came A-pe'si the Coyote. A-pe'si was limping, badly. "Ne-sa (brother)," he said to the Old Man, "I am so hungry. Will you give me some food?"

Na-pe saw that the Coyote was carrying a sea-shell, a big one, hanging on his neck. "Give me that shell, and I will give you some food."

"No," said the Coyote. "I can't give you this shell. It is my Medicine — my power from the Above Spirits — and I should never have good luck again if I give it away. You have more food here than you need; it will rot before you can use it all. Give me a little."

"No," said Na-pe. "But I will race you for it round the lake. If you win, you may have a meal. If I win, you must give me that holy shell."

"Oh, Ne-sa," said A-pe'si. "Have some pity! I am so lame, and so hungry!"

But Na-pe insisted. At first, he outdistanced the Coyote, but A-pe'si gained, bit by bit, till at last he left Na-pe far behind. When he reached the place where the meat was, he sat down and howled loudly.

At once, all the four-footed animals gathered. Quickly, they ate every single scrap of meat, the mice running up the pole to eat the insides of the tongues. Then they ran away, and hid. And when Na-pe arrived there was not a morsel left, and he was very angry.

But the next time he was not so mean.

Creatures

Canadians Sight Hairy Creatures
Article from The New York Times

NORDEGG, Alberta (Canadian Press) — Many residents in this area believe a band of hairy humanoid creatures is roaming in the nearby foothills of the Rocky Mountains.

And George Harris, a 54 year old retired bulk fuel dealer here is planning an expedition to track them down.

"There have been so many sightings and other kinds of evidence in the last year that I'm convinced there is something there," he said.

The latest sighting was reported by five workmen at the Big Horn Dam construction site on the North Saskatchewan River west of this community 120 miles southwest of Edmonton.

Floyd Engen of Eckville, one of the workers, said the creature appeared to be 15 feet tall with round shoulders and dark in color, perhaps from hair covering its body.

In Agassiz, British Columbia, John Green, editor-publisher of the weekly *Agassiz-Harrison Advance,* said the description led him to think of a Sasquatch that would weigh about four tons.

Mr. Green has made a study of Sasquatch — the Pacific Northwest's version of the Himalayan Abominable Snowman.

Many town residents, Indian families and guides in this area believe the creatures are roaming the district.

Edith Yellowbird, 16, living with a band of Indians, said she had seen four strange figures. She said they were tall and that two had been walking around and the other two had been going bending down.

Mark Yellowbird, 62, her father, said he had seen a figure in the same area near Windy Point.

Guy L'Heureux, 19, of Rocky Mountain House, a technology student at the Northern Alberta Institute of Technology in Edmonton, was working on a pump house with Harley Peterson, 17, a cement finisher from Condor.

They spotted the figure on a point above the dam site and were joined by Mr. Engen, a back-hoe operator, Dale Boddy, 21, of Ponoka, an education student at the University of Saskatchewan, and Harley's father, Stan, 46.

"The figure sat for about 15 minutes and then it stood up, looked around and walked off," Harley said.

"It looked enormous. It's head was bent slightly forward and it looked very hefty. We watched it for about three quarters of a mile as it made its way around a ridge."

Dale Boddy said the creature could not have been a bear, because it was too tall and its legs were too thin.

"A bear couldn't have walked that far on its hind legs — and not at that speed," he said. "It looked as if it was taking 6 foot strides and covered the distance in about two minutes."

A group of men went to the spot the following day to try and find tracks, but apparently the ground was too hard to show prints.

Vern Saddleback, 28, an Indian, said "many people have seen the tracks" and that the creatures had come within 200 yards of the Indian camp.

Mr. Harris said it is believed the creatures were fascinated by noise, which he said could explain why they were attracted to the dam construction site.

However, Mr. Engen said he had jumped up on a tractor, waved his hard hat and yelled at the creature moving on the ridge.

"It didn't seem to notice," he added.

Skeleton of Giant Found Near Vernon Arousing Interest

Article from The Colonist, *1931*

Ethnologists and archaeologists in British Columbia are interested in the discovery, by a road gang, of a group of skeletons near Vernon. It is believed that they may prove to be the remains of a race that preceded the native races that met the first coming of the white men to the Interior valleys 120 years ago.

The particular skeleton that is causing much speculation is that of a man. It measures six feet six inches, but the man in life must have measured at least one inch, or possibly two inches more than the length of the bones which have been recovered. The skull formation is much larger and of different shape to those uncovered in other excavations in the district.

The find was made by a road gang on the Vernon-Kamloops Highway about four miles out of the former place. Six skeletons were uncovered. One was that of a woman, three boys in their teen ages, and a fifth that of a young man who had not yet attained his full growth, possibly of a youth of nineteen or twenty. Nearby was located the frame of the man of gigantic proportions.

In close association with the human remains were found stone implements, differing but little from the type of implements used by natives on the arrival of the white man. This, however, does not give any indication as to the period in which the aborigines lived as there is practically no difference known to exist that definitely marks phases of the Stone Age west of the Rockies. Different localities might vary, to some extent, the types of stone cutting tools, but these passed from one part of the country to another where there was inter-communication between tribes.

It is the exceptionally large and differently-shaped skull,

and the gigantic proportions of the skeleton of the man, that creates especial interest among scientists.

Among modern Indians there are legends of the existence in prehistoric or mythical times, of a race of giants who inhabited the country before the coming of the peoples of Mongolian extraction.

Some years ago, it is reported, half a dozen skeletons of men of tremendous proportions, were uncovered in the Columbia Valley. One of these skeletons, it is said, measured considerably over eight feet, while the smallest would correspond in height to the latest discovery, that of a man who stood nearly seven feet.

It is possible, according to those who have examined the recent discovery, that the skeletons are those of a family that lived in the Okanagan country four thousand years ago.

J. B. Munro, deputy minister of agriculture, examined the skull several days ago at Vernon, where it is in the custody of the coroner, Dr. O. Morris. Mr. Munro says that it does not bear resemblance to skulls of other Indians who lived in the locality before the coming of the White traders.

Ethnologists estimate that the first wave of Mongolian or Asiatic immigration crossed the Arctic ice bridge about 6,000 years ago. This was followed by two other distinct immigration waves, separated by spaces of 2,000 years. There is a tendency, until more scientific information can be attained, to place the giant with the second of these penetrations — or 4,000 years ago — as the last wave of Orientals did not come to the Interior, but settled on the coast.

Coyote and the Monster
of the Columbia
Ella Elizabeth Clark

In the old "before people days" when animals were giants,
Coyote was the most powerful of all. Being powerful did not
mean that he was always wise or good. On the contrary he was
often vain, boastful, and greedy. Occasionally he did help the
lesser animal people and, good or bad, he was responsible for
making the world the way we people found it.

One time on his travels, Coyote learned that a monster was
killing the animal people as they travelled up and down Big
River in their canoes. So many had been killed that some of the
animal people were afraid to go down to the water, even to
catch salmon.

"I will help you," promised Coyote. "I will stop this
monster from killing people."

But what could he do? He had no idea. So he asked his
three sisters who lived in his stomach in the form of
huckleberries. They were very wise. They knew everything.
They would tell him what to do.

At first his sisters refused to tell Coyote what to do.

"If we tell you," they said, "you will say that that was your
plan all the time."

"If you do not tell me," said Coyote sternly, "I will send
rain and hail down upon you."

Of course the berries did not like rain and hail.

"Do not send rain," they begged. "Do not send rain or hail.
We will tell you what to do. Take with you plenty of dry wood
and plenty of pitch, so that you can make a fire. And take also
five sharp knives. It is Nashlah at Wishram that is killing all
the people. He is swallowing the people as they pass in their
canoes. You must let him swallow you."

"Yes, my sisters, that is what I thought," replied Coyote. "That was my plan all the time."

Coyote followed his sisters' advice. He gathered together some dry wood and pitch, sharpened his five knives, and went to the deep pool where Nashlah lived. The monster saw Coyote but did not swallow him, for he knew that Coyote was a great chief.

Coyote knew that he could make Nashlah angry by teasing him. So he called out all kinds of mean names. At last the monster was so angry that he took a big breath and sucked Coyote in with his breath. Just before entering his mouth, Coyote grabbed a big armful of sagebrush and took it in also.

Inside the monster, Coyote found many animal people. All were cold and hungry. Some were almost dead from hunger, and some were almost dead from cold.

"I will build a fire in here for you," said Coyote. "And I will cook some food for you. While you get warm and while you eat, I will kill Nashlah. I have come to help you, my people. You will join your friends soon."

With the sagebrush and the pitch, Coyote made a big fire under the heart of the monster. The shivering people gathered around it to get warm. Then with one of his sharp knives Coyote cut pieces from the monster's heart and roasted them.

While the people ate, Coyote began to cut the cord that fastened the monster's heart to his body. He broke the first knife, but he kept cutting. He broke the second knife, but he kept cutting. He broke his third and fourth knives. With his fifth knife he cut the last thread, and the monster's heart fell into the fire.

Just as the monster died, he gave one big cough and coughed all the animal people out on the land.

"I told you I would save you," said Coyote, as the animal people gathered around him on the shore of the river. "You will live a long time, and I will give you names."

Coyote went among them and gave each creature a name.

"*You* will be Eagle, the best and the bravest bird. *You* will be Bear, the strongest animal. *You* will be Owl, the big medicine man, with special powers. *You* will be Sturgeon, the largest fish in the rivers. *You* will be Salmon, the best of all fish for eating."

In the same way Coyote named Beaver, Cougar, Deer, Woodpecker, Blue Jay, and all the other animals and birds. Then he named himself. "I am Coyote," he told them. "I am the wisest and smartest of all the animals."

Then he turned to the monster and gave him a new law. "You can no longer kill people as you have been doing. A new race of people are coming, and they will pass up and down the river. You must not kill all of them. You may kill one now and then. You may shake the canoes if they pass over you. For this reason most of the canoes will go round your pool and not pass over where you live. You will kill very few of the new people. This is to be the law always. You are no longer the big man you used to be."

The law that Coyote made still stands. The monster does not swallow people as he did before Coyote took away his big power. Sometimes he draws a canoe under and swallows the people in it. But not often. Usually the Indians take their canoes out of the water and carry them round the place where the monster lives. They do not pass over his house. He still lives deep under the water, but he is no longer powerful.

The Windigo Spirit
James R. Stevens

The dreaded windigo is the most horrible creature in the lands of the Cree and Ojibwa Indians. Nothing strikes more terror in the hearts of the Anishinabek than the thoughts of windigo.

The cannibalistic windigos strike from the north during the five moons of winter and restlessly haunt our lands searching for food as far to the south as the snow belt extends. Windigos have been known to attack during the summer but this is very rare.

The windigo was once a normal human being but has been possessed by a savage cannibalistic spirit. When a human is possessed by windigo, ice forms inside the human body, hair grows profusely from the face, arms and legs and an insatiable craving for human flesh develops.

When the ugly creature attacks, it shows no mercy. This monster will kill and devour its own family to try and satisfy its lust for human flesh. The windigo is inhuman because of the powerful spirit of cannibalism and destruction residing in its body. When a windigo has destroyed its own people it will travel in a straight line across the forest until it finds the next group of victims. Usually high winds and blizzards accompany the windigo in its travels. It is said that the scream of a windigo will paralyze a man, preventing him from protecting himself. Sometimes an attack by a windigo can be turned away by a powerful medicine man and this has occurred.

There is a place at Sandy Lake called Ghost Point that was marauded and destroyed by a windigo in the old days. The remains of the village are still there today.

The Windigo at Berens River
James R. Stevens

The mighty Berens River flows westerly from the country of the Swampy Cree into Lake Winnipeg — Winnipeg means dirty water in our language. In the old days the Berens River was an important fur-trading route. Our people paddled down the river in canoes laden with valuable furs that were traded at the Hudson's Bay post at the mouth of the Berens.

About a hundred years ago a small camp of Indians were living near the post. One of the Indians from this camp went out trapping with his wife and children. After a few days the people in the camp heard the trapper screaming and howling in the forest. They knew from their own strange feelings that the man had turned into a windigo. One of the Indians from the camp went to the man's trap line and found the half-devoured corpses of his wife and three children. When the people heard what had occurred, they were panic stricken. It would only be a short time before the windigo would be attacking their camp and something must be done before the monster was upon them.

Meeting together in the council circle, the people chose their most powerful ma-mandowin-ninih, Rotten Log, to destroy the windigo.

"I must have a man to accompany me on this venture and he must be a man without fear," Rotten Log told the frightened people.

One man rose from the council circle after a long silence. He was a half-breed, or wessa-ko-day-wininih, who had been accepted by the people.

"I am a man without fear of man or beast," the half-breed stated softly.

The great council dispersed and Rotten Log and the half-breed were left alone to plan the destruction of the windigo. After much discussion, they decided to capture the windigo alive.

The half-breed went around the scattered lodges of the camp and captured eight of the largest and strongest dogs that he could find and returned with them to the council circle where the ma-mandowin-ninih had constructed a huge wooden toboggan. They hitched the snarling dogs to the great sled and loaded it with lengths of thick braided ropes and other provisions for their journey.

With eight brutish dogs howling, the two brave men trekked into the frozen snow-clad forest toward the camp of the murderous windigo. The men crossed one large lake, then through a portage to the edge of a smaller lake. Here they camped because darkness began to cover the land. They built a huge fire, using eight-foot logs to feed the flames. On two sides of the roaring fire they made soft beds of green pine branches on the snow. During the night tibikigeesis crawled across the frozen sky and the two men huddled close to the fire.

In the morning, the half-breed went out on the ice and laid a trail of branches across the lake in order to lure the windigo to their camp. When all was prepared, the two Indians sat beside the fire and waited nervously.

"Do not be afraid unless you see I have fear," Rotten Log told his partner. They threw more logs on the fire because the intense cold was making their bodies turn numb and stiff.

Then, across the lake, they saw the windigo striding boldly over the branch trail toward them. As the hairy monster approached, they noticed it had chewed off its own lips. Its face was hideous; the teeth and gums of the creature were caked with blood. The fingers of the creature were also gone; it had eaten them to satisfy an insatiable craving for flesh. The windigo sat down opposite the two stunned men at the campfire. It sat there muttering, watching the men across the roaring fire. Suddenly the creature leaped over the flames, pouncing on Rotten Log. Windigo wrestled him, trying to bite his throat, but Rotten Log called on his guardian spirit, the great turtle, mis-qua-day-sih, to help in the struggle. Mis-qua-day-sih did not fail the Indian; he gave him the supernatural power and physical strength to subdue the windigo.

The half-breed and Rotten Log tied up the windigo and rolled it on the sled. The dogs started to drag the raving windigo back to the settlement. Pulling the toboggan through the deep snow was a difficult task for the animals, because of the weight of the struggling windigo. Again the ma-mandowin-ninih called on his guardian, mis-qua-day-sih, and his sacred turtle gave him strength to shove the heavy load. The huge dogs strained in their harnesses several more times and the toboggan stopped; but each time the sacred turtle gave them the power to continue with their prisoner. Finally, they reached their camp by the Berens River with the lunatic windigo.

At the camp the people placed the captive in a large building and built a huge fire to melt the ice from his body. After several hours near the heat of the fire, the windigo finished sweating the ice from his body. Then he vomited. In front of him, in his own spew were the eyes and hair of his wife and children.

This windigo never regained normality and it died in the camp. The people there burned the corpse to destroy its windigo spirit.

The Animals Climb into the Sky
Ella Elizabeth Clark

The theme of a visit to Sky Land by the mythological people of the earth is found in the myths of many tribes in British Columbia and in the State of Washington. The following is from the Kootenays; the Okanagans and the Shuswaps relate almost the same story. About forty versions have been recorded; in them the part played here by the two Hawks is played by Chickadee, Wren, Woodpecker or Boy Sapsucker.

Long ago, the animal people decided to make a journey to the Sky World. When they wondered how they could get up there, Grizzly Bear, who was their chief, told them he had a plan. He called all the people together and said to them, "Each of you — each animal, bird, and fish — will shoot an arrow upward until a rope of arrows reaches the sky."

All agreed with his plan. Coyote shot the first arrow toward the sky, but it fell down without reaching the spot. Fish, Toad, and Snake tried, but their arrows also fell back. One animal after another tried to hit the sky, but none succeeded. At last two Hawks took their turn. They had already visited the sky and were known to be skillful with the bow and arrow.

For a day and a night their arrows whistled through the air before the animals heard them strike the sky. The two Hawks continued to shoot. Their second arrow hit the notch of the first, the third one hit the notch of the second, and so on. At last they had a rope of arrows that reached almost to the ground. In order to complete the rope, Raven stuck his bill into the notch of the last arrow and braced his feet against the earth. Thus the animals climbed from the earth to the sky.

"Wait a minute," said Glutton, while the first ones were climbing. "I must look after my traps. Then I will be with you."

But when he came back, all the others had gone up the rope, including Raven. Glutton was so angry at being left behind that he pulled down the arrows and scattered them all over the land. This is how the Rocky Mountains came to be.

Before the other animals had reached the sky, Muskrat had climbed up there on his tail. With his spirit-power he had made a number of houses appear on the seashore. There he awaited the other earth people, eager to play a trick on them. The houses were very dirty. When the animal people arrived, Muskrat shot at them from the houses. As soon as he had shot from one place, he ran through a tunnel into the water and then into the next house. From there he shot at them again. In this way he made them believe that many people lived there and were shooting at them.

At last Woodpecker discovered that only the Muskrat lived in those houses. He watched at the hole until Muskrat came out, and then he killed him.

When the animal people were ready to return to the earth, they were surprised at not being able to find the rope on which they had climbed. Their chief thought of a plan and said to them, "Let us make a noose and catch Thunderbird. Then we will put his feathers on ourselves; with their help we will fly down to the earth."

Soon they saw a flash of lightning and heard the Thunderbird coming. Quickly they caught him in a noose and pulled out his feathers. Eagle took the best feathers. The others were divided among many creatures, but there were not enough for all. Those that took feathers flew down and became birds. Others leaped down and became fish or land animals. Coyote used his tail to steer with so fell gently to the earth. Sucker fell on a rock and broke his bones. He had to borrow new ones, and since then he has been full of bones.

Some people say that the creatures that did not return from the Sky Land were killed by the Sky People and were changed into stars.

Sightings from the Deck
Mary Moon

People who were fortunate enough to see Ogopogo from the decks of ships and motorboats often got a good close look at him; some even tried to chase him. Others, however, were frightened when the creature chose to follow in their wake, as no one was quite sure how friendly or unfriendly he was.

In the 1920s, Ogopogo was frequently seen by captains, crews and passengers on board the sternwheel steamships and tugs that plied Okanagan Lake before the roads were improved and highway vehicles began to carry people and freight.

Captain Joseph B. Weeks, who served on a number of the lake's steamboats, used to blow the ship's whistle to alert the attention of passengers and crew whenever he sighted the lake creature during 1923 and 1924. This I learned from a letter written to me from Montreal by William B. Folkard, who worked as a fireman on the lake boats in his youth. He added that Angus McKinnon, pilot of the diesel tugboat *Naramata,* also blew the whistle at the first sight of Ogopogo during the same years.

The results of this hooting and tooting were most unfortunate. Ogopogo, who apparently cannot stand loud noises, would promptly dive for the bottom of the lake and stay there while the ship was in the area.

Captain Weeks, whose destiny was tied up with the lake creature as well as the lake, chose to have his ashes scattered near Ogopogo's home at Squally Point. After his death on 23 February 1969, this was done from the deck of the tugboat *Naramata* — the sternwheelers he had skippered having glided into the pages of history. Mr. Folkard also told me: "In 1923, Captain Matt Reid of the S. S. *Okanagan* used to see Ogopogo occasionally in the early evening on hot summer days, as we were going southwards round Rattlesnake Point, directly across from Peachland." This is near Squally Point, the creature's home. "Captain Reid had also seen it near Westbank, about forty feet in length with a head like a horse," he added.

"A brown crocodile body about fifty feet long, with the same diameter as an auto wheel," was the description given by Mr. T. M. Thompson of Peachland, when he viewed Ogopogo in October 1926. At that time, Mr. Thompson was standing on the deck of the Canadian Pacific Railway's famed stern-wheeler, *S. S. Sicamous,* "The Great White Swan" that served Okanagan folk for over twenty years and now is permanently moored on the lakefront at Penticton as a tourist attraction. She was among the largest sternwheelers in British Columbia and is one of only two left in the province.

As the *Sicamous* was approaching Westbank wharf early in the morning, Ogopogo appeared about a hundred yards away, said the accounts in the *Kelowna Daily Courier* on Thursday, October 7. In the 1920s everyone knew everyone else in the Okanagan Valley, so one of the passengers who also saw Ogopogo on this occasion is identified only as a Mrs. Cooper of Summerland. Another, unnamed, witness said Ogopogo did "a gigantic nose dive in a swirl of water" as he submerged.

In 1926, the idea of equipping the B. C. government ferryboat plying between Kelowna and Westbank with "devices designed to repel the attacks of Mr. Ogopogo and family" was seriously considered. Under a Victoria dateline on August 31, the *Daily Province* reported:

> The public works department will call for revised tenders for this ferry within a day or two, in an effort to give the people of the Okanagan a thoroughly satisfactory service across Okanagan Lake. It was denied that the ferry plans were being revised to cope with the sea serpent menace, but officials indicated that as a revision had been ordered they would seize the opportunity to arm the new vessel adequately. They are rather puzzled to know, however, just what kind of weapons should be used for fighting the Opopogo tribe.

A cartoon in the *Vancouver Sunday Province* of 5 September 1926 showed a ferry boat armed with a small cannon pointing at Ogopogo who was swimming alongside. Four men were apparently engaged in loading the cannon. "It has been unsuccessfully engaged by artillery," said the caption.

On 18 August 1925, four boys — William Andrews, Allen Butler, Bob Butler and Ken Booth — were riding on rafts on Okanagan Lake. They saw what they thought was a log, six feet long, floating on the water. When it began to wriggle about, they realized that they were watching a peculiar-looking animal. People on the shore also noticed the swell of the waters, although the surface was otherwise as smooth as a mirror, and thought it due to the movement of some large creature under the surface. The boys said later that the whole lake seemed to sway as the waves rushed over their rafts. "It must have been as big as a whale," they added. The creature's head was submerged and the body resembled a large stovepipe. It travelled at a speed which caused their rafts to rock considerably when the swell reached them.

John C. Robson, principal of Rossland Public School, was the grandfather of two of the boys. He was on a nearby wharf and confirmed that the surface of the lake all that afternoon was as still as a pond. A young lad who was with him drew his attention to "a very decided swell coming in toward the wharf", and with no boat in sight, Mr. Robson later concluded that the swell was the same as that which rocked the boys' rafts.

Mr. H. Neill suddenly grabbed for his field glasses on Thursday 16 August 1928. He was aboard the S. S. *Pentowna,* captained by James Roe, as it was backing out of Naramata on the way to Summerland, on the other side of the lake. Between Mr. Neill and the brilliant sun was something strange in the lake. He watched it for a while, then handed the glasses to his wife.

"Before the other passengers could look through their own field glasses, the *Pentowna* had disturbed his lordship and he disappeared," said the account in the *Summerland Review* on Friday, August 17. "Only the head of the beastie was visible on this occasion, but residents about the lake will have their field glasses at hand for another appearance of the much wanted creature."

The reason why travellers in the Okanagan Valley carried field glasses and why householders living on the shores were equally well prepared was that Ogopogo was most active in the 1920s and often written about in the newspapers of the valley.

In 1970, Mrs. Mary Gartrell Orr of Summerland wrote to the Kelowna Chamber of Commerce: "My uncle, David Lloyd-Jones of Kelowna, said Ogopogo rolled up beside the Kelowna Sawmill tugboat, *Orchard City,* while it was crossing the lake, sometime in the 1920s. Before the crew could realize what was happening, Ogopogo disappeared. Uncle David was a real disbeliever, until then."

Some lake boat captains shared Mr. Lloyd-Jones's scepticism. Captain Jack McLeod, skipper of the CPR tugboat

Okanagan, did not believe a word of the Ogopogo stories. "I'm a sceptical sea captain and I've travelled the waters of Okanagan Lake for twenty-seven years without seeing any signs of a monster," he declared emphatically to the *Penticton Herald.* But on Saturday, 16 July 1949, he was on the CPR wharf at Kelowna when he noticed what appeared to be a head of a swimmer and a long black log near the now vanished Aquatic dining room complex on the lakefront. He paid little attention at first. A second glance revealed that the "log" was moving quickly through the water, much too fast to be a log or even a human being swimming, and it certainly was not a boat. As it moved rapidly across the lake towards Westbank, it left a considerable wake behind. "At last I've seen Ogopogo, and this is no second-hand story, as I saw it with my own eyes," exulted Captain McLeod.

A moonlight encounter with Ogopogo at a distance of only fifteen feet was recalled by a Vernon man who wishes to remain anonymous. He was replying to an appeal in 1970 by the Kelowna Chamber of Commerce for details on sightings of Ogopogo.

The meeting with the lake creature took place on a clear, moonlit Tuesday evening shortly before the international regatta at Kelowna in either 1934 or 1935. Two young men and two girls were seventy feet out on the lake in a rowboat about a hundred feet north of the mouth of Mill Creek, which empties into the lake near the bridge at Kelowna. As they rowed slowly along in the calm water, someone said: "Look out, there's a log ahead of us!" Someone else said: "Maybe it's Ogopogo." All four of them laughed. One of them suggested they get close enough to hit the log with an oar, so they rowed nearer to the object. It was fifteen or twenty feet long, about sixteen inches in diameter, and it just disappeared into the water at each end. The rowers froze.

"We were about fifteen feet from the object by this time," said the Vernon man. "The girls were getting uneasy, as were we — although we would not have admitted it at the time. I had some kitchen matches in my pocket and I struck several of these and threw them at the object. As the matches flared briefly, they revealed something dark and shiny.

"During all this time the object was completely motionless. Suddenly we became aware that it was moving. Since we were in a direct line between it and deeper water, the object slowly and silently moved in a semicircle around our boat and disappeared from sight. There was a tremendous splashing and then silence."

The two men decided against telling the local press their story. Two days later, the newspaper contained a report of a sighting of Ogopogo on the morning after the four of them had seen him by moonlight. This man said he had seen the lake creature at five in the morning at more or less the same place, while out practising sculling so that he could compete in the regatta.

The anonymous Vernon man wondered if he and his three friends had the distinction of having been closer to Ogopogo than anyone else. Well, yes and no. Up to that time, the mid-1930s, they might have been able to make that claim. In the 1970s, Ernie Lording of Kelowna, who has seen Ogopogo several times, said that he once came within three feet of the creature.

On Sunday, 6 October 1935, Edward Grahame, a Vernon farmer, was fishing with his father-in-law, Jim Ripley from England, and his brother, Charles B. Grahame. They were all alone about a mile or so from the north end of the lake when, without warning, Ogopogo slid his snakelike length up out of the calm depths. It was a clear afternoon about two o'clock, so there was no mistaking what they saw scarcely two hundred feet from their rowboat. For five or six minutes they watched him moving at fifteen miles per hour towards the shore. They saw humps, each about a foot above the surface, undulating along the top of the water. Because so much of him remained below the surface, they could not estimate what his total length might be.

Two pairs of Kelowna businessmen chased Ogopogo in 1951 on two separate occasions, but to no avail. The lake creature was simply too fast-moving for their motorboats to keep up with.

The first pair of pursuers, Cedric McNair Stringer, a director of the Kelowna Chamber of Commerce, and Vic Cowley, were out fishing on the lake on the clear and cloudless morning of May 19, when they saw Ogopogo on the east side of the lake, going north at first. Mr. Stringer was impressed by the sight of three or four humps in the water about three quarters of a mile away, but could not be sure the humps were undulating. Ogopogo was making a rolling movement, but no waves. The color of the fifteen or so feet of the object which appeared above the water was an odd grey-black. The two men hastily reeled in their fishing lines and revved the motor of their powerboat to chase Ogopogo. At 20 to 25 knots they sped to the exact spot where they had seen the head, but Ogopogo had vanished. Forgetting all about fishing, they cruised up and down for an hour hoping to see Ogopogo again, but had no luck. Mr. Stringer added that the experience had changed him abruptly from a nonbeliever to a believer in the existence of Ogopogo.

The second chase took place on 8 July 1951, as dusk was falling. Monty DeMara, a Kelowna insurance man, and Bill Fisher were travelling north to Kelowna in a motorboat when a "thing" suddenly appeared in the water, crossing thirty-five yards in front of the boat from left to right, moving toward the shore near Squally Point. "It was like a great moving log, but alive, moving up and down a little in the water," Mr. DeMara told me. "Then the thing moved parallel with the shoreline as it went south, so we turned the boat around and chased it." The object seen by both men for almost a minute was dark brownish green and forty feet long. No head was visible and it did not make any waves or any sounds. But the men yelled with excitement as they chased the lake creature — which must have startled him because he submerged.

"If I'd only had a camera!" lamented James Shelley who, with Bob Derker and Jerry Huffman, pursued Ogopogo in an outboard motorboat on Tuesday, 9 July 1957, and approached within twenty-five feet of the lake creature. They were close enough to see four humps, dark green to black, about four feet apart. Apparently, there were fins on each hump. The diameter of the coils was about two feet and they saw about fifteen feet of Ogopogo's body.

Before his adventure at 7:30 in the evening about a half mile off Gyro Park public beach in Kelowna, Mr. Shelley had thought Ogopogo was "strictly a mythical creature", but he was now convinced it was no fish story. His lack of a camera at the time was particularly unfortunate, as that year the Canadian Tourist Association had offered a reward of five thousand dollars for the first genuine photograph of Ogopogo. As no one came forward to claim the reward, the Canadian Tourist Association withdrew it some years later.

Some people chase Ogopogo and some are chased by him. The people in the following three stories belong in the second category.

On the evening of 17 July 1959, Mr. and Mrs. R. H. (Dick) Miller, Mr. Pat Marten (Mrs. Miller's brother), Mrs. Marten and six-year-old Murray Marten were in a cruiser returning home to Vernon. Dick Miller, editor of the *Vernon Advertiser,* was the first to notice Ogopogo following about 250 feet in the boat's wake. He estimated that the lake creature was travelling at approximately seventeen miles an hour and gaining on the cruiser which was doing only ten.

"Pat Marten, who was at the helm, turned the boat around and headed in Ogopogo's direction, so we got a magnificent view of him (or her or it)," wrote Dick Miller in the *Advertiser* on July 20. Ogopogo was still travelling at the same speed and was only 175 feet away by this time. Dick Miller made a quick sketch of how the snake-like head with the blunt nose appeared to him at the moment. Everyone else in the boat was frantically passing the field glasses around for a close-up of the dark greenish serpentine form.

"Our excitement was short-lived (we watched for about three minutes). Ogie did not appear to like the boat coming at him broadside, so very gracefully he reduced the five humps which were so plainly visible, lowered his head and gradually submerged," wrote Dick Miller.

A snake when swimming in water gets its forward propulsion by moving its body in a sideways motion. This sea serpent does not. It glides very gracefully in a smooth, direct forward motion. This would lead me to believe that in between the humps it possibly has some type of fins which it works together, or possibly individually, to control direction," Mr. Miller concluded.

Two fourteen-year-old girls burst into the newsroom of the *Kelowna Daily Courier* at 1:30 on a Sunday afternoon in November 1970. Shaking and out of breath, they blurted out that Ogopogo had followed their motor-equipped rowboat off Strathcona Park south of Kelowna bridge. Only a hundred feet from their boat, a three-humped darkish Ogopogo had pursued them in circles for about ten minutes.

"We were scared to death, he was so close," exclaimed one of the girls. Neither would give her name, afraid of being ridiculed although this was the eighth sighting of 1970 — at least the eighth reported to the press. Many sightings are never told to the public but just discussed with family and friends.

Rita Bridges and Louis Guidi of Kelowna on Sunday 10 July 1949 were in a rowboat close to the west shore of the lake opposite the Aquatic dining and athletic complex when Miss Bridges noticed Ogopogo less than a hundred yards away from the rowboat, which he seemed to be following. Three undulations appeared above the water, but his head was not visible. She turned deathly pale, and almost fainted, then pleaded with Louis Guidi to turn towards the shore, which he did. Ogopogo proceeded on his way south, no doubt going home to Squally Point.

Hundreds of little fish leaping up in the air as though frightened attracted the attention of the then Brenda Briese when she was driving a motorboat along Okanagan Lake one hot mid-July evening between six and seven, in 1967. She was towing Brian Bocking on water skis and was accompanied in the boat by his sister Candy, now Mrs. Dirk van Hees of Kelowna.

Brenda (now Mrs. Robert deRoos) told me the story in Vancouver where she teaches school: "We were quite a distance from shore, about one third of the way across the lake. I saw hundreds of little fish leaping up, the way they do in other places to catch flies at night. But they don't ordinarily jump like that in Okanagan Lake. Something was scaring those fish."

Then she saw what appeared to be a big log in the water, ahead of the motorboat and to the right. "It looked as I would imagine the back of a whale would look — greyish, blubbery and smooth with no humps. It was just lying there in the water, not moving, about a hundred feet away from us. I saw twenty feet of it, a curved shape with no head and no fins, just like a whale resting under the surface of the water. I had to swerve the boat to the left to miss hitting it, and I glanced back to make sure I *had* missed it. Whatever it was had disappeared entirely. If it hadn't disappeared like that, I really would have thought it was a log. There were very few ripples. . . ."

She headed the boat back to shore at once and explained her action when they reached the Briese family's dock, for although Candy too saw the monster, Brian Bocking on the skis did not. "It scared me so much I didn't go water skiing again all that summer."

One year later, another party of water skiers had a thrilling encounter with Ogopogo. Sheri Campbell, daughter of E. A. (Fred) Campbell of Kelowna, was already a believer in the existence of Ogopogo, because both her parents had seen him, but Sheri's four companions were sceptics. At approximately 5:45 p.m. on Tuesday, 23 July 1968, Willie Walls, Bruce and Gwen Johnson and Rennee Bliss all became believers.

The youngsters, who ranged in age from fourteen to twenty-one, were motorboating seven miles north of the Kelowna Yacht Club on the east side of the lake when all of them noticed big waves. Willie Walls wondered why waves of such a size should occur just there. There was no wind, no other boat anywhere near them, and the rest of the lake was smooth as glass.

"The waves were large rollers ranging from three to five feet and without origin," Miss Campbell told me. "There was no one around but us and someone fishing in a small rowboat. I crossed the boat's wake and was skiing on the right side when I saw the Ogopogo floating on the surface without his head or tail being visible. From the surface of the water, he appeared to be six feet in depth and about twenty feet in length of body. He was just resting there without movement, for about two minutes.

"I became a little hysterical. Panic is the word — I had no idea where his mouth was! I dropped the rope. They came around to pick me up. By the time they had picked me up, Ogopogo had begun moving. His blue-green-grey scales glistened like a rainbow trout as the sun shone on him. That's the funny thing . . . it looks more like a snake and doesn't have those "things" that stick up on the back of the statue at the foot of Bernard Avenue in Kelowna.

"After we were all in the boat, we decided we wanted to get closer. We got quite close to him, within five feet or so," she said.

"Willie Walls saw him as close as anyone did, but he couldn't see the head as it was in the shade cast by a mountain.

Willie could see the neck, however, and estimated the total length at about twenty feet. Ogopogo submerged then and started heading north towards Vernon at a terrific speed, with the waves parting on either side."

Sheri Campbell continued: "The first time Ogopogo dived, he came up five hundred yards away, two minutes later. The second time he surfaced and was visible for about thirty seconds. When he swam beneath the surface, he made waves which streamed behind him in vee shapes."

For two minutes, the five youngsters chased Ogopogo at forty miles an hour, but he was too fast for them. Sheri Campbell estimated the lake creature's swimming speed at more than forty-five miles an hour because "it was all we could do to keep up with him."

"The experience hasn't really changed my life, just opened up my mind a little. But it *did* happen and it was terrifically exciting," she concluded.

The Okanagan Indians Knew Him Well

Mary Moon

The land of the prehistoric Okanakane Indians stretched from just north of Vernon, in the province of British Columbia, across the international border to where the Okanogan River joins the Columbia River near Brewster in Washington State. The area is spelled Okanagan in Canada and Okanogan in the United States.

Around the eighty-mile length of Okanagan Lake, scores of small prehistoric Indian settlements have been found by farmers, construction workers and archeologists. The floors of some of the Indian winter housepits, called *kikulis* or *kekulis,* are three thousand years old. A whole hillside covered with these stone-lined dug-outs, roofed with hide or thatch, is commemorated by the name Kick Willy Loop in Vernon.

The Okanagan Indians, whose language belonged to the Interior Salish group, had much personal freedom, with a minimum of leadership, and lived in bands of self-governing villages. Territorial rights in fishing, root-digging and hunting grounds could be shared with other bands. They moved seasonally in search of food — which included deer, elk, mountain sheep, goats, salmon, berries, seeds and many plants. They dried or smoked their winter supplies and either buried them in stone-lined cache pits or stored them on scaffolds too high for wild animals to reach.

In September, when the kokanee salmon spawned in Mission Creek (which they called N-wha-que-sin) in what is now South Kelowna, the Indians camped along the banks to catch, clean and smoke-cure thousands of fish for the winter. Then, as now, the lake monster hung around the mouths of creeks to eat spawning fish. The Indians called him Naitaka. When Indians were forced to pass by Squally Point, or even cross the lake anywhere, they took along a small pig, a dog or a chicken to drop in the water. Sometimes the offerings included venison or wild berries. These were supposed to distract the water god and allow the Indians to escape.

Primrose Upton opened her book, *The History of Okanagan Mission,* with the words:

First were the Indians . . . they have left their mark upon our civilization. A great many of our place names are Indian in origin and the famed lake monster — Ogopogo — has his beginnings in Indian folklore.

It is a pity that the Indians had no written language and, although pictographs have been found along many of the well-known trails, it is not known if they have a story to tell. However, stories were handed down from father to son, and one of the best-known of these is that of the Demon of the Lake, who lives in the depths between Squally Point and the island between Okanagan Mission and Naramata.

No Indian would fish near there, and if perchance the bait were taken by the monster, a wise Indian would certainly let N'hahtik have it, line and all. They believed that the Demon's anger could be appeased by throwing a live dog to his lair. (In his journal for 1827, Sir Walter Scott mentioned that Scottish Highlanders killed dogs to use as bait in the hope of catching what they called "the water cow".)

All Indians rushed for shelter when the dark ridge of rising water showed that N'hahtik was abroad. He churned the waters into a fury with such speed that one minute there was breathless calm and the next the wind was howling and the white waves racing and clawing at one another, sinking back exhausted only to be smashed by the next wave.

An Indian legend about the origin of Naitaka or Ogopogo

came into my hands in Kelowna recently. I asked John F. Lund of Regatta City Press if it was an authentic Indian legend, and he consulted Noll Derriksan, former chief of the Kelowna and Westbank Indian Band. Mr. Derriksan thought the story could have been handed down from generation to generation through the band. He wondered if the white people had picked up the legend somewhere along the line and laid claim to it — which has happened, on occasion.

Whoever "owns" the legend now, it is a good story:

Many moons ago there lived in these hills an old Indian known to all of us — The Old Man of the Mountains. A friend of all animals and a kind counsellor to his people, he was called by them Old Kan-He-Kan.

There came one day to the valley an evil man named Kel-Oni-Won who was possessed with the Devil Spirit. He murdered the vulnerable old man with a club. In memory of Old Kan-He-Kan, his people named the beautiful lake in the valley Okanagan.

They called upon the gods to avenge his death and punish his murderer. The gods, unable to decide on a punishment, let the murderer brood on his sin until a council could be held.

The gods later decided to change Kel-Oni-Won into a lake serpent — a restless creature who would be forever at the scene of the crime, where he would suffer continued remorse.

He was left in the custody of the beautiful Indian Lake Goddess, and was known from that time as The Remorseful One. The only beings who would tolerate his company were the water creatures and the hated rattlesnake. (Today's Ogopogo Island, his legendary home at the lake's big bend, was formerly called Rattlesnake Island.)

So if you wish to see him and cannot get near him

you will know his conscience still bothers him and he is ashamed to show his face, the legend ends.

Another tragic legend about Ogopogo was told by some older Indians to historian Frank Buckland, who studied the Okanakane Indian culture for nearly fifty years. The story is dramatic:

Chief Timbasket, a member of the southern tribe of the Okanagan nation, was visiting with his family the Indian village which stood where Westbank is now. The villagers, of the Tisn-stip-ep-tinsub tribe, had spent several days preparing to travel down the lake to the southern end, to attend the usual summer gathering on the site of the present city of Penticton. The Indians called the area Pentk-tn, meaning "always place", a permanent camp.

The Westbank tribe's medicine man had made "big medicine" to protect the voyagers from the lake demon. Each canoe had a mystic sign painted on its bow with a mixture of fish oil and the paint called tulameen, meaning "red earth". (The same paint, used by them in their rock paintings, was found to the west of the Okanagan Valley, where the word survives as the name of a community and a river.)

Timbasket, the Indian cynic, watched all these preparations and declared his disbelief in the existence of the lake demon. He was told that the Westbank Indians intended to sacrifice a live dog to the water god as they passed Squally Point, but he was quite unimpressed. He knew too much to concern himself with outmoded customs.

The Westbank Indians paddled their canoes cautiously at what they considered a safe distance from shore as they passed Squally Point. Timbasket defiantly chose to travel closer to the rocky headland. Suddenly, the lake demon arose from his lair and whipped up the surface of the lake with his long tail. Timbasket, his family and his canoe were sucked under by a great swirl of angry water.

Years later, a hunting party stalking deer high up on the same shore found a wrecked canoe, splintered and rotting. Two daubs of yellow ochre on the shattered bow identified it as the property of the vanished Timbasket.

How did it get there, so high up on the mountain, the legend asks, for its position was far beyond the reach of any wave in the lake. Had the lake demon dragged the canoe and the Timbasket family half-way up the slope before devouring them?

Unknown artists of the Okanakane Indians in centuries past may have left us three or even more portraits of Ogopogo painted on rocks. Two of these have been preserved in drawings by two Okanagan Valley women.

Primrose Upton told me: "The pictograph we saw is on a granite rock face, with lichen intruding, at McKinley Landing. It faces southwest, can be reached only by boat and can be seen only from the water. McKinley Landing is on the east side of the lake, north of Kelowna and a few miles south of Okanagan Centre. The painting was done in red ochre and was very dim in June 1965, when we recorded it."

The Indian rock painting was too faint to be photographed, so Mrs. Upton sketched it. Her drawing shows two portraits of Ogopogo from different angles. The one lower down on the rock depicts a horse-like left profile with horns or upstanding ears, one hump and a forked tail. In the upper left-hand corner of the pictograph, the lake creature appears to be stealing away through the weeds, looking rather rodent-like in shape.

Historian Frank Morgan Buckland described another Indian rock painting of Ogopogo: "Up near the headwaters of Powers Creek (a stream in Westbank) there is said to be an Indian painting of Naitaka in red ochre on the smooth surface of a huge rock that stands abruptly out of a small mountain tarn. It is a bit of tangible evidence that the Indians believed in and worshipped some lake demon."

Mr. and Mrs. Upton searched for Buckland's rock painting in vain and concluded that it has faded completely.

Toward the end of the eighteenth century, long before the sa-ma, or white man, came into Okanagan Valley, the Okanakane Tribe presented a dugout canoe eighteen feet long and five feet wide to Chief Halka-wan-cheen. "At each end was a huge carving of Na-ha-ha-itkh, (Ogopogo) the water god," says Mrs. Louise Gilbert, an Okanakane Indian writer in Penticton. Her tribe still occupied the land from the north end of Okanagan Lake (they called it Tee-khwat) to the south part of the river of the same name, in today's Washington State.

Fear of the lake creature continued among the Indians into the present century. According to Leslie Kerry, a Kelowna newspaperman, "All the Indians used to talk about Ogopogo in the twenties, when there were more Indians around the lake than there are now. It was common knowledge among them around 1926, when Ogopogo was frequently discussed. The Indians spoke to me of their fears of him, and of taking a chicken or a piglet aboard their canoes with which to propitiate him, if necessary."

Today, opposite Squally Point on the edge of the modern Highway 97, stands an official marker put up by the Department of Recreation and Conservation, which reads:

"OGOPOGO'S HOME: Before the unimaginative, practical whiteman came, the fearsome lake monster, N'ha-a-itk, was well known to the primitive, superstitious Indians. His home was believed to be a cave at Squally Point, and small animals were carried in the canoes to appease the serpent. Ogopogo still is seen each year — but now by white men!"

The "Little Men" of Long Ago
B. A. McKelvie

The legend of the Sasquatch — a giant race that once roamed this country, and survivors of which are believed to exist in the mountain wilds of British Columbia — is well known. But the public is not so well acquainted with the fact that there is a wide-spread belief amongst the native peoples of the province in the existence of leprechauns. These "little men" appear in the stories of Interior as well as Coastal tribes. That the stories may be founded on prehistoric fact is admitted by such eminent authorities as A. E. Pickford, Provincial Government anthropologist.

Very little is known of the race or races that preceded the Indians of British Columbia, and Mr. Pickford says that it is possible that there was a people here of short stature, like Japanese, who were driven into the hills by the ancestors of the present Indians, and native women warned their children against the "little people" of the forest. So the story may have survived.

In any event, Mr. Pickford is recording whatever he may learn in respect of the leprechauns.

I first learned about them from Captain Charles Cates, of North Vancouver. He was seeking information from an old Squamish friend about the Sasquatch — or, as the giants are known to them, the "Smy-a-lichk." "He said he had never seen one, but he had seen a strange thing when he was young," the Captain related. "He said that an old man had told him of a 'Squolk-ty-mish' or pygmy that was in the district around Woodfibre.

"It had the habit of tapping on trees with a stick, as it scurried through the forest.

"Then one day, my friend said," the Captain went on, "he was far back in the mountains when he heard a rhythmic tapping. He remembered the story of the Squolk-ty-mish, and crept quietly towards the sound.

"After a while he saw a queer little man. He was naked except for a little green hat that looked as if it was made of moss. The little fellow had a stick and would skip around and seemed to get a great delight in finding a hollow log on which to drum.

"My friend said he got within about twenty-five feet before the little fellow saw him. Even then he was not very scared and kept skipping about like a squirrel and chuckling to himself. He worked his way gradually farther away from my friend and then suddenly disappeared."

Captain Cates said that from another old Indian friend he had learned that an old woman stated that she had seen a Squolk-ty-mish up in the hills that border Lynn Valley. He had not told this informant anything of the story he had previously heard, the Captain said, and was interested to find that the description of the little man with the green hat was similar. Now the Captain has one carved on a totem pole, matching a pole bearing the likeness of a Smy-a-lichk, or giant.

Andy Paull, president of the North American Allied Tribes, says that such stories are common among the Indians in the Burns Lake region, where he made inquiries for me recently. The natives of the Central Interior, he said, were quite familiar with tales of a race of small men who were reported to live in the woods, and dwell in mountain caves. He says that the correct pronounciation is "Stut-ko-mish".

Jimmy John is a fine type of Nootkan. He is an expert wood carver, and maker of masks and totems, and therefore well acquainted with the lore of his people. Carvers are like ancient minstrels who preserve the past. He has lived at Nanaimo for many years past, but was brought up on the West Coast.

His statement made the other day at the Provincial Museum was that the Nootkans have a belief in "the little people". They call them "Win-a-chist". They are about two feet in height. He carved masks to represent them. These masks had a sharp, white snout, and were adorned with an eagle feather. Only one family was permitted to use this mask or to have the Win-a-chist dance.

Rev. Peter Kelly, captain of the United Church Mission boat *Thomas Crosby,* who is proud of his Haidah lineage, states that when he was a boy on the Queen Charlotte Islands, he heard stories of the "little people".

So, it would appear that there is a general inclusion in the mythology of British Columbia of leprechauns, and that like those of Ireland, at least some of our little people sported on the green.

The Black Bonspiel of Wullie MacCrimmon

W. O. Mitchell

CHARACTERS

MRS. BUTTON	PIPERS
MRS. SLANEY	AIDES
THE DEVIL	MALLEABLE CHARLIE BROWN
WULLIE MACCRIMMON	CROSS-CUT CHARLIE BROWN
THE REVEREND B. G. PRINGLE	JOE HARRINGTON
PIPE-FITTING CHARLIE BROWN	JUDAS ISCARIOT
ANNOUNCER	GUY FAWKES
GOVERNOR GENERAL	MACBETH

SETS

EXTERIOR: Wullie's shop and Funeral Parlour
INTERIOR: Wullie's shop
Curling-rink

ACT I

MUSIC: *Simple but macabre and threatening theme of original radio play continuing background through:*

FADE IN: *The year's first snowflakes are lazily feathering down, if this can be done without viewers assuming that their sets are giving them faulty reception. Through the snowfall we see street of typical small-town Alberta store fronts.*

We see that one of their false fronted stores is "Barney's Vulcanizing". Camera goes from sign to sign: "Chez Sadie's" — in angling neon, like a signature across the face of the building — finally "W. MacCrimmon — Harness and Shoe Repairs". Pause, then down and along the street

we see two women engaged in earnest con-
versation before Chez Sadie's. Then on to: the
door of the mortuary, which is simply a white,
square wooden building; on it, the sign:

STEVE HAZZARD

LICENSED EMBALMER

FUNERAL DIRECTOR

MUSIC OUT:

The door opens and a man in a dark fall coat —
tailored kind with a velvet collar — steps out. He
wears a dark homburg hat, and carries in his
hand a small case such as travellers have for
samples of literature. He closes the door
carefully behind himself. He walks down the
board walk, his steps deliberate and distinct.
They continue through: We see MRS. BUTTON *and*
MRS. SLANEY, *the women who were in conversation*
before Chez Sadie's.

MRS. BUTTON . . . and I said to her — you may think you're the
whole Home and School Association, Lucy
Tregillis (SOUND: *footsteps nearing)* . . . but as far
as I'm concerned — *(She turns as* THE DEVIL *comes*
up to them.)

DEVIL 'Day, Mrs. Button — nice crisp day.

MRS. BUTTON Oh — good afternoon — uh — Mr. — ah —
(stares after DEVIL *as he walks on, then turns to*
MRS. SLANEY) — but I happen to know, I said to her,
what kind of language has been heard on these
school grounds and I don't — *(full stop)* Who was
that anyway? Stranger. But he did call me by
name. Oh — well — I happen to know, I said, that
Mr. Langley's car has been parked outside Mame
Harris's house three nights in a row now — he did
seem familiar — as though I'd seen his face before

The Black Bonspiel of Wullie MacCrimmon 213

— oh — probably a travelling man of some sort
. . . *(She looks right down the street.)*

THE DEVIL *has stopped before the shop of W.
MacCrimmon. He looks up at the sign — opens
the door and enters.*

*Interior: MacCrimmon shop. A counter runs
halfway along the front. Behind it and to the left*
WULLIE *is seated at his shoe last. He is bent over
the shoe there as he hammers in tacks. Almost
centre, behind the counter, stands a pot-bellied
heater with a mica belly-button, the stove-pipe
angling in anguish up and across the ceiling, then
up and at right angles and out the side wall.
Before* WULLIE *and his last is a shoes-to-be-
repaired counter in which are tumbled various
pairs of ticketed shoes, boots, and slippers.*

THE DEVIL *enters — pauses within the door, which
he closes behind himself.*

WULLIE *looks up from the last. He lays his
hammer down. He gets up with the care and
preciseness of the rheumatic and walks towards
the counter.* WULLIE*'s face has a full, pursed look.
His eyes still on the visitor, he lifts his hand and
spits out the cargo of tacks. He places them on the
counter, then:*

WULLIE	Aye-he?
DEVIL	Mr. MacCrimmon. *(This is a statement.)*
WULLIE	Aye-he?
DEVIL	My curling-boots. I would like a resole job done on them.
WULLIE	*(He looks down to the parcel. The visitor's hand rests beside it. It is a small hand, almost fleshless, sinewy, dextrous-looking — its back coarse with jet wiry hair that grows almost to the base of the nail. We travel up the arm to the first*

sight of THE DEVIL's *face with its black brows that have an upward flare at their outer ends.* WULLIE *lifts his eyes, now suspicious and a little — just a very little — worried.)* When — ah — when would you want them done?

DEVIL　My next trip through. Two weeks . . .

WULLIE　You curl. (DEVIL *nods.*) At the Glencoe? In the city?

DEVIL　*(shakes his head).* No. *(Pause.)* When could you — could I have them in two weeks' time?

WULLIE　*(shrugs to the shoes-to-be-repaired shelf).* I'm behind on my repairs. *(He picks up the boots and turns them over thoughtfully.)* Nice boots — yes — uh — afraid you'll have to resort to buckled overshoes for — uh three weeks?

DEVIL　*(calculated pause as he looks at Wullie).* Three weeks then.

WULLIE　Best I can do. *(He sets boots down again — looks up.)* You travel? (DEVIL *nods.*) Aye-he. *("I thought so.")* You ah — *(about to ask a question; thinks better of it.)* Aye-he.

DEVIL　I had detail work planned for here in two weeks. I can move it ahead a week — take a run down the East line and into Southern Saskatchewan. *(Pause.)* That's always a good territory. Three weeks.

WULLIE　*(a little dazed-looking — his eyes down on the boots on the counter).* Aye-he. Three weeks.

SOUND: *Tinkle of bell over the front door.* WULLIE *looks up to the door, then down to the counter again. He picks up the tacks from the counter and puts them into his mouth. He turns away to the last, sits, begins the crooked rhythm of his hammer. He stops. He gets up and comes back to the counter, looks down at the curling shoes.*

WULLIE's *hand picks one up and as it does a white card flutters out . . .*

WULLIE Warm — warmer than it would be — if he'd just taken it off. *(Pause as* WULLIE *turns over the boot.)* But he must have carried it a distance through cold winter air. *(Lays boot down, picks up white card. The business card held in* WULLIE's *hand:*

Mr. O. Cloutie
WHOLESALE SOULS/RETAIL SINS
Business & Home Address: Sulphur Blvd.
Hell

He picks up THE DEVIL's *boots — looks down at them. Shrugs.)*
Ah, well. *(He moves over to the shoes-to-be-repaired shelf.)* A boot's a boot for all that. *(Carelessly, and with contempt for all people in high places, even though their title be the Prince of Darkness, he negligently tosses the boots onto the shelf. He walks to the last, sits, takes up his hammer, and begins the crooked rhythm of shoe repairing.)*

On the shoes - to - be - repaired shelf: we see labourers' felt boots, high-heeled riding-boots, somehow pathetic little child's boots, boots with great bunion bulges — and on top, where WULLIE *has tossed them,* THE DEVIL's *curling boots. As* WULLIE's *hammer continues its tapping impatience* THE DEVIL's *curling-boots almost seem to glow. Imperceptibly at first, they steam, then from them lifts a definite drifting wraith of smoke.*

SOUND: *Tinkle of the doorbell —* WULLIE's *hammer breaks off its sound.*

THE REVEREND B. G. PRINGLE *is just closing the door.*
He is a progressive United Church minister. He
is thirty-five — still plays a little hockey with the
young people. He is a quite nice, straight young
man — not the "precious spinster" caricature on
radio and in the movies.

PRINGLE   Good day, Mr. MacCrimmon.

WULLIE   Good day. *(If anything, he had been warmer*
           toward the earlier strange visitor.)

PRINGLE   Crisp.

WULLIE   *(around the tacks in his mouth).* Aye-he.

           He goes on with his cobbling through the next few
           lines — not rude, mind you, but just so that the
           young minister will understand that he's a busy
           man and can have no time for United Church
           matters!

PRINGLE   Dropped in — are you busy?

WULLIE   Some. You're not the first.

PRINGLE   First?

WULLIE   Visitor. *(Looks up at* PRINGLE. *)* I had your
           opposition in a while back. (PRINGLE*'s eyebrows lift*
           slightly in surprise.)

PRINGLE   Oh — oh — was Father O'Halloran here to
           visit . . .

WULLIE   No — no. *(Pause.)* What had you in mind, Mr.
           Pringle?

PRINGLE   *(he is obviously embarrassed).* Oh — a moment
           — just a moment of your — time. Ah — called
           on Mr. Clayton and uh — Mr. Thompson — Mr.
           Bolley.

           WULLIE *lays down the boot he's been working on —*
           stares hard at MR. PRINGLE.

WULLIE   All members of your congregation.

PRINGLE   Yes. *(Not important really.)* Yes — they are.

	(Awkward pause.) Mr. MacCrimmon — *(Clears throat.)* I know you aren't a member of Grace — of our church.
WULLIE	That's right.
PRINGLE	Still — I am calling on you as I did on the others — uh — in regard to the new church.
WULLIE	Aye-he. *(He puts the boot over the last, puts tacks back into his mouth, picks up the hammer.)*
PRINGLE	We hope to break — uh — ground on it early this spring.
WULLIE	Do you. *(He knows what's coming — he begins to hammer on the shoe. Continues through:)*
PRINGLE	When we have managed the necessary funds. *(Pause.)* When we have managed — uh — the necessary funds. *(Quite pointed.)*
WULLIE	Mmmmmmmmm-mmh. *(He is still tapping on the boot.)*
PRINGLE	*(brightly).* So far we have done very well — almost better than we expected. And — ah — I see one of my fondest dreams very near to coming true. The thing I've directed all my energies towards since coming to Khartoum.
WULLIE	*(drops the hammer with a clatter).* That an' prohibition . . .
PRINGLE	Yes. In the matter of temperance I have taken a firm stand.
WULLIE	*(half rising from his seat).* The prohibition of Sabbath curling.
PRINGLE	Oh — yes — that — yes. *(Awkward pause.)* I've always felt that there should be one day set aside for the spirit.
WULLIE	You could say curling was as much for the spirit as for the flesh. . . .
PRINGLE	Well — for — for — contemplation. One day out of seven for — uh — I — well, I suppose we do

	not see eye to eye on that, Mr. MacCrimmon.
WULLIE	No — we do not.
PRINGLE	*(slides around the end of the counter and starts towards* WULLIE). But you must admit that we did have a — the approval of the majority of the townspeople — More were against Sunday curling than were . . .
WULLIE	More do not curl than do . . . or have wives that do not. Not one curler voted for your by-law prohibiting Sabbath curling.
PRINGLE	For their own good, Mr. MacCrimmon. For their own good.
WULLIE	You can't.
PRINGLE	Can't what?
WULLIE.	You can't determine for other people what's for their own good. It's a judgement they must acquire for themselves.
PRINGLE	Oh now . . . it often helps to have a little outside help now and again. No harm in stiffening the moral . . .
WULLIE	If it needs outside stiffening, it is then a false morality. You could patch up the outside from now till the resurrection and you would still have a poor thing, Mr. Pringle. *(Swinging around towards* PRINGLE.) Have you tried to work from the inside out, Mr. Pringle?
PRINGLE	*(he is reaching inside his coat)*. We do that — we do that too.
WULLIE	Do you now.
PRINGLE	*(as he unscrews the cap from his fountain pen)*. Now — I know you are not a member of our congregation but — I — have — I would like to put your name down.
WULLIE	Mr. Pringle!
PRINGLE	*(looking up but with the pen-nib poised)*. Yes?

WULLIE	You know I was born Presbyterian.
PRINGLE	Yes . . .
WULLIE	As you were.
PRINGLE	Well, I . . .
WULLIE	*(sure he has him on the run now as he advances on him, gesturing at him with the end of the cobbling-hammer).* But with this difference — I still am — Presbyterian. Continuin' Presbyterian.
PRINGLE	*(straightening up).* But we welcome — you're welcome to come and worship with us in Grace United.
WULLIE	No thanks. When it was Grace Presbyterian — that was another thing — but now that it has turned — *(pause for emphasis while* WULLIE*'s face shows his distaste as though the word were sour in his mouth.)* Methodist!
PRINGLE	Not Methodist. It isn't Methodist, Mr. MacCrimmon. United!
WULLIE	I was not born nor was I brought up Methodist. *(Brings down cobbling-hammer smartly on the counter for emphasis.)* I do not intend to live Methodist. *(Final clinching bang of the hammer and* PRINGLE *draws back hand just missed by a hair.)*
PRINGLE	Now — just a minute — you've started out with the wrong assumption . . .
WULLIE	I have been given the choice of your Methodist church and . . .
PRINGLE	*(objecting noises).* Oh, please . . .
WULLIE	*(magnanimously).* All right — all right your United Church — Baptist — Seventh Day Advent, Father O'Halloran's Saint Therese and the Meetings of the Burning Church of Nazareth over the Odd Fellows Hall. *(Pause.)* I have visited them all since, since . . .
PRINGLE	Since the union.

WULLIE   Since the loss of my own church. *(Pause.)* I long
                ago decided to remain what I am — continuing
                Presbyterian with the creed of my fathers and
                what was a good foundation for my father is a
                good foundation for me. (PRINGLE *begins to walk
                towards* WULLIE.)

PRINGLE   But your father lived in a different world. Your
                father believed many things that you don't believe
                in.

                WULLIE *and* PRINGLE *at the stove,* WULLIE *straightens
                up with a chunk of kindling from the wood box.*

WULLIE   No. My faith and my convictions are the same as
                my father's — the same as the day I set beside him
                in church — hearing the minister's voice soaring
                and dipping grand as he painted for his
                congregation the hell that waited all sinners. *(He
                bends to open the stove front.)*

PRINGLE   We believe in a religion of love today, Mr.
                MacCrimmon.

WULLIE   *(he throws it over his shoulder as he squats before
                the stove).* Aye — of love and no Hell.

PRINGLE   Well . . .

WULLIE   . . . and no Devil.

PRINGLE   Symbolically speaking.

WULLIE   *(to his feet and facing* PRINGLE *with the wood
                chunk still in his hand).* I mean actually speaking.
                Hell and the Devil. *(He brandishes the wood
                chunk in his enthusiasm.)* There's the foundation
                for a religion — the skeletal requirements you
                might say. Mr. Pringle, when you begin to preach
                sermons with some bones in them — when you can
                show me something besides the wishy-washy
                symbolical hells and symbolical devils — then
                Wullie MacCrimmon will be right alongside the
                other members of your congregation — taking

	communion with — in your new Methodist Church!
PRINGLE	But it's not Methodist — its Unite — oh all right, Mr. MacCrimmon. *(He turns back to the counter — picks up the list and begins to fold it up.)* I'll — I won't bother to put your name down.
WULLIE	Hold on now. Don't be too hasty. Half a loaf is better than none. I don't mind . . .
PRINGLE	*(arrests his hand with the folded list halfway to his breast pocket).* Half a loaf!
WULLIE	How much had you in mind putting me down for?
PRINGLE	Twenty dollars.
WULLIE	I see. *(Pause.)* A church is a church. *(Pause.)* Methodist or not.
PRINGLE	But it's . . .
WULLIE	*(turning back to the stove).* Twenty dollars. An indirect blow.
PRINGLE	*In*direct blow!
WULLIE	Mr. Pringle. *(He advances on him still with the wood chunk in his hand.)* Will you tell me one thing.
PRINGLE	Yes?
WULLIE	Do you or do you not believe in a Devil?
PRINGLE	*(finds this question a rough one).* Well — *(long pause)* I do believe there is a force for evil abroad in the world.
WULLIE	*(advances on* PRINGLE, *backing him towards the counter).* That does not answer my question. *(He has lifted the wood chunk now and is holding it loosely out from him — wrist turned up like a duellist about to engage his opponent.)* Do you believe in a personal Devil?
PRINGLE	Well — *(longer pause)* I — *(clears his throat)* No.
WULLIE	Do you believe in Hell?
PRINGLE	*(his back to the counter — long pause — clears his throat again).*

WULLIE	Do *(poke with wood chunk in* PRINGLE's *breastbone)* you *(poke)* Believe *(poke)* in Hell? *(poke)*
PRINGLE	I believe we make a hell for ourselves through our . . .
WULLIE	Ah! *(He turns away in disgust and takes a few quick steps to the stove — there he turns about.)* Do you believe in a three-dimensional, crackling, actually burning Hell to which we may or we may not go when our time comes? *(With the end of the wood chunk he flips open the door in the front of the Quebec heater and we see the glint of the flames leaping within.)* Where we may roast

We see the flames within the heater while WULLIE *goes on with hell.*

	. . . in blazing fire from everlasting to everlasting? *(Pause.)* Do you? *(Pause to give* PRINGLE *a chance to answer.)* Shrieking and writhing in torment and exquisite pain beyond all human comprehension while the Lord — in His infinite compassion and mercy — looks down from the dew-washed heights of Heaven above.
PRINGLE	*(finds this utterly repugnant to his notion of a Heavenly Father and true Christianity).* No! Mr. MacCrimmon, no. I do not!
WULLIE	*(bangs home the wood chunk into the flames).* Aye-he. *(He clangs the door shut and turns back to* PRINGLE.) And what would you say, Mr. Pringle, if one day you sat in your study with the King James version of the Bible in one hand — your thumb and finger in the Concordance — and there came a ring at the door bell? What would you say if you went to it and found there a lean, dark gentleman — black brows, that turned upwards at

	their outer corners? If you saw that he had hoofs . . .
PRINGLE	Oh — now — now . . .
WULLIE	And he announced himself as the Devil come to have a short talk with you between his routine calls in the town of Khartoum, Alberta?
PRINGLE	I'd say I was having hallucinations.
WULLIE	Then you would be wrong. *(He advances to* PRINGLE *at the counter.)* Now there is where Father O'Halloran and I come a little closer to understanding each other. I remember his explaining to me about a year ago the meaning of a Black Mass.
PRINGLE	Black Mass!
WULLIE	Then you've heard of it.
PRINGLE	I believe that in more backward countries — ignorant and superstitious people . . .
WULLIE	A ceremony devoted to the worship of the Devil — everything backwards — robes worn backwards — crucifix upside down — prayers backwards. Black Mass.
PRINGLE	Superstition!
WULLIE	'Tis an old superstition then.
PRINGLE	It's still . . .
WULLIE	As old as time. *(He goes towards the last.)* As old as the flesh. As old as Adam. *(He sits down at the last.)* And you think you'd be having hallucinations if you saw Old Cloutie . . .
PRINGLE	Yes — I certainly . . .
WULLIE	*(bringing cobbling-hammer down smartly on boot sole).* Then you would be wrong. *(Bangs boot again.)* I know. *(Bang again.)* He called on me today.
PRINGLE	What!

WULLIE	In the shop here. Brought me in a pair of his curling-boots for me to mend.
PRINGLE	That's ridic—
WULLIE	Oh, no it isn't. *(Gestures with his hand towards the shoes-to-be-repaired shelf.)* They lie over there on top of the shoes to be repaired . . .
PRINGLE	*(laughing).* A devil bringing in curling-boots.
WULLIE	Aye-he — it's unusual — most curlers just use overshoes. You don't find many custom-made curling-boots.
PRINGLE	Nor devils who curl. What would bring him here?
WULLIE	He tells me he's a regular visitor here in Khartoum. He'll be back in three weeks' time.
PRINGLE	I knew you were a stubborn man, Mr. MacCrimmon — I knew you were — uh — old fashioned — in your beliefs — but I never ever did you the — I never for a moment accused you of being superstitious.
WULLIE	And I'm not. *(He gets up from the last, walks silently to the cash register on the end of the counter. He punches it, looks up as he puts his hand into the drawer.)* Now — twenty dollars.
PRINGLE	*(rounding the corner of the counter).* Eh?
WULLIE	Towards your new Methodist church. If he's a regular visitor to our town we could use another church — new church. You may put me down for twenty dollars. *(He looks down as he thumbs over the bills in his hand.)* I'm going to need all the support I can get . . . *(sticks out the twenty dollars at* PRINGLE *who takes them numbly)* however unpromising it may look. Here.

PRINGLE *will never understand the dark ways of the heart of a dour Scot. Bewildered, he slowly, sadly shakes his head.*

The Black Bonspiel of Wullie MacCrimmon   225

ACT II

A riding-boot inverted over the shoe last. WULLIE *over the riding-boot.* PIPE-FITTING CHARLIE BROWN *smoking his pipe, sits in a wooden chair, leaning forward with his elbows across the back . . .*

PIPE   . . . five times she's called me up there. Five times I unplugged her — an' five times I told her all she's got to do is stop little Byron from droppin' his plasticine down an' she won't get plugged an' I won't have to haul my tools up there an' unplug her. That's the trouble with plumbing, Wullie — all the time dealing with the public — the female public.

WULLIE   Aye-he.

PIPE   That's where Malleable Brown has it all over me — black-smithin' you don't get many women walkin' in an' askin' you to do a job for 'em with them breathin' down your neck. Or take Cross-cut Brown — don't find him tanglin' with the female public way I do. Some. But not one hundred per cent the time. Gets a person's nerves . . .

WULLIE   Aye-he.

PIPE   Look at me — how many years I bin curlin' second for you?

WULLIE   Twenty-two.

PIPE   An' I should of bin skippin' a rink for twenty-two years — just one reason why I didn't — nerves — plumbers' nerves. Loose as the fringe on an Indian jacket. I say you can't have iron nerves an' be a plumber — an' you can't skip unless you got iron nerves.

WULLIE   You're a good second, Pipe-fitting.

PIPE   We're all good, Wullie. You're skippin' the best rink in Alberta, Wullie.

WULLIE   *("Why argue — it's the truth")* Aye-he.

PIPE   Malleable Charlie Brown's a nice third — never gets to thinking he's skip — Cross-cut Charlie Brown's a dandy lead an' we all bin curlin' together for over twenty years. An' this year we're better'n we ever bin before. Why, look at last night — after the fourth end Doc didn't have no more chance than a gopher through a thrashing machine. Way we're curlin' this year, we could take the Macdonald Brier. *(He tilts the chair forward towards* WULLIE.*)* How'd you like to curl the Macdonald Brier, Wullie?

WULLIE *stops the cobbling-hammer in mid air. Slowly slowly he lowers it. He lifts his head and his gaze becomes distant.*
MUSIC: *Sneak in Governor-General - Macdonald-Brier music. Dreamy background through:*

WULLIE   The Macdonald Brier. *(This is almost whispered with reverence.)* Aye-he — the Macdonald Brier . . .

PIPE   I seen 'em once. 'Twenty-one — Time they played off at the Granite Club . . .

WULLIE *is smiling gently. Slowly — slowly he closes his eyes.*
MUSIC: *Coming up as* PIPE-FITTING*'s voice fades.*

PIPE   — I never thought I'd ever seen 'em but I did — in 'twenty-one at the Granite Club . . . *(Out.)*

FADE

Interior: Curling-rink stylized. The ends are to right and left. We see the boards separating the rinks but not the ice. This set will serve also as the Khartoum curling rink. Bare roof girders stretch above. Lighting suggests a misty dream quality.

MUSIC: *Full band which has been playing "The Maple Leaf Forever".*

Announcer dressed in dinner jacket in empty space raises his arms and slowly turns this way and that like the ring announcer at the wrestling matches or the boxing matches in Madison Square Garden . . .

ANNOUNCER Ay-nouncing thee winner . . . Grand Champeens of the Macdonald Brier Play-offs . . . champeens by one rock of thee Dominyun of . . . Canada . . . and . . . therefore of thee world . . . *(long pause.)* . . . Skip . . . Wullie . . . MacCrimmon and his rink made up of . . . Lead: Cross-cut Charlie Brown . . . Second: Malleable Charlie Brown . . . Third: Pipe-fitting Charlie Brown . . . all of Khartoum, Alberta . . .

CAST *(Cheers.)*

ANNOUNCER And now . . . by His Governor-Generalship, the Governor General of Canada . . . thee presentation of the Macdonald Brier Cup and special souvenirs . . . for each man a gold spittoon from the Senate . . . engraved with their names . . . *(Pause.)* The *(with a broad wave of his hand to the* GOVERNOR GENERAL*'s corner) Governor General!*

MUSIC: *Up the pipes and into the band bouncing away at "The Maple Leaf Forever", and keep it through:*

GOVERNOR GENERAL and AIDES . . . GOVERNOR GENERAL *rises and clasping both hands, raises them aloft to the throng. He turns to each of the* AIDES, *who step forward from either side of the throne, present brooms, then, raising them aloft, cross them before the* GOVERNOR GENERAL, *who steps majestically down the throne steps and under the arched brooms. He pauses while the* AIDES *smartly*

*bring down brooms and come before him to sweep
ahead of him as curlers would for a rock going
down the ice.*

We see PIPERS *piping . . .* AIDES *sweeping just ahead
of the* GOVERNOR GENERAL *as he parades down the
rink to make the presentation. To:*

WULLIE *and his men with tams and with brooms
held at attention. They are lined up:* WULLIE, *then*
PIPE *then* MALLEABLE, *then* CROSS-CUT. GOVERNOR
GENERAL *presents Cup to* WULLIE *. . . shakes his
hand. Turns back to the* AIDES *and takes in
succession from them, or someone else in his
retinue, a gold spittoon. Gives* WULLIE *his first,
then* PIPE-FITTING, *then* MALLEABLE *. . . shakes hands.
Same procedure with* CROSS-CUT, *who at the end
makes a self-conscious curtsy.*

*We see the returning parade (holding parade long
enough to let* PIPE *and* WULLIE *get back to the shop
set).*

*Pipes continuing, cross-fade the pipes and
dissolve:*

WULLIE *with his eyes closed and head back.*

PIPE   *(his voice coming on).* . . . straight down the ice.
She come straight down the ice, Wullie — no
in-turn — no out-turn — straight as a ree-vival
meetin' cough through a curtain rod! The winnin'
rock of the 'thirty-four Macdonald Brier Play-
offs!

WULLIE   *(he opens his eyes — shakes himself a bit as he
realizes he has been dreaming).* Pipe-fitting —
(Pause.) I would give anything *(low — reverent —
almost whispered)* utterly anything — for to skip
the winning rink in the Macdonald Brier Play-offs
— I would . . .

SOUND: *Tonk tonk of the bell over the front door.*

The Black Bonspiel of Wullie MacCrimmon   229

WULLIE *starts and looks over that way.*
SOUND: *Door closing — three distinct steps across the floor.*

WULLIE *(shaken — repeating numbly).* I would — give —

DEVIL *(loud — clear — decisive).* That's a bargain, Wullie MacCrimmon!

PIPE-FITTING's *mouth has dropped open — his chin resting on his arms on the back of the chair.*

PIPE Huh!

DEVIL *(as before).* That is a bargain — Wullie MacCrimmon!

All of them in arrested positions. THE DEVIL *just inside counter.*

WULLIE *(long long pause).* Would you mind — giving a bit of a twist to yon damper on the stove pipe?

THE DEVIL, *with* PIPE-FITTING's *and* WULLIE's *eyes following him, steps to stove — reaches up and twists protesting damper.*

WULLIE — wee bit close in here. *(In the pause* THE DEVIL *chuckles.)* Pipe-fitting — meet Old Cloutie.

PIPE *(half risen from his chair).* Old Cloutie?

WULLIE Beezalie Bub — Satan — Old Scratch — Old Nick — the Devil — Old Cloutie. *(As he has done this enumeration,* PIPE-FITTING *has been descending back to the chair one notch for each title.)*

PIPE Oh — *(pause)* him. *(He relaxes into the chair — then up out of it.)* Pleasure. *(Tight-lipped, but giving* THE DEVIL *a chance to be a good guy.)*

DEVIL *(slight bow).* All mine.

PIPE *(standing by his chair)* How's things?

DEVIL Things are all right.

PIPE *(suddenly remembering his manners — shoves chair at* THE DEVIL). Take my seat. *(Awkward*

	pause.) You — ah — two got business — I'll — I'll *(he's headed around* THE DEVIL *towards the open end of the counter)* be goin'. *(He stops as the thought strikes him.)* It *was Wullie* you wanted to have a talk with . . .
DEVIL	*(nods).* That's right.
PIPE	*(in a burst of speed rounds the end of the counter — back over his shoulder).* Never did get around to finishin' up Mrs. Harrison's waste-and-overflow — *(fading to the front door).* Guess I better get hold of my wrenches *(yanks open the front door so that the bell tinkles violently)* an' skin over there. *(Slams the door as he goes out.)*
WULLIE	*(slight pause).* You're early.
DEVIL	Came through on an unscheduled trip — *(he turns* PIPE-FITTING*'s chair around to face* WULLIE*)* involving an ungraded-school teacher and some beer.
WULLIE	*(he has turned sideways on the last.)* That would be Miss Sparrow — been going into the "Ladies and Escorts Room" of the Royal Hotel with the new Royal Bank cashier.
DEVIL	That's right.
WULLIE	Small matter — isn't it?
DEVIL	In itself — yes. *(He sits in* PIPE-FITTING*'s chair.)* Mrs. Annie Burbidge saw her go in — she mentioned it to Mrs. May Whittaker, who, in turn, got on the Gladys Ridge party line the greater part of yesterday. *(He tilts the chair easily back — lifts one leg and puts it over the other — looks up pensively.)* Mrs. Whittaker looks interesting to me.
WULLIE	Aye-he.
DEVIL	*(he is idly swinging his toe in the air).* Most interesting.

WULLIE	Just argy-bargy — isn't it?
DEVIL	In itself — yes. But this woman — with her it's — the accretion that counts.
WULLIE	I see.
DEVIL	For the most part nothing very flashy in the way of sin goes on in the West here. My more regular calls are the Blue Bird Cafe — penny ante in the little back room. Mame Harris's little brown cottage by the CNR depot is a routine call of mine — then there's the pool hall.
WULLIE	Aye-he.
DEVIL	The small novelty line. *(Sighs.)* Petty intolerance — lust for tea-pot power — self-indulgence — sins of omission — snobbery — within the family tyranny — *(pause)* that sort of thing — *(deprecatory)* quick turn over.
WULLIE	*(grunts). (Pause.)* About the bargain — *(pause)* you caught me unawares.
DEVIL	I frequently do it that way.
WULLIE	My soul for the Macdonald Brier.
DEVIL	That's the deal.
WULLIE	*(rises from the last).* Mmmh-hmh. *(Walks thoughtfully to the counter.)* Seems a fair enough exchange.

THE DEVIL's *face lights up with eagerness.*

DEVIL	It's a good bargain, Wullie.

WULLIE *is filling his pipe — elbows on the counter.*

WULLIE	As I said — you caught me unawares.

THE DEVIL *has risen from his chair — stands by it.*

DEVIL	I intended to.
WULLIE	*(searching for a match in his vest pocket).* I'd be — ah — within my rights if I refused to consider such a contract binding.
DEVIL	*(long, careful pause — this is important to Nick).* You — would — be. *(Grudgingly.)*

WULLIE   What makes you *(his eyes careful on the bowl of his pipe as he puffs it alight)* — so fussy about a MacCrimmon soul?

THE DEVIL *moves over to* WULLIE *on the lines:*

DEVIL   I might as well be frank with you. I need a good third for my rink.

WULLIE *and* THE DEVIL *are at the counter —* WULLIE *still resting on his elbows. He has not thrown the dead match away.*

WULLIE   Do you now. Just for curiosity's sake — how — *(tosses aside dead match)* in hell — *(pause)* do you keep your ice?

DEVIL   Artificial.

WULLIE   *(a lift of the eyebrows).* Oh.

DEVIL   We curl what you might call shirt-sleeves bonspiels on sheets of polished volcanic deposit. *(Pause as he regards* WULLIE — *it is obvious that his mind is not on this chit-chat but on the bargain.)* Gives us a fast knock-out game.

WULLIE   I see. *(He straightens up as though to move away.)*

DEVIL   *(impulsively putting his hand to stop* WULLIE*).* You've wanted to curl in the Macdonald Brier. For generations now I've had my — *(make him a little sympathetic)* — I've wanted to win a championship bonspiel — the Celestial Brier Play-offs. I *can* win it — with you curling third for me.

WULLIE   *(this is a new side to* THE DEVIL — WULLIE *returns to leaning on his elbows — contemplating the bowl of his pipe and turning over in his mind the bargaining possibilities of this new information).* Would you entertain a sort of counter-proposition, Mr. Cloutie.

DEVIL   *(wary).* Let's hear it.

WULLIE   *(takes his time — with his thumb he presses down the tobacco in the pipe to get a more even burn).* You might call it a condition to the first offer. *(He draws a deep breath —* THE DEVIL *gets down on his elbows.)* I have a fair rink of my own. I can't say I'd care to curl third on a rink that couldn't beat the one I now skip — I'd be willing to curl for you in Hell — only on the condition that your rink is a far better one than mine — the one made up of Cross-cut Brown — Malleable Charlie Brown — Pipe-fitting Charlie Brown. *(He looks up at* THE DEVIL.)

DEVIL   *(still wary).* And your proposition?

WULLIE   You curl us a match. *(Pause.)* If we lose then I curl third for you at no price — when my time comes . . .

DEVIL   *(straightening up).* At no price!

WULLIE   Aye-he. You need not deliver me the Macdonald Brier Play-offs. But — if we win — then you must deliver according to the terms of your first offer — I will skip a winning rink in the Macdonald Brier Play-offs — but again — at no price.

DEVIL   *(he is smiling.)* You retain your soul.

WULLIE   I retain my soul, intact.

DEVIL   *(a couple of quick, jubilant steps).* Well — well — *(swings back to the wooden* WULLIE*)* do you really mean that?

    MUSIC: *Sneak in "Devil" theme background here:*

WULLIE   I do.

DEVIL   You — you're willing to be a party to such an agreement? *(He is slightly incredulous.)*

WULLIE   I am. The match to be curled on our own ice, of course.

DEVIL   That's all right.

WULLIE   It isn't binding to any other members of my rink, you understand.

DEVIL	That's right.
WULLIE	*(facing the* DEVIL*).* It'll have to be on a Sabbath evening.
DEVIL	I curl *only* on the Sabbath.
WULLIE	I'll get to your boots immediately. *(Straightens up.)* Say — next Sabbath.
DEVIL	*(also straightening up).* You've exchanged a good bargain for a bad one, Wullie MacCrimmon.
WULLIE	*(back to his elbows on the counter).* We'll see — in four days. *(He blows a cloud of smoke out before him.)*
	MUSIC: *Up full with "Devil" theme.*
	FADE OUT.

ACT III

Interior: Wullie's shop
SOUND: *Tinkle of bell above door.*
PIPE-FITTING *is back again — at the door he peers anxiously, sees* WULLIE.

PIPE	You — you all right, Wullie?
WULLIE	Aye-he. He's been gone an hour.
PIPE	*(to the counter).* That's nice. *(Sigh of relief.)*
WULLIE	*(turning away to the shoes-to-be-repaired shelf).* And how's Mrs. Harrison's waste-and-overflow?
PIPE	Fine — just fine. *(Heads for his chair.)* Now. *(Clears his throat.)* You — uh — finished with you — with what you was doing?
WULLIE	*(at the shoes-to-be-repaired shelf. Picks up* THE DEVIL*'s curling boots and idly turns them over in his hands.)* Aye.
PIPE	*(pause).* Dripping.
WULLIE	Oh.
	PIPE-FITTING *has his chin in his arms over the back of the tilted wooden chair.*
PIPE	Wasn't nothin' had to be done. C'rossion.

The Black Bonspiel of Wullie MacCrimmon 235

C'rossion would of taken care of her. *(Looks speculatively over to* WULLIE.*)* Funny thing about plumbin'. Time. C'rossion. Take care of just about fifty per cent of your leaks. *(Still marking time and waiting for* WULLIE *to say something about the visitor.)* Why — I seen new jobs — sprayin' at every joint — I seen 'em tighten up by themselves — without a wrench — *(Long pause.)* C'rossion.

WULLIE *stares down at the* DEVIL*'s curling-boots in his hands.*

PIPE   You — ah — what — maybe it's none of my business — but just what business did he have with you?

WULLIE *tosses curling-boots to the counter.*

Curlin'-boots?

WULLIE   This was not his first call — couple weeks ago. He left his curling-boots — custom made — wanted the soles mended. Dropped back a wee bit early to — ah — said he had a little business with May Whittaker.

PIPE   *(relieved).* Oh. That all.

WULLIE   Well — no — it isn't, Pipe-fitting. It isn't all. *(Goes to the last — sits.)* It — ah — it isn't all — at all. *(Clears throat.)* He's quite fussy about curling.

PIPE   Is he.

WULLIE   Aye. Says they curl a fast knock-out game in Hell.

PIPE   Do they.

WULLIE   Volcanic deposit — smooth — fast — I imagine it's a lot like this artificial ice.

PIPE   I guess she might be. Did — uh — did you an' him talk curlin'?

WULLIE   We did.

PIPE   Them boots. Was that all he come in for — an' to talk curlin'?

WULLIE　　No. No. *(Picks up cobbling-hammer, tacks —
couple of taps on the boot in front of him.)* He
says he has not a particularly good third. He —
he's looking for a good third for his rink. He likes
my game.

PIPE　　Uh-huh.

WULLIE　　So — it wasna just the curling-boots. He had a
proposition to make me. *(Pause.)* I sort of liked it.

PIPE　　Get into an aitch of a mess takin' the Devil up on
a proposition, Wullie.

WULLIE　　Aye. This one involved a curling-match. *(Pause to
send out a feeler with* PIPE-FITTING.*)* His rink
against ours. *(Assessing* PIPE*'s response.)* Pipe-
fitting — if you're willing I'll be wanting you for
a match this Sabbath evening.

PIPE-FITTING *slowly lowers his chair back —
straightening up.*

PIPE　　Agin — again?

WULLIE　　Against Old Cloutie and his rink from Hell.

PIPE　　*(we see only momentary hesitation on* PIPE*'s face).*
Why — sure. *(He gets up from his chair.)* Look
— I'll tell Malleable for you — let Cross-cut ride.
I figure he'd keep goin' once he got started. That's
the way to do her . . . *(He starts for the door —
stops at the counter and looks back to* WULLIE.*)*
Kind of curious — see who he's got on his rink.
You know — local folks. *(To the door, hand on
the knob.)* Take old man Dowling went West in
'thirty-two just after he diddled Mrs. Fowler out
of that correction line half section . . .

Door opens — bell tinkling — MALLEABLE *enters.*

PIPE　　Oh — Malleable — I was just headed your
way . . .

MALLEABLE　　'Day, Pipe-fittin' — Wullie.

WULLIE   Malleable.

PIPE-FITTING and MALLEABLE come back to the counter.

MALLEABLE   What you Indians been plottin' agin the whites today?

PIPE   Ah — *(Clears throat — lays hand on MALLEABLE's shoulder.)* Ah — Wullie — me an' Wullie was just talkin' over a match — Sunday night.

MALLEABLE   Sunday night. Ain't any Sunday curlin'. Reverend Pringle fixed that.

PIPE   That is just a little pick-up match, Malleable. *(WULLIE has come up to the counter.)* Wullie here made the arrangements. Keepin' it quiet. *(Pause.)* You interested?

MALLEABLE   *(sliding a plug out of his pocket)* Sure. *(He opens his jack knife.)* Who's she agin?

WULLIE   Old Cloutie.

MALLEABLE   *(has the plug between thumb and knife blade — cuts off corner, and as he looks up at WULLIE he raises the segment between thumb and knife blade to his mouth.)* Who?

WULLIE   Old Cloutie.

MALLEABLE   *(getting the chew right).* Who's he?

PIPE   *(with a look at WULLIE).* You ought to know, Malleable. Old friend of yours.

              MALLEABLE 's head is back — he is slowly and ruminatively chewing — trying to remember anybody of that name. Decides not. Shakes head slowly. Stops chewing — considers a moment, then shakes head again.

MALLEABLE   I don't know anybody that name. Now there was a fellow — Coonie — Herb Coonie — lived in the Springbank district — he curled — I remember once in a green bonspiel back in . . .

PIPE   Cloutie. Old Nick . . .

WULLIE	The Devil, Malleable.
MALLEABLE	*(goes on chewing a second — hitch in the rhythm).* Oh. *(Takes up careful chewing again.)* Him.
WULLIE	We have a match on Sunday night — I — uh — I have an agreement with him. A great deal depends on who wins the match.
MALLEABLE	Oh?
WULLIE	It's up to you whether you curl or not. Doesn't concern you — however it turns out. Just me.
MALLEABLE	*(ceases chewing suddenly).* An' if we lose?
WULLIE	If we lose — the Devil has one more MacCrimmon soul — I'd like to depend on you for third.

MALLEABLE *'s mouth is ominously still as he considers the proposition.*

MALLEABLE	Why — *(one slow chew)* sure, Wullie, — *(two slow chews)* sure — *(back in gear and chewing naturally).*
WULLIE	Thank you, Malleable.
PIPE	Now look, Malleable — about Cross-cut . . .
MALLEABLE	Uh-uh. You tell Cross-cut, you tell Father O'Halloran. I wouldn't say nothin' to Cross-cut.
WULLIE	Sunday night.
MALLEABLE	Okay. Sunday night. *(Pause.)* Don't you worry none Wullie.
WULLIE	*(picks up the curling-boots — looks down at them.)* Aye-he. *(Looks up.)* We better get in a couple of practices.

MALLEABLE *and* PIPE-FITTING *are at the opened door.*

MALLEABLE AND PIPE	Okay, Wullie. *(They go out.)*

MUSIC: *Sneak in "Devil" theme background for:* WULLIE *at the counter with* THE DEVIL *'s curling boots in his hands — sighs. Looks up and out. Down at his boots again. Up.*

WULLIE	*(with fervent feeling).* Stand fast, Craigellachie. *(Pause.)*
	MUSIC: *Up full, then out.* And curl to beat hell!
	DISSOLVE TO: *Interior: Wullie's shop.* *Medium close shot —* MR. PRINGLE *is angry.*
PRINGLE	What's this I hear, Mr. MacCrimmon! About a curling match.
	WULLIE *has one of* THE DEVIL *'s boots over his last. The outer and second sole are separated — the outer one turned back.*
WULLIE	There's to be one.
	PRINGLE *has come to* WULLIE *'s side. He looks down at him.*
PRINGLE	When?
WULLIE	Day after tomorrow.
PRINGLE	That's Sunday.
WULLIE	Aye-he. Sunday evening.
PRINGLE	*(pause).* I'm — uh — that's contrary to our local by-law — Lord's Day Alliance . . .
WULLIE	Aye-he.
PRINGLE	I would appreciate it very much it you would call it off. *(Pause.)* As a favour to me.
WULLIE	I canna.
PRINGLE	Oh — now — a curling match. Couldn't you shift it ahead an evening — or back an evening?
WULLIE	I made a bargain. It's important I keep it — *(pause)* to the letter.
PRINGLE	I always thought you were on the side of law and order, Mr. MacCrimmon.
WULLIE	I try to be. This is a special case.
PRINGLE	What's special about it?
WULLIE	You remember a while back we had a conver-

	sation — the day you put me down for twenty dollars for your new church?
PRINGLE	Yes.
WULLIE	This match — it's against — we're curling against the gentleman for whom I'm fixing a pair of curling boots. We — uh — spoke of him.
PRINGLE	What! You're not telling me — you aren't — now just a minute . . .
WULLIE	I and my rink curl Sunday night against the Devil and his rink from Hell.
PRINGLE	*(long pause).* Have you gone out of your mind . . .
WULLIE	No — I have not. I made a bargain with him —
PRINGLE	Look — if a curling-match is that important to you — a Sunday curling match — there's no need to cook up a wild excuse like that to justify . . .
WULLIE	It's no wild excuse, Mr. Pringle. I've told you just how it is.
PRINGLE	*(laughing).* All right — all right. I'll look the other way. You go ahead with your curling-match.
WULLIE	We must. *(Clears throat.)* I'd appreciate it very much if you didna say anything to anybody — what I've just told you.
PRINGLE	You mean — whom you're curling against. Why — of course not — don't worry about that.
WULLIE	How — is the collection for the new church coming along?
PRINGLE	Fine — just fine.
WULLIE	I — uh — I've been thinkin' it over. Ye may — uh put me down for a bit more it you care to.
PRINGLE	Now that's very . . .
WULLIE	A hundred dollars more.
PRINGLE	Oh — you can't afford . . .
WULLIE	— and while you're down here — you might drop in on Pipe-fitting Brown —
PRINGLE	I've already called on him.
WULLIE	It'll do no harm to call on him again. You might

	tell him you've just seen me and I've upped my contribution. Tell him — tell him — considerin' what's at stake Sunday night it can do no harm. *(Pause.)* I think you'll find Pipe-fittin' in a co-operative mood.
PRINGLE	But a hunded dollars — a hundred and twenty dollars — that hardly seems — it's a lot of money for —
WULLIE	Had you attended the Old Country church I did as a boy, Mr. Pringle — had you heard a few of the sermons I did — you would think a hundred and twenty dollars little enough. Be sure to call on Pipe-fitting. Now — if you'll excuse me — I've a call to make myself. Down the street on Joe Harrington's.
PRINGLE	Your watch out of order?
WULLIE	No — no — a wee matter — something to do with our match.

MUSIC: *Brief punctuation seque to "Devil" theme. Fade out for* WULLIE.
Interior WULLIE's *shop.*
A small copper rivet on the counter of the shop.

| WULLIE | I know it's a strange request, Joe. But it's an important one. I want it just like that. |

A hand picks up the rivet.

JOE HARRINGTON *is looking at the little rivet. He looks up.*

| JOE | Looks like a rivet. |

WULLIE *faces* JOE *across the counter.*

WULLIE	It is a rivet.
JOE	Copper rivet.
WULLIE	That's right.
JOE	You want me to make you one up just like it — only silver. Silver rivet?

WULLIE	Aye-he.
JOE	Wouldn't be any trick at all to silverplate this one. Lot easier — a silver rivet would cost . . .
WULLIE	*(tensely)*. Now look, Joe — you must get it right. Exactly right. I want a rivet — like that. Silver — solid silver — sterling silver. It must not be plated. A sterling silver rivet.
JOE	Okay — okay — I'll do it for you. Drop in the — beginning the week.
WULLIE	Beginning of the week's no good to me. It's no good at all. I must have it tomorrow morning.
JOE	Look — I didn't rush you on those boots of mine, I'm a busy man like you are. I got the Husbay wedding — folks coming in to buy china — cut glass — silver — I got way behind on my watch repairing.
WULLIE	Believe me, Joe — it's important.
JOE	All right. All right.
WULLIE	Fine, I'll pick it up a nine o'clock tomorrow morning.

MUSIC: *Brief   punctuation   seque   "Devil" background.*

DISSOLVE TO:

Exterior: Funeral parlour.
The door opens and THE DEVIL *steps out. He carries a curling-broom and wears a tam. He is followed by his third, his second, and his lead — as they move off down the street . . .*

MUSIC: *Replaced by the whine and groan of bagpipes playing "MacCrimmon Will Never Return".*

DISSOLVE TO:

Interior: Wullie MacCrimmon's shop.
WULLIE *and his rink also with curling-brooms and tams. Here inside the shop the sound of the pipes is unmistakable but muted.*

CROSS-CUT	What's that!
PIPE	Kiyoots.
CROSS-CUT	Kiyoots nothin! Bag-pipes! From the direction of the rink.
MALLEABLE	I can't ever tell which direction bag-pipes is comin'. They come at you from all directions at once.
CROSS-CUT	Ain't these fellows awful fussy for a little pick-up game. *(He turns to* WULLIE.) What's that tune, Wullie?
WULLIE	'Tis pibroch. The finest lament ever composed. *(Pause.)* "MacCrimmon Will Never Return". *(Sadly.)*
CROSS-CUT	*(heads for the door).* Sure cheery — come on — let's go.

We see the four figures of WULLIE *and his rink as they come out of the door and start down the street.*

MUSIC: *Wail of the bag-pipes, louder and louder.*

DISSOLVE TO:

Interior: Curling-rink.

THE DEVIL *and his rink — piper pacing the boards between rinks. The last, sad notes of "MacCrimmon Will Never Return" squeezes off as* WULLIE *and his crew enter from the right.*

MUSIC: *Take up the "Devil" theme subtly through:*

DEVIL	Evening, gentlemen.
CROSS-CUT	Evenin'.
MALLEABLE PIPE WULLIE	} Evenin' — how's things — mmmmmh.
DEVIL	The visiting rink's all here. May I introduce my men — first, my third — Mr. Iscariot.

WULLIE MALLEABLE CROSS-CUT PIPE	To meet you. Pleasure. Evening

CROSS-CUT   I didn't quite get the name.

JUDAS is dark and worried — he has a hand in his side pocket.

JUDAS   Iscariot, sir, and yours? *(Nervously he jingles change in his pocket.)*

CROSS-CUT   Brown. Charlie Brown. Just call me Cross-cut so's you won't get me mixed up with Pipe-fittin' and Malleable.

DEVIL   My lead — Mr. Fawkes.

CROSS-CUT MALLEABLE PIPE WULLIE	Pleasure. Glad to know you. How do you do. etc.

CROSS-CUT   Just call me Cross-cut.

GUY   Nice meeting you, old boy. Call me Guy.

CROSS-CUT   *(a bit wonderingly).* Guy? Guy?

DEVIL   And my second — a dependable man with a guard rock. Countryman of yours, Mr. MacCrimmon — Mr. Macbeth.

MACBETH   Tomorrow and tomorrow and tomorrow and tomorrow.

CROSS-CUT PIPE MALLEABLE WULLIE	(Greetings as before.)

CROSS-CUT   You — uh — Mr. Macbeth — you from around these parts?

MACBETH   Fife, sir.

CROSS-CUT   *Beginning to dawn on him that there's something funny here.* Say — what the hell's goin' on here!

The Black Bonspiel of Wullie MacCrimmon   245

DEVIL   Now — have you any preference as to the end of the rink to start . . .

PIPE   Only one end to start from. Scoreboard's there.

DEVIL   As visiting rink would you mind indulging us — starting from the other end first?

WULLIE   All right with us. I have no . . . *(He breaks off to look with surprise . . .* CROSS-CUT *and* WULLIE *look too.)*

GUY FAWKES is walking down the rink with the score board under his arm. We see him walk to the starting end of the rink, lift score board to post, and begin hammering.

MALLEABLE   Hey . . . what's he doin'! Your lead . . . why's he movin' the score board from the other end of the ice?

SOUND: *Hammering off as* GUY *nails up board.*

MALLEABLE   Why'd he take the board down an' bring it up to this end and . . .

DEVIL   Just a slight preparation before we start, gentlemen.

GUY is just stepping back from score board which he has nailed up. He surveys his work . . . We see score board . . . it is upside down.
CROSS-CUT comes into the frame . . .

CROSS-CUT   Startin' the wrong end of the ice! Turnin' the score board upside-down! I don't get it!

GUY FAWKES   *(as he moves carelessly away — over his shoulder to* CROSS-CUT*).* You will soon, old boy.

CROSS-CUT stares after FAWKES *as* PIPE-FITTING *steps up and takes him by the arm.*

PIPE   It's all right, Cross-cut. It's all right.

PIPE-FITTING has CROSS-CUT *by the sleeve — is trying to placate him.*

CROSS-CUT	Weel, it ain't. That long, thin, hungry-lookin' fellow with the blond mustache. One that turned the board around. Somethin' funny about him.
PIPE	An Englishman, that's all . . .
CROSS-CUT	He didn't have any hammer when I shook hands with him. An' his name — uh . . .
PIPE	Fox.
CROSS-CUT	Yeah — Guy Fox — now that name seems kind of familiar to me. The whole outfit seems funny to me. You take that fellow from Fife — mutterin' all about tomorrow an' tomorrow an' tomorrow . . .
PIPE	Farmer. Droughted out six years runnin' — no crop. Kind of got him a bit. Sort of his way of sayin' next year — next year — I'll get a forty-bushel crop next year.
CROSS-CUT	Yeah? *(He's not convinced at all.)* That other fellow — the visiting third. He . . .
PIPE	He's all right, Cross-cut.
CROSS-CUT	Always jinglin' silver in his pocket — what was his name?
PIPE	I didn't get it either, Cross-cut. I think he's a cattle buyer from out Gladys Ridge way — just a minute — got to toss for first rock with him . . .

MUSIC: *Up with the "Devil" theme while:* PIPE *and* JUDAS ISCARIOT *toss for first rock. We see* ISCARIOT *throw piece of silver in the air, then all the men look down to see what it is . . .*

The coin. Shows an obviously Roman head with laurel wreath. The players move into position.

CROSS-CUT *takes his first rock, puts his toe in the hack —*

Looks up along the rink to the other end where WULLIE *and* THE DEVIL *stand.*

WULLIE	*(calling to* CROSS-CUT*).* Straight handle, Cross-cut!

CROSS-CUT *swings back and releases the rock — he glides forward a bit as though following the rock down the ice . . .*

MALLEABLE *and* PIPE *sweep fervently ahead of the rock . . . halfway across the stage they stop and watch the passage of the invisible rock to the end . . .*

CROSS-CUT *is dusting off his knees and stepping back from the hack.* THE DEVIL, *rock in hand, has come up to him. We see astonishment on* CROSS-CUT*'s face. He steps forward with protest as* THE DEVIL *prepares to curl his rock.*

CROSS-CUT   Hey — hold on there — just a minute . . .

THE DEVIL *pays him no attention. Slowly, carefully, he crouches and brings the rock back for the swing. He curls his rock.*

CROSS-CUT   That ain't right — he's skip — skips don't — *(looking wildly around for someone to hear his protest)* skips don't curl first. Skips got to curl *last!* Where's their third — that fellah . . .

He stops with mouth open as he looks down the ice. THE DEVIL*'s men are sweeping madly — but in the wrong direction. They come from the opposite side of the stage — sweeping to meet* THE DEVIL*'s rock from the far end.*

CROSS-CUT   An' look at them sweepin'. Down to *meet* the rock instead of with her! Backwards! Skip first! Lead last! Score board upside down! Judas! *(Realizes what he's said.)* Yeah! Judas Iscariot! A third name of Judas Iscariot! *(He throws his broom on the ice.)* The visitin' rink's from Hell. Boys! *(All out in sheer terror.)* You're riskin' your immortal souls in a black bonspiel!

WULLIE	*(calling reassurance from the other end of the rink).* It's all right, Cross-cut — all right! You're curling on the right rink, Cross-cut!
	PIPE-FITTING *holds* CROSS-CUT, *trying to soothe and restrain him.*
CROSS-CUT	All right for you Protestants. But there ain't *any* rink — a right rink in this sort of a match! *(Panic shows on his face.)* I wouldn't curl another rock...
PIPE	Wullie's got an understandin' with the visitin' skip, Cross-cut.
CROSS-CUT	*(turning on* PIPE*).* You said his third was a Gladys — a cattle-buyer from Gladys Ridge way.
PIPE	Pull yourself together an' get your next rock — it's just Wullie he's interested in — nothin' to do with the rest of us . . .
CROSS-CUT	How can you! How can you be sure it's only Wullie . . .
PIPE	Look, Cross-cut — you're in the same boat as me — you got nothin' to lose in the first place.
	THE DEVIL *listens to this exchange with lifted eyebrows. He smiles and inclines his head slightly to* CROSS-CUT.
DEVIL	That's right. Quite right, Mr. Brown.
	CROSS-CUT*'s face shows shock. Then instantly — anger. "Got me in the bag, has he!"*
CROSS-CUT	Is that so. Is—that—so! *(He turns to* PIPE-FITTING.*)* Gimme that there rock! (PIPE-FITTING *does so.*) All right . . .
	CROSS-CUT *looks down the ice to* WULLIE.
CROSS-CUT	What you want, Wullie!
WULLIE	*(calling back to him).* Straight handle again, Cross-cut. Knock-out!

The Black Bonspiel of Wullie MacCrimmon 249

CROSS-CUT, *toe in the hack, kneels — arm comes back slowly, then forward to release the rock. His face has grim determination and a grimace almost of pain as he releases the rock.*

PIPE-FITTING *and* MALLEABLE *sweep furiously in front of the rock. Two-thirds of the way they stop and stare anxiously as the rock pursues its way . . .*

SOUND: *The lambasting crack of* CROSS-CUT*'s rock as it strikes* THE DEVIL*'s rock, followed by the hollow bump seconds later as* THE DEVIL*'s rock hits the back boards. Perhaps* WULLIE *had to jump to get out of the way.*

TWO SHOTS: THE DEVIL *and* CROSS-CUT.

DEVIL	Nice rock, Mr. Brown.
CROSS-CUT	*(contemptuously).* Better'n a kick in the tail with a frozen boot.

FAWKES *comes in from right, carrying rock. Prepares to deliver it. Close in on rock.* FAWKES*'s face very determined.*

WULLIE*'s solemn (at south end),*

MALLEABLE*'s grim (at centre), and*

JUDAS*'s concerned (right of* MALLEABLE).

The score board shows: only team names on it,

> Home:
> Hell:

THE DEVIL *writes in score to make it read:*

> Home: 0
> Hell: 3

PIPE	Don't you worry, Wullie. We'll make her up. Just a bad break Malleable had to blow his first rock, but we'll make her up . . . we got eleven ends to make her up in.
WULLIE	If it's the kind of knock-out game I think it's going to be, Pipe-fitting, eleven ends are few enough to do it in.

He turns away. Hold PIPE-FITTING. DISSOLVE TO:
THE DEVIL *writes in score end by end to make it read:*

Home: 0 0 0

Hell: 3 4 5

We see THE DEVIL *turn his head, smiling, and* PIPE *as he walks left to join* WULLIE.

PIPE	I still say we'll pull up on 'em Wullie.
WULLIE	I don't know, Pipe-fitting, I don't know.
PIPE	Three ends from twelve leaves nine, Wullie. We got nine ends to pull up on 'em, and nail their hide to a fencepost.
WULLIE	Aye-he.
PIPE	An' we will, Wullie. We will! (WULLIE shakes his head.)

Score board: FAWKES *writes in end by end to make it read*

Home: 0 0 0 4 4 4   4

Hell: 3 4 5 5 6 7 10

DEVIL	Now, that's the brand of curling we have in Hell, Mr. MacCrimmon. *(He is smiling delightedly.)*
WULLIE	Aye-he.
DEVIL	Looks to me as though we count three more this end.
WULLIE	Aye-he.
DEVIL	Four to ten, Mr. MacCrimmon. I had expected a better match from your rink.
WULLIE	Aye-he.
DEVIL	Seven ends gone now — only five to go — six is a pretty healthy lead.
WULLIE	Aye-he.
DEVIL	If — ah — if you'd care to concede . . .
WULLIE	We're conceding nothing!
DEVIL	I'd be willing to — I wouldn't hold you to the

The Black Bonspiel of Wullie MacCrimmon   251

	second offer you made — I would honour my first offer.
WULLIE	I'll keep my bargain — if you win you may have your price at no cost to you. *(He looks up at* THE DEVIL. WULLIE*'s mouth tightens with determination.) Five more ends to go, Mr. Cloutie. Do not count your souls before they're hatched! (He goes.)*

THE DEVIL *has quiet and satisfied amusement on his face. He lifts his eyebrows and shrugs. So be it.*
MUSIC: *up loud.*
CROSS-CUT *delivers rock with great care.*
PIPE *at center begins to smile as rock looks good.*
WULLIE *watches rock in, then triumphant broom aloft.*
PIPE *beams.*
MALLEABLE *gets away a rock carefully.*
PIPE *is anxious, then smiling.*
WULLIE *watches rock in, then triumphant and broom up.*

PIPE	Hot dog!

MALLEABLE *and* CROSS-CUT *smile and nod at each other.*
MUSIC *down to background.*

MALLEABLE	That's more like it, Cross-cut.
CROSS-CUT	Yeah.
MALLEABLE	Holdin' our own anyways. (FAWKES *into frame.)* You don't score this end, mister.
FAWKES	Nor you, old boy. You'll never win a bonspiel on bald-headed ends.
CROSS-CUT	She ain't gonna be bald-headed this end coming up. Jist watch.
FAWKES	I will, old boy.

MACBETH *enters frame with rock. He delivers his rock. Stands up and mournfully mutters:*

MACBETH	Tomorrow and tomorrow and tomorrow.
PIPE	*(anxiously).* What do you think, Wullie?
WULLIE	*(shaking his head).* Aye-he.
PIPE	Six-ten. Can we do her, Wullie?
WULLIE	All we can do is curl, Pipe-fitting. Out-turn Malleable! (*To* PIPE.) I can't understand it. It's not working out. Not working out at all.
PIPE	What's not working out?
WULLIE	Nothing — nothing — I had a wee trick — but it's not working. I doubt it can with only two more ends to curl and four to catch up. *(Pause.)* I doubt it can.

THE DEVIL *twists the bottom of his rock on his broom head. There is a new tenseness on* THE DEVIL'*s face — almost a frown. He brings the rock back and just lets it go. An unmistakable grimace of pain brightens his face . . .*
CROSS-CUT, MALLEABLE, *and* PIPE-FITTING *clap each other on the shoulders — whoops of joy.*

THE THREE	He's cracked! Hogged his rock! Not worth a whoop! Old Cloutie hogged his rock! We count — we count!

WULLIE *at the other end tosses broom into the air.*

WULLIE	*(shouting to them).* Aye, we count — two — two! She's eight to ten boys, and we got the Devil by the tail on a down-hill pull!

THE DEVIL — *same procedure, only on this rock he falls to the ice clutching at his foot. He gets up amid the whoops and shouts of the MacCrimmon rink to hop with one foot cradled in his arms — slips on ice and goes down again.*

The Black Bonspiel of Wullie MacCrimmon 253

The MacCrimmon rink — tossing brooms aloft — dancing.

CROSS-CUT *is dancing and playing his broom like a banjo.* MALLEABLE *is swinging his wide around his head.*

MUSIC: *Triumphant finale swelling.*

MACCRIMMON
RINK
Devil blowed up! We win by one rock! Match is over! We nailed his hide to the fence post!

WULLIE's *rink has brooms tenting above* WULLIE, *who stands in their centre; they are doing a "Round and Round the Mulberry Bush" or Maypole dance.*

MUSIC: *Into tremendous roll of drums building. The rink erupts in smoke and steam wreathing and misting.* THE DEVIL *and his crew vanishing as it clears.*

MUSIC: *With the clearing of the mist to reveal the figures of* PIPE-FITTING *and* WULLIE *— goes into faint "Loch Lomond" background.*

PIPE The Devil's a poor loser.

WULLIE Aye-he.

PIPE His own fault. He'd of had her in the bag if he hadn't blowed up himself in the twelfth end.

WULLIE *(his broom under his elbow while he does things with his pipe).* Aye-he. His own fault. *(Puffs with head down, then looks up.)* His feet.

PIPE His feet!

WULLIE A man cannot curl a fine knock-out match with his mind on his feet. You mind I mended his curling boots?

PIPE Yeah.

WULLIE   I put a wee sharpened rivet between the inner and outer sole of his hack foot — ah — hoof — it was to work through about the third end as near as I could figure. Was not until the twelfth. *(Pause.)* Close call. *(Takes broom from under his elbow and starts to walk away — turns back remembering.)* Oh — Pipe-fitting, I'll be wanting you to curl again for me — soon.

PIPE   Return match?

WULLIE   Macdonald Brier *(Pause.)* Pipe-fitting — how old a man are you?

PIPE   Fifty-two.

WULLIE   Ever heard of the Celestial Brier Play-offs?

PIPE   No. *(Pause.)* I ain't.

WULLIE   You'll curl third for me in that — but not for a while yet.

PIPE-FITTING *slowly rubs his hand over his face, his jaw — snuffs — spits —*

PIPE   If she's what I think she is, Wullie — that's one I kind of think I'll be curling agin you.

MUSIC: *"Devil" theme for finale but sliding into the bouncy "Maple Leaf Forever".*
WULLIE *and his rink of three tried men and true — brooms aloft — arms over each other's shoulders as they walk down the rink through the swirling mist and steam . . .*

Happenings

Divers Probe Old Wreck

Norman Hacking

At the bottom of Lynn Canal, near Juneau, Alaska lie the rusted remains of the Canadian Pacific liner *Princess Sophia,* the most tragic wreck in the history of navigation on the north Pacific coast.

She slipped off Vanderbilt Reef into deep water on the night of October 25, 1918, with the loss of all the 343 souls aboard.

Only recently, with modern techniques, have divers been able to recover relics of that disaster of 58 years ago. A report of their findings appeared recently in *Alaska Magazine,* published in Anchorage.

Few of those who are alive today can be aware of the terrible impact that this shipwreck had on the citizens of Vancouver and Victoria. They had suffered four years of dreadful war casualties. The influenza epidemic was at its height. And then came the loss of the *Sophia,* which struck much closer to home than the loss of the *Titanic* six years earlier.

An elderly friend of mine lost three brothers in the same month. One died on the western front, one died of the 'flu, and the third went down in the *Sophia.*

One of the divers who has explored the *Princess Sophia* wreck is Juneau fisherman Mike Heard. He reports that the

Sophia is a jagged, white mound on the bottom. Virtually no part has escaped the attachment of the large sea anemone.

The effect is eerie. Thousands of white anemones slowly and silently extend and contract their tentacles, sweeping the water for the tiny bits of food on which they live.

Because of the dense covering of anemones and the broken and twisted conditions of the hulk, the lines of the ship are so indistinct that it was only after many trips to the reef that Bill and the other divers agreed on what they were seeing.

The *Sophia* lies on her side, gradually settling into the bottom, with her bow in about 60 feet of water and her stern at about 100 feet. Hull plates lie twisted and broken, pieces of her masts and superstructure are strewn about. There are gaping holes in her sides, all testimony to her last violent moments and years of slow decay.

Not far from the wreck of the *Princess Sophia* lie the remains of another Canadian Pacific liner, the *Princess Kathleen,* which sank at Lena Point on Sept. 7, 1952, fortunately without loss of life.

A writer in *Alaska Magazine* reports that the vessel now rests on a steep slope of from 70 to 200 feet of water, lying on her port side, masts pointing out towards mid-channel. The entire vessel is heavily overgrown with marine life, chiefly hydroids and algae.

Most of the windows of the wheel house are smashed. Inside the bridge-area, voice tubes are still intact, and communication equipment lies strewn about, wires extending in all directions. Just behind the wheelhouse, the mast and its stays extend out over blackness towards mid-channel. Behind the mast are the funnels, still intact and little changed.

The divers report that the *Princess Kathleen* with her many living inhabitants is an intriguing scene, but as the wreck steadily deteriorates it might scarcely be recognized as a man-made object in 20 years.

Remember . . .

Dennis Bell

SKAGWAY, Alaska — Capt. Louis P. Locke, veteran skipper of the Canadian Pacific steamship *Princess Sophia,* thrust his hands into the pockets of his greatcoat and took a quick turn around the gleaming deck of his ship.

Below him, a stream of passengers wrestled suitcases and trunks up the gangplank. Orders bellowed by his officers at dock workers left dancing clouds of frozen breath suspended in the night air.

Stewards guided passengers, including some drunken miners, to sumptuous cabins below.

Outside, deckhands fought for control of the last of 50 head of horses, guiding them to shipboard stables deep in the liner's holds.

As the din of boarding activities quietened, Capt. Locke listened for the deep throb of his vessel's engines.

The sound shattered the eerie silence of the arctic night, echoing off the gloomy cliffs that loomed above the Skagway docks.

Capt. Locke unbuttoned his greatcoat as he entered the wheelhouse. It was 10:45 p.m. on a Wednesday night, Oct. 23, 1918.

A few minutes later he yanked the ship's whistle. The *Princess Sophia* slipped her lines and churned noisily into the Lynn Canal, a 65-mile stretch of water separating Skagway from the Pacific Ocean.

The captain had been at sea most of his life. He had shipped as a boy out of Halifax aboard his father's windjammer and had a distinguished record of service on steam vessels plying Atlantic waters.

For the last 27 years he had been sailing the waters off British Columbia and Alaska.

He was reputed to know the whereabouts of every shoal, reef, current and eddy emanating from the jigsaw coastal outline.

His career would soon end. He was 65 and due to retire shortly. Just a few more runs between Skagway and points south and he could leave the sea for a comfortable pension on dry land.

However, Capt. Locke's dreams of retirement were shattered some three hours later when the *Sophia* ran hard aground on Vanderbilt Reef.

The ship clung precariously to the reef for the next two days, then went down with all hands the night of Friday, Oct. 25.

It was the worst maritime disaster in the history of the west coast — and no ship would ever again bear the proud name *Princess Sophia*.

The loss of life was appalling — 33 women, 17 children, 218 male passengers, Capt. Locke and his 74 officers and men, for a total of 343 victims.

There was no thought of tragedy as the six-year-old passenger vessel steamed toward the Pacific that Wednesday night.

The ship's orchestra struck up a lively tune and men chatted of such things as Christmas at home and the impending end of the First World War.

The passengers included William Scouse, the man credited with scooping the first pan of gold from Eldorado Creek in the Yukon's Klondike rush. Several of the most colorful Eldorado Kings were with him.

Mr. and Mrs. J. A. Sehgers were aboard. They ran the famed Yukonia Hotel on Dawson City's Dancehall Row and were making a long-awaited trip to the outside world.

The Sehgers swapped mining yarns with the dashing Capt. James Alexander, a towering 200-pound former cavalry officer who had headed north in search of gold after a distinguished career in Her Majesty's Dragoon Guards in Africa.

Capt. Alexander, a living legend in the Yukon, was also owner of Engineer Mine at Atlin, B. C., worth an estimated $2,500,000.

Vancouver hotel owner Charley Queen was returning home after checking on his lucrative Yukon mining properties.

Tickets on the *Sophia* were scarce by the time Charley reached Skagway, and the former Vancouver alderman had to use all his influence to get a berth.

Eighty rough-and-tumble riverboat men — the crews from all the White Pass and Yukon boats on the Yukon River — added to the merriment. They were to return north in the spring of 1919 following the breakup of ice on the river.

The conviviality quieted as midnight approached. Most of the passengers were in their bunks when the *Sophia* hit the reef at 2 a.m. with a grinding crash.

The impact threw passengers from their berths, left luggage strewn about the holds, panicked the horses below the decks and dumped cutlery and china from galley shelves.

The exact sequence of events in the early morning hours of Thursday, Oct. 24, will never be known, but investigators said later it appeared the ship had strayed from her course in a snowstorm.

What had been merely flurries and light winds when the *Sophia* left Skagway had developed into a storm by the time she reached Vanderbilt Reef.

Capt. Locke was on the bridge as damage reports started coming in. The vessel was not shipping water, though steel plates along her keel were badly bashed in, and the rudder was damaged.

The big passenger ship was perched in a V-shaped crevice

in the reef, her stern dangling over the whitecapped waves.

Capt. Locke's verdict: She was in no immediate danger of sinking.

Letters found on the bodies of *Sophia* passengers several days later indicated there was little panic among the passengers following the grounding.

"We struck a reef in a blinding snowstorm," wrote a young Englishman. "A number of passengers were thrown out of their bunks and great excitement prevailed.

"Boats were made ready to lower when information was received that the boat was not taking water. The passengers became quiet. Owing to the storm, the boats were not lowered.

"The next morning Thursday we were surrounded by a number of small boats, but it is too rough to transfer the passengers.

"In the realism that we are surrounded by grave danger, I make this my last will and testament . . ."

First to reach the scene was the United States lighthouse tender *Cedar,* which battled its way through towering seas to get within 400 yards of the *Sophia.*

Capt. Locke exchanged shouts with Capt. Leadbetter of the *Cedar* through megaphones and assured him that everything was under control.

More boats were on the way from Juneau and Skagway.

The day ended without any further attempts to get the passengers off the *Sophia.* In addition to the *Cedar,* three fishing vessels also offered to help transfer the passengers.

That night the passengers bedded down apprehensively.

The snowstorm reached gale proportions during the night, and by Friday morning the gale had turned into a blizzard.

"The ship is hard and fast on the reef with her bottom badly damaged, but she is not taking water," Capt. Locke said in a wireless message to company headquarters in Victoria.

"She is unable to back off the reef. The main steam pipe is broken. The passengers are normal."

By noon the ship was taking a terrific pounding. The reef rocks were rapidly eating through the *Sophia's* bulkheads. It was impossible to transfer passengers though the *Cedar* and other vessels remained nearby.

The storm increased in ferocity in the late afternoon and waiting rescue ships were forced to retreat to sheltered coves some distance away for fear of being beached or themselves pushed into the reef.

At 5 p.m. the *Cedar* picked up a wireless message from the *Sophia,* — the first indication she was going down.

"We are foundering on a reef. For God's sake, come and help us."

"Coming full speed but cannot see on account of thick snow and heavy seas," Capt. Leadbetter replied.

Half an hour later the *Sophia* sent its final message: "Just in time to say good-bye. We are foundering."

The *Cedar* heard nothing further from the *Sophia* that night, nor was she able to find any trace of the liner.

The next morning she steamed back into the area amid the appalling wreckage the breakup of the ship had left.

The crew of the *Cedar* recovered 17 bodies, stiffened by the sea spray into grotesque positions. A giant oil slick marked where the big steamer had gone down, stern on one side of the reef, bow on the other.

Her forward masthead was all that remained above water. It was obvious that the *Sophia* had gone down in a matter of minutes — none of the lifeboats or rafts had been properly cleared.

Bodies littered the beaches on both sides of the channel and on nearby islands. Three hundred coffins were rushed to Juneau and Skagway from Seattle.

The body of William O'Brien, a member of the Yukon Territorial Council, was found lashed to a raft, his arms frozen around the corpse of one of his five children who died with him.

Four women, their open eyes glazed with frost, were found lashed and frozen to one another.

One *Sophia* passenger swam 15 miles from the wreck, then died of exposure on a desolate beach. He was found frozen solid in a sitting position, his coat pulled over his head.

Frank Gosse, the *Sophia's* second mate, may also have reached shore alive. Footprints were found near his ice-coated body.

Rescuers also learned that many of those who went over the side in the last fateful minutes tried to take their valuables with them.

One woman had $8,000 in cash tucked in a money belt around her; others had bags of jewelry or gold dust in little sacks around their necks.

There was, however, one survivor — a brown-and-white English setter that dragged itself into a nearby town two days after the disaster, its coat matted with ice and fuel oil.

Even among people hardened by the rigors of world war, the *Sophia* tragedy landed like a bombshell. Newspapers talked of nothing else until Armistice Day, Nov. 11.

Inquiries were held, and Captains Locke and Leadbetter were absolved of all blame.

No responsibility was ever fixed — there was no one left to tell the tale except the English setter.

Months after the disaster — even after the dog recovered its health — residents reported it was terrified of water.

The Ghost Train
Ken Liddell

Andrew Staysko, who retired in 1955 after 48 years in Canadian Pacific train service, pulled his treasured engineer's watch from his shirt pocket, where he had carried it since vests went out of style.

It was time to catch the ghost train.

You can believe or disbelieve the story, but Mr. Staysko produced documented evidence that something mighty strange happened on two occasions amid the cutbanks at Medicine Hat in the summer of 1908.

Bob Towhey was the engineer and Gus Day the fireman on an engine travelling light from Medicine Hat to Dunmore about 11 o'clock one night in June of that year.

At Dunmore they were to couple to the Spokane Flyer. It was a fast CP train that ran from St. Paul to Spokane on the Candian lines, via Portal, Moose Jaw, Lethbridge, Cranbrook and thence south from Yahk to Spokane. The Spokane Flyer did not enter Medicine Hat proper and the crews that took it westward into the Crowsnest Pass, or brought it back, finished their duties at Dunmore junction.

This night Towhey and Day were two miles out of Medicine Hat when, before them, appeared a train approaching on the single line that wound around the hills as the tracks climbed a steep grade from the valley to the tableland of prairie.

As Gus Day recalled many years later, the headlight of the approaching train seemed to be the size of a wagon wheel. The reflection ahead was as though the firebox was open on the locomotive of the approaching train and it lit the dark sky of the night.

Day shouted to Towhey and made for the gangplank to jump. Towhey reached for the brake valve, but his hand stopped in mid-air. The approaching train whistled a warning signal for the curve around which Towhey's train had just come.

Day stood at the cab doorway, Towhey's hand remained suspended before the brake valve and the minds of each man were suspended by emotions.

Then a string of phantom coaches sped past.

The windows were lighted and crew members of the

phantom train waved a greeting from places where crew members would be expected to be found to wave greeting as trains passed.

Then the phantom train disappeared.

Towhey and Day, each fearful of what the other may have thought had they expressed feelings, said nothing. They continued to Dunmore, coupled to the Spokane Flyer and finished the night without further incident.

Two weeks later the two railroaders met on the street in Medicine Hat. Perhaps feeling safer with passage of time, they found the courage to ask each other about what each had seen, or thought they had seen, that startling night.

Each was thankful to learn the other had witnessed the same sight and had experienced the same eerie feeling of having seen a ghost engine pulling a string of cars.

But it had worried Towhey more than Day. Towhey had been to a "reader", he told Day, meaning a fortune teller, and he had been told that he would die within the month.

"I'm going to lay off for a couple of trips," Towhey told his fireman.

Day stayed on the job.

A few nights later, Day was on the same engine going about the same duties. This time the engineer was J. Nicholson, replacing Towhey who had booked off.

At exactly the same spot the phantom train again appeared, headed straight for them with whistle blowing and headlight burning. And again it simply evaporated into the darkness as its crew members again waved greetings from their positions on its engine and cars.

On the morning of July 8 Day reported for duty and found he was assigned to yard service. H. Thompson took his place as fireman on the engine that made a morning trip to Dunmore to pick up the Spokane Flyer, this time to take it eastward to Swift Current.

Thompson's engineer was J. Nicholson.

They left Medicine Hat and headed into the hills. About 100 yards from the spot where the phantom train had been seen on two different nights and by two different crews, another train appeared around a curve, headed straight for them.

But this time it was daylight and it was for real.

It was No. 514 the passenger train coming in from Lethbridge.

And the man at the throttle was Bob Towhey, who had overcome his fears and had returned to work.

The inevitable happened. The outbound engine and inbound passenger train collided. The wreck took the lives of Towhey and Nicholson, the engineers, both of whom had earlier seen the phantom train at almost the same spot.

It also took the lives of a fireman named Grey and a conductor named Mallett, on the inbound passenger train, and seven of the passengers.

Thompson, fireman on the outbound engine escaped by jumping. He recalled later that just before the crash he had seen a farmer standing on a hill, waving his arms. The farmer could see both engine and passenger train approaching each other around the curves and he realized a crash was inevitable. Thompson had mistaken the farmer's arm waving for a friendly greeting.

Some years later *The Locomotive Engineer,* a weekly newspaper of the Brotherhood of Locomotive Engineers, published in Cleveland, printed a story about a phantom train in Colorado.

By this time Gus Day had retired from the railway and was living in Victoria. He read *The Locomotive Engineer,* of course. The story of the phantom train in Colorado brought vivid memories of the strange sights he had seen on two occasions years before on the line between Medicine Hat and Dunmore in Alberta.

He told his story to C. Moriarty, who turned it into an article for a Vancouver newspaper.

When he got to the part about the collision that followed the two trips of Alberta's phantom train, Mr. Moriarty wrote with personal knowledge.

He had been a Canadian Pacific telegrapher at Calgary at the time and had handled a press story about the crash.

First, Give the Chicken a Shot of Home Brew
Agnes Copithorne

In the early days when neighbors were few and far between, I had occasion to accompany my father to the home of a Ukrainian family. And as was the custom in those days, we were invited to share the noonday meal — a memorable repast I have never forgotten.

We were consuming an especially tender roast chicken which had arrived at the table in an earthen dish, succulently imbedded in brown rice. I remarked that the chicken was very good indeed, and our hostess agreed, saying further that the fowl had been killed in a fashion which made the meat more tender.

"You mean there is such a method?" I asked.

"To be sure," she replied. "When a chicken is seized to be killed, it becomes hysterical with fear and tenses its muscles, and the glands become active just as they do in human beings and animals when danger is at hand. A chicken killed in such a manner is not good to eat."

"So," she said, "when we plan to kill a fowl . . ." she looked across at my father, "We give it a little home brew, two or three spoonsful, depending on size."

"What happens?" I asked.

"Oh," she said, "then we let the chicken go. Soon it is flopping around happily, entirely unconcerned. When picked up, it squawks and tries to crow, quite unsuccessfully. Soon it relaxes and hangs limp and now is the time to dispatch it quickly, without difficulty. There is no flexing of muscles, no pumping of the adrenal glands and the meat is more tender to eat."

While considering this, I had another helping of chicken. It was indeed very tender.

Some time later, we were in a position to return this neighbor's hospitality. It was a cold winter's day and father brought out the rum bottle he kept for special occasions.

As I watched them sip their toddies I was reminded of the gastronomical delights of which we had partaken at this man's dinner table.

"About this fowl-butchering," I inquired. "I've been wondering, do all you people kill your chickens in such a manner?"

"Ah, no," he answered sadly. "Not all, by any manner of means."

"Why not all?"

"Many have not the . . . anesthetic to render the fowl insensible. And even those who have, they are likely to look at the bottle and then at the chicken, and to decide that if they drink the stuff themselves, they will not notice if the chicken is tough."

"But in your house, is it always done? Tomorrow, for instance?"

"Well now," he said, wiping his moustache with the back of his hand, "If your father would spare me the few drops left in the bottle, it will be surely so. Tomorrow we have the tender chicken."

It cheered me then, the next day, to think that our good neighbors were eating tender, relaxed drumsticks.

But my father said he had doubts. It had seemed to him that our visitor's wistful look suggested thirst rather than hunger, and I wondered if the chicken got its tot.

First, Give the Chicken . . . 269

Acknowledgements

The editor wishes to thank the authors and publishers for permission to include the following in this anthology:

B.C. Indian Language Project for "How the Animals and Birds Got Their Names" by Charlie Mack from *Sound Heritage Magazine,* Aural History Programme of the Provincial Archives of British Columbia.

The Book Society of Canada Limited for "The Legend of the Thunderbird" by Gail Ann Kendall from *First Flowering.* For "The Cathedral Trees of Stanley Park" and for "The Legend of the Twin Sisters" by John S. Morgan from *When the Morning Stars Sang Together* (1974).

Calgary Power for "Where There's Smoke . . ." by Jacques Hamilton from the radio broadcast *Our Alberta Heritage.*

The Canadian Publishers, McClelland and Stewart Limited for "The Animals Climb Into the Sky", for Children of the Moon", and for "The Creation of the Northern Rocky Mountains" by Ella Elizabeth Clark from *Indian Legends of Canada.* For "How the Raven Brought Light to the World" and for "The Owl and the Raven" by Ronald Melzack from *The Day Tuk Became a Hunter.* For "The Windigo Spirit" and "The Windigo at Berens River" by James R. Stevens from *The Sacred Legends of the Sandy Lake Cree.*

John W. Chalmers for "My Friend Mike" from the *Civil Service Association of Alberta Bulletin.* For "No Mean Country" from the *Alberta Poetry Yearbook, 1965.* For "A Legend of the Rockies" from the *Alberta Poetry Yearbook, 1964.*

Cheam Publishing Co. Ltd. for "Canadians Sight Hairy Creatures" by John Green from *On the Track of the Sasquatch.*

Clark, Irwin & Company Limited for "Munchausen in Alberta" by Elizabeth Brewster from *Sunrise North* (1972). For "The Drover's Tale of the Flying Bull" by Watson Kirkconnell from *The Flying Bull and Other Tales* (1949).

Charles E. Tuttle Co. Inc. for "Spike Drew" by Robert E. Gard from *Johnny Chinook.*

Charles Scribner's Sons for "The Race" by George B. Grinnell from *Blackfoot Lodge Tales.*

Agnes Copithorne for "First, Give the Chicken a Shot of Home Brew".

Dodd, Mead & Company (Canada) Ltd. for "Kathleen" by Robert W. Service from *Songs of a Sunlover*.

Douglas and McIntyre Ltd. for "The Okanagan Indians Knew Him Well" and for "Sightings From the Deck" by Mary Moon from *Ogopogo* (1977), J. J. Douglas Ltd.

Denise Fair for "Avalanches".

Garrard Publishing Company for "A Magic Bear" by Edward W. Dolch and Marguerite P. Dolch from *Stories from Canada: Folklore of the World* (1964) by Marguerite P. Dolch.

T. W. Gee for "The Chair".

Gray's Publishing Limited for "Ko-ishin-mit and Son of Eagle" by George Clutesi from *Son of Raven: Son of Deer*.

Hodder & Stoughton Limited for "The Ballad of Yaada" and for "The Pilot of the Plains" by E. Pauline Johnson from *Flint and Feather*.

Hurtig Publishers for "At the Sign of the Buffalo" by J. W. Grant MacEwan from *Tatanga Mani, Walking Buffalo of the Stonies*. For "Kajortoq and the Crow" by Maurice Metayer from *Tales from the Igloo*.

J. A. Jackson for "Din's Back Room" from the *Quarterly Review of the Missionary Association of Mary Immaculate.*

Macmillan Company of Canada Ltd. for "The Bear Who Stole the Chinook", for "The Girl Who Married the Morning Star" and for "The Old Man" by Frances Fraser from *The Bear Who Stole the Chinook and Other Stories*. For "The Dancing Lodge of Chief Little Mouse", for "The Eagles' War-Bonnet", and for "The Moon and The Seven Singers" by Frances Fraser from *Wind Along the River*. For "Baldy Red" by Robert E. Gard from *Canadian Myths and Legends (Themes in Canadian Literature)*. For "The Grey Archway" by E. Pauline Johnson from *The Role of Women in Literature (Themes in Canadian Literature)*. For "How Coyote Stole Fire" by Gail Robinson and Douglas Hill from *Canadian Myths and Legends*. For "The First Totem Pole" by Hugh Weatherby from *Tales the Totems Tell*.

Manitoba Pageant for "The Golden Boy" by Irene Craig (September 1956).

Lillian A. Maze for "Chinook" from the *Alberta Golden Jubilee Anthology.*

Mrs. Margaret McCourt for "Dance for the Devil" by Edward A. McCourt from *Tigers of the Snow.* For "The White Mustang" by Edward A. McCourt from *Wild Rose Country.*

W. O. Mitchell for "The Black Bonspiel of Wullie MacCrimmon" from *Three Worlds of Drama.*

McGraw-Hill Ryerson Limited for "This May Hurt a Little" by Eric Nicol from *Sense and Nonsense.*

The Province (Vancouver), for "Divers Probe Old Wreck" by Norman Hacking (November 26, 1976).

Nancy Thompson for "St. George" by Nancy Senior from *I Never Wanted to Be the Holy Ghost.*

University of California Press for "Coyote and the Monster of the Columbia" by Ella Elizabeth Clark from *Indian Legends of the Pacific Northwest.*

Van Nostrand Reinhold Ltd. for "Akers and Purcell, Whiskey Traders" and for "Tale of a Gunman" by Andy Russell from *Men of the Saddle, Working Cowboys of Canada,* 1978.

The Vancouver Sun for "Remember . . ." by Dennis Bell (November 22, 1968).

Norman Ward for "Mice in the Beer".

Western Producer Prairie Books for "The Ghost Train" by Ken Liddell from *I'll Take the Train.*

While every effort has been made to trace the owners of copyrighted material and to make due acknowledgement, we regret having been unsuccessful with the following selections:

"A Fishing Story", article from *Crag and Canyon*
"The 'Little Men' of Long Ago" by B. A. McKelvie
"The Dinosaur" by Bert Leston Taylor
"The Most Stupid Boy" by Ruth Young